Applied
BIOLOGY

Applied
BIOLOGY

VOL. IV

Edited by

T. H. COAKER

*Department of Applied Biology, University of Cambridge,
Cambridge, England*

1979

ACADEMIC PRESS

LONDON · NEW YORK · SAN FRANCISCO

A Subsidiary of Harcourt Brace Jovanovich, Publishers

ACADEMIC PRESS INC. (LONDON) LTD.
24/28 Oval Road,
London NW1

United States Edition published by
ACADEMIC PRESS INC.
111 Fifth Avenue
New York, New York 10003

Library of Congress Catalog Number 76–1065
ISBN: 0–12–040904–6

Text set in 11/12 pt, Monotype Baskerville, printed by letterpress,
and bound in Great Britain at The Pitman Press, Bath

Contributors

BRADSHAW, A. D. *Department of Botany, P.O. Box 147, University of Liverpool, UK.*

CLIVE JAMES, W. *Canadian International Development Agency, Ottawa, Canada.*

FIELD, C. R. *UNESCO Arid Lands Project, P.O. Box 30592, Nairobi, Kenya.*

JOHNSON, M. S. *Department of Botany, P.O. Box 147, University of Liverpool, Liverpool, UK.*

PIRIE, N. W. *Rothamsted Experimental Station, Harpenden, Herts., UK.*

STEELE, JOHN H. *Woods Hole Oceanographic Institution, Woods Hole, Massachusetts, USA.*

TENG, P. S. *Department of Agricultural Microbiology, Lincoln College, Canterbury, NZ.*

Preface

The main purpose of this series is to draw together subject matter selected from currently important fields of Applied Biology to produce a synthesis for students, teachers and specialists from other fields. The widely diversified and multidisciplinary nature of Applied Biology emphasizes the importance of the series since interdependence of the various subjects it embraces cannot be ignored especially if the fruits of research are ultimately to be applied for the benefit of man.

Contributions to the series are written by specialists in their field, some with a biological background, others with chemical or physical qualifications, each presenting his subject matter in his own style. As outlined in the Preface to the earlier volumes, each article should, nevertheless, seek to achieve four aims: to review generally the state of the subject; to select one or more aspects for particular critical discussion; to summarize what is known to be of practical importance and to indicate the greatest need for future work.

It is the editor's view that it would be difficult to mould contributions in a particular volume into a homogeneous unit resembling a monograph. It is the aim, however, that the volumes accumulate to provide the individual with the material he needs to synthesize his own views on Applied Biology as a whole.

T. H. COAKER

January, 1979

Contents

Leaf Protein as a Source of Food

N. W. PIRIE

Rothamsted Experimental Station,
Harpenden, Herts., UK

I. Introduction and Terminology

The reasons for thinking of leaves as a useful potential source of protein can be stated simply. Leaves are the part of a crop in which protein is synthesized and not a part to which it is translocated after synthesis. Because translocation losses are eliminated, a forage or other leafy crop should, in a suitable climate, yield more protein per hectare and year than other crops given similar conditions of husbandry. The advantage should be even greater if a species is used that can regrow several times after harvesting and so keep a photosynthetically active cover on the ground throughout the growing season. These points seemed reasonable many years ago; they have been largely borne out experimentally.

Trustworthy and reasonably complete amino acid analyses, made by Chibnall (1939) and others, suggested that the mixture of proteins in leaves should have good nutritive value. This was probable even without the analyses because many non-ruminant animals, i.e. animals in which the alimentary tract is not a site of extensive microbial amino acid synthesis, live almost exclusively on leaves. Furthermore, the great metabolic and synthetic capacity of leaves depends on a more extensive array of enzymes than is present in any animal tissue. It seemed unlikely that the same amino acid deficit, or excess, would characterize all these different enzyme proteins. Seeds and other storage organs contain fewer individual proteins and so are more likely to be nutritionally inadequate. Hence the well-known nutritional inferiority of the protein in seeds compared to that in animal tissues. The expectation that the mixture of proteins in leaves would be as good as, if not better than, the proteins in animal tissues arises for purely statistical reasons; it does not depend on the invalid assumption, which has crept into some articles, that enzyme proteins are in some way "better" than storage proteins—there are simply a greater variety of them in an active organ. This generalization is not invalidated by the fact that milk and eggs, which contain few individual proteins, are nutritionally excellent. Milk and egg proteins are the end product of respectively about 50 and 400 million years of selection for feeding young animals.

Though not always explicitly stated, the expectation that extracted leaf protein (LP) could be the most abundant source of protein, and that it should have good nutritive value, stimulated the early work on LP. Those who doubted the value of the research, or who were actively hostile to it, seem always to have paid too little attention to the basic propositions: they did not contest them, they simply disregarded them. Undoubtedly difficulties could be forseen, otherwise LP production would not be a research theme. It may not be possible to maintain a suitable photosynthetically active cover on the land in a practical farming system. It may not be possible to extract the protein without an economically unrealistic expenditure on machinery and energy. Other components of leaves may combine with, or damage, the protein in the course of extraction so that some essential amino acids are destroyed or made unavailable to non-ruminants, and so on.

Rouelle described in 1773 the extraction of leaf protein and its heat coagulation in two stages, first the protein associated with chlorophyll at 50–60°C and then a paler protein at 70–80°C. I have published (Pirie, 1971a; 1978) translations of that paper and described the history of work on large-scale production (Pirie, 1978). A symposium (Pirie, 1971a) organized by the International Biological Program (IBP) surveyed what was then known about crops suitable for protein extraction, the quality of the product, and the manner in which it could be presented for the table. This review will therefore deal mainly with observations made since that symposium.

There is some disagreement about the most suitable names for the three products of leaf fractionation. There is no disagreement about the equivalent words "juice" and "extract". The coagulum separated from leaf juice, but not fractionated, is called leaf protein in this article. It is sometimes called leaf protein concentrate (LPC). That is misleading because it suggests that it is a more refined form of some parent material that contains less protein. It can be argued that it should be called leaf lipoprotein because it contains 20–30% lipid. But most of that lipid is simply mixed with the LP and not combined with it. Preparations of LP contain 50–70% of true protein. All the values given in this paper for protein yields are calculated from the amount of nitrogen (N) appearing as extracted protein and are therefore values for dry 100% protein. The fibrous residue from which LP has been extracted should not be misleadingly named. "Fibre" is brief, "extracted residue" is descriptive. "Pressed crop", which is sometimes used, is misleading because it perpetuates the illusion that pressing alone is sufficient to extract protein. The fluid from which coagulated protein has been removed is often, unambiguously, called brown juice or deproteinized juice; "whey" is brief and the metaphor is obvious.

II. The Effects of Agronomy and Species on Yield

Early studies on small samples in the laboratory showed, as was to be expected, that young, lush, protein-rich leaves extracted better than mature and dry leaves. Mixed grasses harvested at 10–20 cm, and lucerne (*Medicago sativa*) harvested before coming into flower, proved satisfactory. Most studies on large-scale production have therefore been made with these crops. There is however no reason to assume that they are ideal sources for bulk production of LP and they have some obvious disadvantages. For example: because of the ability to fix nitrogen, legumes are preferable to grasses, but LP from lucerne has a strong flavour and extracts have an inconvenient tendency to froth.

The annual yield of LP depends on the amount of leaf that can be harvested in a year, the amount of protein in the leaf, and the percentage of this protein that is extractable by techniques that are feasible on a large scale. The last two factors are related because, in general, the greater the protein content, the greater the percentage extractability. A striking example of this relationship was the observation (Arkcoll and Festenstein, 1971) that the yield of LP m^{-1} from a plot of kale (*Brassica oleracea*) given phosphorus (P) and potassium (K) was smaller than from an unfertilized plot because, although the dry matter (DM) yield was increased 68%, the N in the DM was diminished 56%. Obviously, this relationship holds only for comparisons between different treatments given to plots of the same species; species containing more protein do not necessarily extract better than others. It does however follow that there is a disproportionate advantage in harvesting leaves that are young, well manured, and well watered. They will not only contain more protein, but more of that protein will be extractable.

Species differ in the extent to which extractability diminishes with maturity, there are also differences between varieties. Crook and Holden (1948) could extract protein from one variety of strawberry (*Fragaria vesca*) but not from another. Byers and Sturrock (1965) compared five maize (*Zea mays*) varieties and found that the differences were not the same in successive years. Wheat (*Triticum aestivum*) varieties also differ (Arkcoll and Festenstein, 1971). Differences in the date at which haulm of different potato (*Solanum tuberosum*) varieties dies are well known and they affect the amount of protein that can be extracted from haulm if that is taken as a by-product when the tubers are lifted (Carruthers and Pirie, 1975). Fat hen (*Chenopodium album*) shows extreme variability. Arkcoll (1971) singled it out as a species which continued to give good protein extraction after flower development; the variety used by Heath (1977) matured more abruptly than three other species with which it was compared; Carlsson (1975) found one variety yielding more than three times as much m^{-2} as another; from an Austrian variety, 80% of the protein was extractable, compared to 50% from a Swedish variety. The yields of extractable protein from 15 varieties of fenugreek (*Trigonella foenum-graecum*) differed by a factor of five (Chandramani et al., 1975b).

The ratio of protein-N to non-protein-N differs between species, it also varies in a species with the conditions of husbandry, atmospheric temperature and possibly the time of day at which the leaf is harvested (cf. Hill-Cottingham and Lloyd-Jones, 1979). Because non-protein-N will be more difficult to use in commercial practice than nitrogen in LP, or associated with the fibre residue, species and conditions should be chosen in which non-protein-N is as small a fraction of the total-N as possible.

Species that appear to extract well in laboratory conditions may be almost impossible to handle on a large scale because the extract is glutinous (e.g. comfrey, *Symphytum asperrimum* and *officinale*, or sweet potato, *Ipomoea batatas*). By contrast, some of the grasses that extracted badly when put through domestic mincers, extracted well when disintegrated in high-speed pulpers.

It follows from all this that a satisfactory basis for commercial LP extraction will not be established until there has been much more agronomic, or plant physiological, research. Sowing dates, fertilizer treatments, time of harvest, and ability to re-grow after harvest will have to be studied with many more species and varieties. There is also scope for plant breeding. The crop-plant varieties used so far were all selected according to criteria such as the ability to yield abundant seed; these may well be inimical to LP yield. Crops grown for LP production will probably have flowering delayed or prevented by sowing them at unusual times, or in unusual latitudes, or by genetic manipulation, or through use of growth regulators, so that senescence is delayed and there is a prolonged period of vegetative growth. No attempt has so far been made by plant breeders to use LP yield as a desirable quality. In selecting candidates for research on breeding, the point already made should be borne in mind i.e. there should be abundant, lush, protein-rich leaf. Three more factors should be borne in mind. The leaves should not be carried on a very fibrous stalk or the energy needed for pulping will be excessive unless some form of scutching is possible; the leaf should be neutral or slightly alkaline (acidity can be partly counteracted by pulping with added alkali, but this complicates the process); the presence of tannins and phenolic substances diminishes protein extraction.

To give an impression of the potentialities of LP production, it is worth while surveying some of the results that have been published on protein extractability and yield although often little information is given about the antecedents of the plants used, and the most suitable varieties may not have been chosen. It is convenient to group possible sources of leaf arbitrarily into the categories: species used in conventional agriculture; leaves available as the by-product of a conventional crop; tree leaves; water weeds and leaves not at present used in conventional agriculture.

A. CONVENTIONAL SPECIES

In the period during which extraction equipment was being designed and improved at Rothamsted, conventional crops grown in the conventional way were used. Latterly, cereals were sown two to four times more quickly than usual and fertilizer was used on some plots unusually liberally, but the plots were not irrigated although in this region there is a water deficit in four summers out of five. Cereals were sown in autumn so as to use winter sunshine and ensure an early start in spring. Three or four harvests could be taken from wheat and two or three from barley (*Hordeum vulgare*); second harvests were uncertain with rye (*Secale cereale*). About the beginning of June the land was ploughed and resown with crops such as mustard (*Sinapis alba*), fodder radish (*Raphanus sativus*) or tares (*Vicia*). Yields of LP exceeded 2t ha^{-1} i.e 334 kg of protein-N ha^{-1} (Arkcoll and Festenstein, 1971; Pirie, 1978). To get yields as large as this, it is important to harvest the leaf before maturity causes the percent extractability to diminish.

In all these experiments, increasing the amount of N fertilizer up to 264 kg ha^{-1}, increased the yield of LP although there was little increase in the yield of DM after about 132 kg ha^{-1}. Very large doses of N are, however, used inefficiently. Thus the largest added yield of LP resulting from 264 rather than 132 kg nitrogen was 76 kg, i.e. only about 10% of the additional N was recovered in LP. It is probable that it would not, as a rule, be economic to aim at these very large yields. The maximum yields from legumes depending for N on their root nodules were 1247 kg ha^{-1} from red clover (*Trifolium pratense*), and 1009 kg ha^{-1} from lucerne, each harvested three times. The yields would probably have been larger with irrigation.

Working with cocksfoot (*Dactylis glomerata*), ryegrass (*Lolium perenne*) and fodder radish, Heath and King (1977) found that true protein accumulates mainly in the leaf laminae, and accumulation diminishes or stops, when stem growth supercedes laminar growth. The density at which a crop should be planted, the amount and timing of fertilizer application, and the frequency of cutting, should all be managed so as to ensure maximum formation of leaf rather than stem. The inclusion of large amounts of stem in material from which LP is being extracted, contributes little extra protein, and it acts as an absorbent mass within which the laminar protein gets lost. Heath (1978) contrasts the extra trouble and expense of repeatedly sowing annual crops, with the apparent economy of using perennial crops: he concludes that annuals give more flexibility, can probably be managed so as to give a more even supply of material throughout the season, and should in the conditions of commercial farming yield 840 kg of LP ha^{-1}. This is more protein concentrate than any other system of farming produces, and it does not take into account the value of the fibre residue and the non-protein-N in the juice.

With irrigation, but without N fertilizer, lucerne in New Zealand yielded 2t of LP ha^{-1} during the seven summer months; there was little difference in LP yield between four-week and five-week harvests though the latter gave larger DM yields (Allison and Vartha, 1973). During the New Zealand winter, rye grass (*Lolium multiflorum*) yielded 1·2t ha^{-1} from six harvests taken during 4·5 months. As at Rothamsted, the extra yield when more than 180 kg ha^{-1} of nitrogen fertilizer was applied was gained wastefully (Vartha and Allison, 1973).

Other temperate zone conventional crops have been less thoroughly studied. Byers and Sturrock (1965) compared five clover (*Trifolium* and *Melilotus*) varieties. Apart from their ability to fix N, they seemed no better than the other species that were being used at the time; 40–50% of their protein was extractable. Tares came in the same range. An unsuccessful attempt was made (Byers and Jenkins, 1961) to increase the yield by spraying tares with gibberellic acid immediately after the first harvest had been taken. When given 132 kg of N ha^{-1}, mustard yielded 10·6 kg of LP ha^{-1} day^{-1}, and rape (*Brassica napus*) a little less (Arkcoll and Festenstein, 1971). Sunflower (*Helianthus annuus*) produces very large yields of both DM and protein if given enough N, but this protein does not extract well from mature plants (Lexander *et al.*, 1970). These measurements were made on leaves that had been frozen. It is possible that freezing coagulated some of the protein and so made it unextractable, but earlier (unpublished) experiments at Rothamsted, made on material pulped while fresh, were essentially similar unless very young plants were used.

In India, lucerne given irrigation water and some N fertilizer yielded more than 3t of LP ha^{-1} year^{-1} in spite of an aphid attack (Dev *et al.*, 1974). More than half the yield was from six to eight harvests taken between October and March. Irrigation was essential to get such yields (Savangikar and Joshi, 1976). In some experiments, growth regulators such as "Simazine" have increased the protein content of leaves: Simazine did not increase the LP yield from lucerne (Dev *et al.*, 1974) or hybrid napier grass (*Pennisetum typhoideum* × *P. purpurea*) (Gore and Joshi, 1976b). In some parts of India, lucerne does not survive well; it is treated as an annual rather than as a perennial crop. Until the reason for this poor survival has been found, and possibly corrected, lucerne lacks one of the merits that it has elsewhere.

Byers (1961) noted good extraction of LP from cowpea (*Vigna sinensis* or *unguiculata*). It has many merits; LP made from it has a pleasanter flavour than LP made from lucerne, and its associated rhizobia do not waste 40–60% of their metabolic energy, as those associated with soy and lucerne do, in making hydrogen rather than fixing N (Schubert and Evans, 1976). Cowpea responded consistently to inoculation (Deshmukh and Joshi, 1973). Nevertheless, it was usually given farmyard manure and 20 kg N ha^{-1}; more N gave no extra yield. When grown in summer with that treatment, it yielded 895 kg of LP ha^{-1} from three harvests during 80 days, i.e. it accumulated 11·2 kg of LP ha^{-1} day^{-1} (Deshmukh et al., 1974). An earlier experiment (Deshmukh, PhD thesis) gave 16·9 kg ha^{-1} day^{-1}; if this can be repeated it will be a world record for LP production. These yields should be borne in mind if any attention is being paid to a discouraging forecast of the potentialities of LP (Jamaica, 1965) based on the ludicrous daily yield from cowpea of 0·5 kg ha^{-1}.

Tetrakalai, the tetraploid form of *Phaseolus aureus*, grows well in the wet season in West Bengal where it is used as fodder. It produces LP at rates that would correspond to an annual yield of 1760 kg ha^{-1} if growth had been maintained by irrigation during the dry season. The crop was studied for three years with different harvesting rhythms and spacings of the plants. Bagchi and Matai (1976) conclude that it is an admirable crop which, on better soil than they have access to, would give large yields. Berseem (*Trifolium alexandrinum*) does not yield as well as cowpea, lucerne or tetrakalai, perhaps because its extractability declines unusually rapidly as the crop matures (Shah et al., 1976; Mungikar et al., 1976a). This legume may however become important because it is already familiar in India and Pakistan, and its soft leaf favours economical extraction. At Aurangabad, yields from hybrid napier grass varied from 2·2 to 0·6 t ha^{-1} in spite of liberal use of N fertilizer (Gore et al., 1974). This variation probably depends on the precise interval between successive harvests; the crop quickly becomes fibrous which, as already explained, wastes energy during extraction and diminishes extractability. The yield of DM is greatest with 50-day intervals between harvests, the yield of LP is greatest with 18- to 23-day intervals. Their largest annual yield of LP was 0·98 t ha^{-1}, but reasons are given for thinking that 2 t would be attainable. Yields in West Bengal (Matai et al., 1976) were consistently smaller than at Aurangabad. Yields from the three grasses, *Bracharia mutica*, *Cenchrus glaucus* and *Panicum maximum*, grown further south at Coimbatore (Chandramani *et al.*, 1975a; Balasundaram *et al.*, 1975), depended on the frequency of cutting. *P. maximum* gave 1·3 t of LP ha^{-1} year^{-1} when cut every 30 days, with a daily yield of 15·8 kg during one month, whereas the yield was only 0·5 t when the interval between harvests extended to 45 days.

Although the efficacy of green manuring is doubtful in regions with high soil temperatures, the technique is widely used. Species are chosen which give an abundant yield of N-rich foliage quickly; these are the basic characteristics of a good source of LP. Where green manuring is considered desirable, it would seem better to plough in only the two by-products from LP extraction. Some of the crops already discussed, e.g. lucerne and mustard, are used, a few others, e.g. kudzu (*Pueraria phaseoloides*) (Byers, 1961) and *Sesbania sesban* (Gore and Joshi, 1976a) have been tried as sources of LP. The latter extracted well but was not thought preferable to lucerne or cow pea. However, the extensive range of tropical legumes commonly used as green manures, cover crops, or hedge plants has not yet been adequately studied. This is a promising group of species because the techniques of husbandry are already familiar.

B. BY-PRODUCT LEAVES

The idea of using as a source of LP, leaves that are the by-product of some conventional crop has an obvious appeal. Unfortunately, the range of potential sources is limited. When a dry seed such as maize, rice (*Oryza sativa*) or wheat is harvested, the leaf is withered. Sugar cane (*Saccharum officinarum*) is a possible source. The tops are now usually burnt because, by removing trash, hand-cutting is made easier, and, by removing snakes and scorpions, pleasanter. With mechanized cutting these advantages of burning lose some cogency; furthermore, burnt cane deteriorates rapidly, so that the sugar yield diminishes if there should be an unexpected delay before processing. Even in regions so humid that the tops are still green and moist at the time of harvest, they seldom contain more than 1·2% N (on the DM). That, however, corresponds to at least 0·5 t of protein ha^{-1}; Balasundaram *et al.* (1974a) extracted 108 kg of LP ha^{-1}. Cane tops are so fibrous that the energy expenditure on extraction would be large. If they were used as fibrous material with which to mix leaves such as those from sweet potato and water hyacinth (*Eichornia crassipes*), which are so soft that they are not easily handled in existing machines, some protein would be extracted from the cane tops as well.

The area devoted to cassava (tapioca, manioc, or yuca, *Manihot esculenta* or *utilissima*) is so large, and there are such extensive plans for increased production for food and industrial alcohol, that thorough study of its leaf would be worthwhile. Varieties differ; this may explain why Byers (1961), Singh (1964) and Balasundaram *et al.* (1974a) extracted little protein from it, whereas Balasundaram *et al.* (1974b) and Fafunso and Oke (1977) were more successful. Unfortunately, these papers do not state that the leaves were a genuine by-product taken at the normal time for harvesting the tubers. On the other hand, efficient extraction equipment was not used in these experiments and cassava leaves, when mature, are dry and tough. Other by-product leaves from which LP is not likely to be economically extracted, are those cultivated for the sake of essential oils or perfumes; they are usually subjected to drying or steam distillation, and these processes coagulate protein *in situ*.

Sugar beet (*Beta vulgaris*) and potato leaves are the two most abundant by-products in the temperate zone. Yields from the former, which is largely wasted in Britain though not in Germany or Poland, depend on the weather and the date of harvest; the largest yield during casual trials at Rothamsted was 500 kg LP ha^{-1}. However, even if the yield in commercial practice were only half our experimental yield, the 193 000 ha on which sugar beet is grown in Britain would produce 48 000 t of extracted protein as well as a fibre residue that would be a more attractive cattle fodder than the untreated tops. More research is needed to find out whether the usual technique of separation (Morrison and Pirie, 1961) removes oxalate adequately from the LP.

The outstanding photosynthetic efficiency of sugar beet is due in part to the vertical disposition of its leaves (cf. Monteith, 1977). Towards the end of the growing season, the leaves bend over so that there is more mutual shading and a decline in efficiency. A few experiments suggest that part of the leaf can be harvested early in the year with little diminution in sugar yield—presumably because the new growth keeps more nearly vertical. The idea that some leaf can be harvested from a crop without affecting the yield of the primary product deserves fuller investigation.

As a safeguard against blight, and to facilitate tuber-lifting later, potato haulm is usually destroyed mechanically or with a herbicide at the beginning of September. The main reason for the neglect in Britain of potato haulm as an animal feeding stuff, is fear of poisoning by solanin and other glycoalkaloids. These are separated in the "whey" when LP is made. LP has been made regularly from potato haulm at Rothamsted since 1952, it has also been made in India, Pakistan and

Poland. In nutritive value for rats it resembles LP from other sources (Henry and Ford, 1965; Hanczakowski, 1974).

The yield of LP depends on the potato variety and the date on which the haulm is taken (Carruthers and Pirie, 1975). Some early varieties yield 600 kg ha^{-1}, maincrop can yield 300 in late August, but yield diminishes to 100 or even less by mid-September. Once the idea has been accepted that something valuable could be extracted from potato haulm, prudent farmers would probably harvest haulm a little earlier than usual so as to prevent blight. But tuber weight is still increasing at the beginning of September, and it would therefore seldom be worth-while to take the haulm early simply because of the increased yield of LP. In Britain, early potatoes occupy 30 000 ha and maincrop 230 000 ha. It is reasonable to conclude that about 50 000 t of LP could be extracted from the haulm.

Mobile viners now drop pea (*Pisum sativum*) haulm in the field. The whole crop used to be carted to the viner, and the haulm was sometimes used. From haulm grown on experimental plots, 600 kg LP ha^{-1} can be extracted: that is more protein than is in the peas. Haulm collected from a factory 30 km from Rothamsted did not extract as well as fresh haulm —perhaps because there was an interval of about 3h before the bruised and battered haulm was pulped. The percentage of haulm N that was recovered as protein N varied from 22–47% (Byers and Sturrock, 1965). If we reverted to the old method of vining in a factory, protein could be extracted from the haulm without delay. However, peas may not ultimately be a useful source of LP because there is little leaf on some new varieties.

When maize is allowed to ripen completely, the leaves are too dry and depleted of protein for satisfactory extraction. From some varieties, harvested at the end of August, only 20% of the protein was extractable (Byers and Sturrock, 1965). When harvested earlier, i.e. at the sweet-corn stage, nearly half the protein was extractable and the yield of extracted protein reached 480 kg ha^{-1}. The area devoted to sweet-corn in Britain is too small for it to be an important source of LP.

Open air vegetables occupy 0·17 M ha in England and Wales—the brassicas alone occupy 60 000 ha. Raymond (1977) quotes 4·6 M t as an estimate of the total fresh weight of discarded material. That probably contains nearly 0·1 M t of protein and half of it would be extractable. Material discarded in the field would be fresh and worth using as a source of LP. Much of it is already being collected and some market gardeners pay to dispose of it. Discards at the retail level will probably be too damaged to be worth extracting.

Tekale and Joshi (1976) point out that vegetable-growing gives

Indian farmers a better income than other types of farming, and that recent improvements in vegetable varieties are as sensational as those with the widely publicized new cereal varieties. A survey by FAO (1971) found that vegetable consumption in India was almost the smallest in the world. It is therefore likely that market gardening will soon increase greatly, and it is fortunate that several by-product leaves have already been studied there. Yields of LP from the brassicas were 90–160 kg ha^{-1} (Matai *et al.*, 1973; Deshmukh *et al.*, 1974; Tekale and Joshi, 1976). LP made from cauliflower leaves, taken as a by-product, was a useful supplement to wheat in a rat diet and contained 0·6 mg β-carotene g^{-1} (Goel *et al.*, 1977). Other useful by-product leaves from market gardens were chicory (*Cichorium intybus*) (Mahadeviah and Singh, 1968), sweet potato (Byers, 1961; Balasundaram *et al.*, 1974a, b; Deshmukh *et al.*, 1974), and radish (Tekale and Joshi, 1976). Hussain *et al.*, (1968) estimate that 60 000 t of LP could be extracted from by-product leaves in Pakistan, half coming from radish. The potentiality of groundnut leaves (*Arachis hypogaea*) depends on the rainfall in the period before the seed is harvested. In Ghana they extracted reasonably well (Byers, 1961); in India and Nigeria poorly (quoted in Pirie, 1971a).

Plants are grown on such a large scale as sources of fibre that these leaves deserve careful study. LP has been extracted from cotton (*Gossypium hirsutum*), but it would be difficult to collect leaves after the usual procedures of chemical defoliation. The leafy upper part of ramie (*Boehmeria nivea*) is cut off and left in the field before the stem is harvested (Byrom, 1956), and the various tall species from which jute and similar fibres are made, usually have to be scutched in the field before retting. Some of these leaves are inconveniently mucilaginous; this may be a varietal matter and so could be avoided. Some of the other fibre-plants are less probable sources of LP. Sisal (*Agave sisalana*) has an acid leaf, that defect could be partly counteracted by scutching in dilute sodium carbonate. Abaca (*Musa textilis*), like banana (*Musa sapientum*), contains phenolic material that will probably interfere with extraction. Although these difficulties may be overcome, it would be unwise to assume that every protein-rich leaf is a potential source of LP.

C. TREE LEAVES

Few tree leaves have been studied; elder (*Sambucus niger*) is the only one from which LP extraction has been satisfactory. With curious uniformity the leaves from other trees, even when thoroughly disintegrated by methods that would not be practicable on a large scale, have given poor percentage extractions. Tree leaves are the main food for many animals, and chemical analyses (Siren *et al.*, 1970; Siren, 1973) show that in protein content and amino acid composition they are similar to conventional crop plants. They therefore deserve thorough study to see whether young leaves taken from coppices would extract better, or whether some changes in the technique of extraction would be effective. Work such as this is important because a food-producing tree crop would be the ideal replacement for tropical rain forest. It is now obvious that ecological disaster follows attempts to cultivate annual plants in regions where there is frequent intense rain. Unless the soil is protected by the roots of perennial plants, erosion is a serious risk. The trees usually thought of as replacements for natural rain forest produce an exportable commodity such as rubber or palm oil, and it would be advantageous if some of the trees produced protein for local consumption.

D. WATER WEEDS

The untended, mixed growth of weeds on land is not a potential source of LP although some individual species from the mixture may ultimately be cultivated as sources. The wild growth is unsuitable because it is unmanured and grows on rough sites from which collection would be difficult—otherwise it would not have weeds on it. The situation is different with water weeds. Obviously they do not suffer from drought, and they are often abundantly manured. When this abundance is supplied by sewage, or the run-off from too heavily manured farmland, it is called eutrophication. The excessive growth of water weeds is harmful for many reasons: it increases the waste of water by evaporation in hot countries, interferes with flow in irrigation ditches, interferes with navigation, and is a health hazard when it harbours disease vectors such as snails. Much effort is therefore expended on attempts at control. Mechanical destruction, herbicides and "biological control" leave the remains of the weed *in situ*. These methods may control growth, but they do not affect eutrophication. The killed plants rot in the water and most of the elements they contain, and the excreta of an unharvested agent of "biological control", are likely to return to the water. When herbicides are used, they and their breakdown products may remain in the water and so make it unsuitable, or less suitable, for irrigation. If water weeds were used, and so removed from the water they infest, that water would not only be freed from infestation, but would be depleted of the elements causing eutrophication. This would economically convert a problem into an asset.

Water hyacinth (*Eichornia crassipes*) is the most abundant, troublesome and decorative of the weeds. It is said to cover 200 000 ha in

India, and similar areas elsewhere. The total area is probably more than 1 M ha with an annual growth of 10–30 t DM ha^{-1}. The DM of the whole floating plant contains about 2·5% N, the leaves contain up to 5%. An impressive amount of protein is therefore potentially available. Unfortunately it does not extract readily unless alkali is added (Ghosh, 1967; Taylor *et al.*, 1971; Matai, 1976); extraction is being commercialized in the Philippines (Monsod, 1976). Pieterse (1974) reviewed the literature on the biology and use of water hyacinth in a perhaps unreasonably pessimistic manner. Two other floating weeds, Nile cabbage (*Pistia stratiotes*) and the fern *Salvinia auriculata*, extract as badly as water hyacinth at their natural pH (about 6) (Byers, 1961; Matai *et al.*, 1971; Matai, 1976; Rothamsted unpublished). The effect of adding alkali to them has not apparently been tried.

It would be easy and economical to collect these floating weeds with equipment mounted on a barge, process the extract on it, and discharge the soluble material. The compact extracted fibre and LP would have to be transferred to land less often than would be necessary with bulky fresh weed. That method of working would obviously not control eutrophication as effectively as processing on land.

Protein appears to extract more easily from rooted than from floating water weeds: there is no obvious physiological basis for this distinction. From mixed weeds collected in Hertfordshire, 47% of the protein was extractable (Pirie, 1959); from a water lily (*Nymphaea lotus*) in Ghana, 40% (Byers, 1961); and from one in Alabama (*Nymphaea odorata*) 61% (Boyd, 1968). Boyd (1968, 1971) lists several other species that extract well, *Justicia americana* yielded 300 kg of LP ha^{-1} when harvested in May or June. Nothing seems to be known about the readiness with which these plants regrow after harvest. Unfortunately the reeds (*Typha* and *Phragmites*), which produce very heavy crops in suitable regions (Dykyjova, 1971), do not extract well.

No measurements seem to have been made of the extractability of protein from algae or angiosperms growing in sea water. If the problem of collection could be solved, the angiosperms seem to have potentialities. Thus turtle grass (*Thalassia testudinum*) is as productive as most conventional crop plants; its rhizosphere fixes 100–500 kg N h^{-1} year^{-1} (Patriquin and Knowles, 1972). Most of the large algae (seaweeds) contain too little protein to make extraction probable. Those species that are rich in protein, e.g. *Ulva* and *Porphyra* are already used as food.

E. MISCELLANEOUS UNCONVENTIONAL SPECIES OF LEAF

Protein extraction has been attempted from about 300 species of leaf.

A fairly complete list of references to papers on them has been published (Pirie, 1978), there is therefore no need to survey this literature again. Furthermore, so little information was given about the antecedents of most of the leaf samples, that it is not possible to calculate the possible annual yield. We have now passed beyond this phase of "Natural History" in which every extraction held some interest. Unsystematic studies may suggest that a species is worthy of detailed study; it is only in exceptional circumstances that it would be worth publishing results on plants that were not cultivated on land of known manurial status, and harvested at several stages of growth.

Of the quarter million species of flowering plant, the conventional crop plants may well be the most suitable when used in conventional ways and grown in climates similar to those of the region in which they originated. Hitherto, we have decided which crops should be grown, and have then extended their range into increasingly improbable regions. The alternative approach is to examine the species that already grow well in a region to see whether some use, in this context the extraction of LP, could be made of them. Attention should first be given to species that are already cultivated on a small scale, though not used as sources of leaf. For example: quinoa (*Chenopodium quinoa*) is cultivated for its seeds in the Andes, its soft texture makes protein extraction economical (Pirie, 1966a), and it was one of the species investigated in detail in the laboratory by Carlsson (1975). Mustard is cultivated mainly as a green manure in Britain, and its relative, *Brassica nigra*, is an oil-seed crop in India. If harvested young it regrows well and gives excellent yields of LP (Matai *et al.*, 1973; 1976). *Brassica carinata*, which is used as an oil-seed crop in Ethiopia, appears to have potentialities in Texas as a source of LP (Brown *et al.*, 1975). A more unexpected suggestion is that *Tithonia tagetiflora*, usually cultivated because of the beauty of its flowers, should be used; it regrows well after harvesting and responds vigorously to N manuring (Deshmukh *et al.*, 1974; Mungikar *et al.*, 1976b).

There seems to be little substance in the argument sometimes advanced that LP would be more acceptable if it were known to be made from leaves already familiar as green vegetables. So few communities eat vegetables to a desirable and physiologically reasonable extent (Pirie, 1975a; 1976a, c), that nothing would be gained by extracting protein from leaves that could be eaten in the natural state by adults. The situation, as will be pointed out later, is different with infants. Instead of extracting LP from edible leaves, it would be better to see whether some forage crops could be used as leafy vegetables, as young lucerne and oats (*Avena sativa*) already are in some places.

Nevertheless, Gunetileke (quoted in Pirie, 1971a) claims impressive yields from *Basella alba*, and Fafunso and Bassir (1976) extracted *Corchorus olitorus*, *Solanum incanum*, *Solanum nodiflorum* and *Talinum triangulare*. The yields of LP were however no greater than those from forage crops.

Areas of water tend to be dominated by one species of plant which persists in spite of regular cutting—hence the earlier discussion of protein extraction from water weeds. A single plant species e.g. bracken (*Pteridium aquilinum*), dominates an area of land only when no adequate use is being made of that land. Regular harvesting quickly alters the composition of the sward, and growth will soon become minimal if the nutrients removed by harvesting are not restored. In the long run therefore, seemingly abundant "weeds", growing untended, are not a probable source of LP. In the short run however, the use of "weeds" may be a valuable step towards eradication. *Parthenium hysterophorus* has recently become a troublesome weed in India; the extraction of LP from it (Savangikar and Joshi, 1978) may be a step towards control. As a result of that work the possibility arises that it may be possible to make LP as a by-product if the related plant, *P. argentatum*, should, as is suggested (Yokoyama *et al.*, 1977), be commercialized as a source of rubber.

Successful exploitation of a wild plant, or weed, necessitates its domestication and cultivation as a new crop. It will not be cultivated unless it is demonstrably superior in some respect to an existing crop. Wild plants have a few common defects that can probably be quickly eliminated. Though some grow vigorously, some seem unprepossessing simply because they are growing on poor soil. Even with good husbandry some, which may extract well in the laboratory, grow slowly. A glance at pictures of the wild ancestors of our crop plants show what improvements skilled selection can bring about. Uniformity in the time of germination is an important characteristic for which conventional crop plants have been selected. Wild plants tend to be much less uniform: this is an understandable aspect of evolution for it ensures that every individual plant of a species will not suffer should there be inclement weather throughout a region at about the time of germination. Uneven germination should not be considered a serious defect in an uncultivated species: uniformity could probably be introduced quickly by deliberate selection.

Many uncultivated plants are poisonous because of the presence of alkaloids and similar substances. This is not a serious defect because alkaloids would be separated from the LP during the process of extraction. Some species, however, are even more strongly flavoured than lucerne and it may be difficult to remove the flavour. An extreme example is *Leonotis taraxifolia* which grows vigorously in Jamaica, extracts well, and gives an unuseable product. It is therefore important to assess the flavour of a carefully made preparation of LP at an early stage in the study of any new species.

The primary reason for suggesting that wild plants should be investigated is that potentially valuable species may have been overlooked 5000 to 15 000 years ago when most of the species on which we depend were chosen. Another reason, stressed by Hudson (1975, 1976) and by Wareing and Allen (1977), is the meteorological situation in Britain and several other countries. In spring, by the time there is abundant light and moisture, and day-time air temperature is adequate for growth, soil temperature is still so low that the roots of conventional crops do not absorb nutrients. But low soil temperatures, at both the beginning and the end of the year, do not stop the growth of many weeds. For purely scientific reasons it would be interesting to know the basis of this physiological difference between crops and some weeds. It is not impossible that the useful ability to grow in cold soil could then be introduced into some conventional crops. At Rothamsted, nettles (*Urtica dioica*) yielded 612 kg ha^{-1} of LP from one harvest; this is more than we got from any other weed (Pirie, 1959). Carlsson (1975) put nettles near the top in his survey of 71 species, but concluded that the Chenopodiums were probably the group most worthy of fuller investigation.

It would be unreasonable to devote more than a small fraction of the total effort put into research on LP to the study of unconventional species. Nevertheless, this study would be a useful piece of academic research. Besides the possibility that the period of active photosynthesis could be extended if more plant species were included in the cropping sequence, diversity, either of species growing together or grown in succession, offers many possible advantages. Suitably designed mixtures would contain species that grew when others were dormant, that exploited the full depth of soil for nutrients and water, and that were not all susceptible to the same pests and diseases.

III. Techniques for Extracting and Separating Protein

A. EXTRACTION IN AGRONOMIC RESEARCH

The feasibility of LP extraction, and the characteristics of leaves from which extraction would be easy, were established by work with domestic meat mincers, food mixers, three-roll paint mills etc. When co-operative work started under the auspices of the International Biological Program (Pirie, 1976b) greater uniformity and repeatability were needed. A pulper and press combination was designed (Davys and Pirie, 1969; Davys *et al.*, 1969) that gave repeatable results on 3-kg samples of leaf—a reasonable quantity considering the non-uniformity of field crops. The pulper is a fixed hammer mill that cannot become clogged with partly disintegrated pulp, the press applies 2–3 kgf cm^{-2} in a repeatable manner. Both parts of the unit can easily be carried. Older methods of pulping, followed by hand-squeezing in a cloth, extract a greater percentage of the protein, but differences in experimental care and assiduity can affect results by a factor of two. Repeatability, rather than completeness of extraction, was the objective in designing this combination. Large-scale extractors, especially if the fibre is re-extracted, may bring out half again as much LP as is brought out by the IBP combination. In quantitative work, especially with crops harvested sequentially so that only a few kilograms can be taken each time, it is probably essential to use separate pieces of equipment for pulping and pressing. Autolytic changes are rapid in pulp; there should therefore be the shortest possible interval between the two processes.

B. SMALL-SCALE ROUTINE EXTRACTION

The IBP pulper, though designed as an agronomic tool, is convenient for small-scale preparative work. It can be hand-fed at 1–2 kg of crop min^{-1}, with a mechanized feed it takes 3–4 kg min^{-1}. Working with a small belt-press (Pirie 1971a; 1978), this makes a convenient unit with which to produce 2–10 kg lots of LP; units such as this are used in several countries.

Extraction in one operation is obviously better when all that is required is a supply of juice and dewatered fibre. Large three-roll sugar cane mills, and conventional screw expellers, have been tried; for various reasons (Pirie, 1978) they are unsatisfactory. A conventional screw expeller applies pressure, rubbing to liberate juice is incidental. It should be possible to design a unit in which the crop is adequately disintegrated while being pushed into the part of a simple expeller in which pressure is applied. The prototype (Pirie, 1977b; Butler and Pirie, 1978) is a perforated cylindrical barrel within which a slow-moving conical rotor carries an interrupted flight, or set of flights. The crop is fed in by an auger at the end where the cone is narrow. The auger is also interrupted so that the crop is extensively disintegrated before it enters the barrel. Because crops vary greatly in texture and DM content, arrangements are made to vary the feeding rate of the auger and the extent to which the cone is inserted into the barrel, i.e. the thickness of the emerging shell of pressed fibre. More detailed description is unnecessary because the unit is still being improved. The protoype takes 1–2 kg of crop h^{-1} and runs on about 300 watts. This is 10–20% the power consumption of the pulper and belt-press combination. Larger units could be made on the same principle.

C. COMMERCIAL PRODUCTION UNITS

A scaled-up form of the pulper and belt-press combination is used to process 5 t of crop h^{-1} at the National Institute for Research in Dairying (Connell, 1975). The various units that are making leaf juice commercially, e.g. BOCM-Silcock and France-Luzerne, use screw expellers designed for pressing other materials. Bruhn *et al.* (1977), in Wisconsin, make leaf pulp on a large scale by extruding the crop through holes in a cylindrical die—as in a pelleting press. They stress that this is an interim arrangement and that much more research is needed on the process of extracting protein-rich juice from leaves.

D. COAGULATION AND SEPARATION

In agronomic work, a sample of the leaf extract is precipitated with trichloroacetic acid. This should be done quickly because of autolysis, but there is no urgency about the subsequent analyses. Heating is the simplest and most widely used method of bulk coagulation: other methods will be described later when fractionation is discussed. Around neutrality, all the protein in a leaf extract coagulates in a few seconds at 70°C. Brief heating is sufficient; sudden heating is, however, desirable because it produces a curd that is hard, granular and easy to manage on a filter (Morrison and Pirie, 1961). It also minimizes enzymic changes. All the juice enzymes are not inactivated at 70°C and they may cause changes in the protein during prolonged storage. With a crop such as lucerne, which contains more chlorophyllase than most crops, heating to 100°C is advisable. Otherwise, the enzyme splits phytol from some of the chlorophyll and the resulting chlorophyllides readily lose magnesium to yield pheophorbides (Arkcoll and Holden, 1973; Holden, 1974). Protein made from a lucerne extract heated slowly to 80°C contained enough pheophorbide to photosensitize rats (Lohrey *et al.*, 1974; Tapper *et al.*, 1975). Preparations heated to 100°C absorb atmospheric oxygen more slowly than those heated to 70°C (Shah, 1968), but there is so much non-enzymic oxidation when dry material is stored without protection that this difference is probably not significant. The only known disadvantage of heating extracts to 100°C rather than 80°C is the extra consumption of steam.

As soon as a leaf is pulped, autolysis begins; the rate at which protein is digested depends on the leaf species (Tracey, 1948; Singh, 1962; Batra *et al.*, 1976) and probably also on the age and nutritional status of the crop. For maximum recovery of protein, there should be no avoidable delay between pulping and heat coagulation: some delay is advisable if nucleic acid in the LP is considered deleterious. As often, incompatible requirements necessitate a compromise. The coagulum can conveniently be separated by pouring the coagulated juice into cloth "stockings" and leaving them to drip for as long as "whey" runs out freely; they are then pressed at $0.3–0.5$ kgf cm^{-1} (30–50 kPa) for a few hours. Pressure is simply applied by means of a weighted lever. It is more important to press thin layers on grids that allow the juice to escape freely, than to press heavily. With larger quantities of leaf, some form of pump-fed filter press will be needed.

Dry leaf powders are used as flavouring agents in many parts of the world, there is therefore no universal dislike of "leafy" flavours. However, during the initial phase of introducing LP as a human food, as much flavour as possible should be removed. Furthermore, some potential sources of LP, e.g. potato haulm, contain water-soluble materials that are slightly toxic, and all contain sugars that will slowly form protein complexes with diminished nutritive value (Maillard reaction). The curd, after being thoroughly pressed, should therefore be washed.

The coagulum from a suddenly heated extract can easily be filtered off; when re-suspended in water, at leaf pH, filtration is difficult. It becomes easy if salt is added to the water or if the suspension is acidified to about pH 4. It is not essential to measure this pH. Different samples of press-cake are so similar that it is safe to assume that 200 ml of 2 N acid will be sufficient for 1 kg (wet weight) of cake, and the pH is not critical. Besides facilitating filtration, acidification ensures freedom from alkaloids and results in a product with the keeping qualities of cheese pickles or sauerkraut. Unfortunately, acidification converts the chlorophylls completely to pheophytins through loss of magnesium. The dull green is less attractive than the bright colour of neutral LP, and the risk of pheophorbide formation is increased. There is more loss of carotene from acid than neutral LP and the unsaturated fatty acids in it are more rapidly oxidized. If LP is regarded as something to be made on the farm, these defects of acid washing must probably be accepted. If it is regarded as an industrial product, it could be washed without acidification, and separated by centrifugation or, if washed by acidification and filtration, the washed, pressed and crumbled coagulum could be neutralized again by exposure to ammonia vapour.

Coagulum containing 40% DM is easily made by pressing. If the residual water contains the amount of soluble material usually found in leaf extracts, about 7·5% of the DM of the LP will be this extraneous soluble material. A less adequately pressed coagulum may contain 80% of water, and soluble material will then account for about 20% of the DM. Similarly, when a well-pressed coagulum is re-suspended in enough water to make the concentration of soluble material <1 g litre^{-1}, and pressed again till it contains 40% DM only 0·15% of the final cake will be soluble. The recommended standard is $<1%$ soluble material (Pirie, 1971a).

IV. PREPARATION OF FRACTIONS

As a prelude to making enzyme or virus preparations from leaf extracts, chloroplasts and their fragments have, for half a century, been coagulated by freezing, addition of calcium salts, judicious addition of solvents such as ethanol, or of weak acids. It is unlikely that these methods could be used in large scale work either because of expense or of the need for very close adherence to precise conditions. The methods that are most likely to be applicable are heating, the addition of water-immiscible solvents, ionized polymers, or high-speed centrifuging. The coagulum is loosely called "chloroplast" protein because it carries with it the chlorophylls and their green breakdown products; the protein that remains in solution is, equally loosely, called "cytoplasm" protein. The "chloroplast" fraction carries out with it components of such structures as nuclei, mitochondria and ribosomes; when made from leaf extracts that have been inadequately strained, or made from inadequately washed leaves, it also carries any fibre and dust present in the extract. For all these reasons, "chloroplast" protein usually contains 6–8% N, unfractionated protein contains 9–11%, and "cytoplasm" protein may contain 16%. "Chloroplast" protein is less digestible both *in vitro* and *in vivo*; the quality of the remaining protein is therefore improved if it is removed. These are real merits and it may be that when LP is produced industrially it will be worthwhile separating the pale "cytoplasm" fraction because it could be presented as a food in more ways than the "chloroplast" fraction. But the separation is not simple enough to be regarded as a farm operation. Whatever method is used for fractionating leaf extracts, the precise conditions that separate the "chloroplast" fraction completely, with minimum loss of "cytoplasm" protein, probably depend not only on the leaf species, but also on its age, fertilizer treatment, and the weather to which it was exposed. Fractionation is unlikely to be satisfactory if a prearranged schedule is followed; instead, some preliminary laboratory examination of each type of extract will probably be necessary.

Most of the protein in a leaf is present initially in the chloroplasts. Even the refined methods used to separate them in the laboratory release some of their contents. The rougher methods used in bulk extraction cause still more damage. One factor that distinguishes species classified as good sources of LP is probably chloroplast fragility. However, it is unlikely that species will be found, or conditions of extraction devised, that will produce extracts in which less than 60% of the protein is in the "chloroplast" fraction. This fraction contains the β-carotene: it will be a pity if it is all used as animal feed in countries where people lack vitamin A.

A. FRACTIONATION BY HEATING

Rouelle's (1773) method of heating in two stages is still the most widely used fractionation procedure. Heat coagulation is so rapid that even momentary overheating must be avoided. About 100 ml of juice can be swirled in a flask while being heated directly. When working on a large scale it is better to maintain one surface of a heat exchanger at the required temperature and to let the juice flow over the other surface while it is being continuously scraped (Pirie, 1964a). The juice should be cooled as it comes out of the exchanger; it must then be centrifuged because the curd is too soft and gelatinous to be collected on a filter. Coagulation begins at 40–55°C depending on the pH (4·5–6·5), the species, and probably the age and physiological state of the plant (Byers, 1967b; Lexander et al., 1970; Carlsson, 1975). "Cytoplasm" protein coagulates when the juice from which "chloroplast" protein has been removed is heated to 80 or 100°C. In spite of the 200 years during which the process has been used, it has been patented (Bickoff and Kohler, 1974).

B. CENTRIFUGAL SEPARATION

Centrifugal separation of "chloroplast" protein on a commercial scale depends on choosing crops with chloroplasts that do not break into small fragments, and on the availability of robust centrifuges that can be run economically at the required speed. Experience from research on plant viruses shows that chloroplasts and their fragments sediment at 8000–50 000 times gravity. For sedimentation in a continuous-flow centrifuge it is usually necessary to centrifuge at 100 000 times gravity. The material removed by high-speed centrifuging is similar to, but not identical with, the material removed by heating to 50 or 60°C; the supernatant fluid after centrifuging usually contains some protein that coagulates when heated to 60°C. If it should prove to be feasible on a commercial scale, centrifuging will be a valuable pre-treatment in making good quality LP from some species. Thus LP made from potato leaf juice that had been centrifuged at 25 000 times gravity contained 11–12% N whereas without that treatment it contaihed only 9–10% (Carruthers and Pirie, 1975).

C. FRACTIONATION WITH SOLVENTS

Material similar to the "chloroplast" protein that coagulates on gentle heating is precipitated more easily than the remainder of the protein by solvents such as methanol, ethanol and isopropanol. But 10–20% of solvent has to be added and solvent recovery would probably be un-economic. Chloroplasts and their fragments are readily coagulated by many water-immiscible solvents. Slade *et al.* (1945) used amyl alcohol; Allison (quoted in Hove and Bailey, 1975) used *n*-butanol. Some of the halogenated hydrocarbons have been used in similar processes: they may be preferable in the laboratory, but they are more expensive. Furthermore, if the "whey" is to be used as a culture medium for micro-organisms, there are advantages in using a solvent that can be metabol-ized by micro-organisms and that acts as a coagulant at a concentration small enough not to inhibit their growth.

D. MISCELLANEOUS METHODS OF FRACTIONATION

Chibnall's original method (1939) of removing the larger particles, including "chloroplast" protein, by filtering leaf extracts through a 3 cm thick pad of paper pulp has occasionally been used by others (e.g. Lugg, 1939; Davies *et al.*, 1952; Yemm and Folkes, 1953; Chibnall *et al.*, 1963). In the original form, it is satisfactory for making "cytoplasm" protein, but the "chloroplast" fraction would be difficult to recover in useable form. Technical developments in the production of smooth surfaced membranes of graded porosity, that can be scraped clear of "chloroplast" protein when they get clogged, may make such a method practicable on a commercial scale.

The "cytoplasm" protein in solutions that have been freed from "chloroplast" protein by any of the methods described above can be concentrated five to ten-fold by ultrafiltration (Tragardh, 1974; Knuckles *et al.*, 1975). Some of the brown pigments and soluble salts are removed so that a pale product containing 93% protein can be made by precipatating, with acid, alcohol or heat, the material retained on the filter. If the temperature is kept near 0°C during acid precipitation, the precipitate will redissolve at neutrality or at pHs <3. Because of its solubility, the product would fit more smoothly than heat coagulated material into the conventional operations of the food industry, but it would cost much more than heat coagulated material.

Before high-speed centrifuges were standard pieces of laboratory equipment, stable and clarified leaf extracts were often made for serological and other studies by adding enough alkaline phosphate to precipitate the Ca^{2+} in the extract. The calcium phosphate precipitate carries out with it all the chloroplast protein: it also carries out the nucleic acid (Pirie, 1974). This procedure deserves fuller investigation. Coagulation of "chloroplast" protein by polyacrylamide resin may depend on a somewhat similar process and could be useful in commercial practice. Concentrated extracts from some plant species, e.g. various tobacco (*Nicotiana*) varieties, deposit crystals containing ribulose diphosphate carboxylase when dialysed (Chan *et al.*, 1972). In spite of the technical difficulty of large scale dialysis, this process is suggested as a means of making edible protein. If this suggestion is being taken seriously, precipitation of "chloroplast" protein by the addition of phosphate would seem to be the most suitable first step.

V. The Composition of LP

The technique used to make the leaf extract, and the species of leaf, affect the gross composition of LP. If the crop is not washed before extraction, surface dust will contaminate the LP. If some form of screw expeller is used for the extraction, rather than the pulper and belt-press combination, there will be more fibre in the LP. Extracts from some species contain so much polysaccharide and phenolic material, which coagulate along with the protein, that the LP may contain only 6% N. The composition of material containing as little protein as this has not been studied in detail.

The most convenient and thorough method of washing is to dump the crop into a tank of water, and drag it out continuously under a fine spray of water at a rate suited to the capacity of the equipment used for extraction. Wetting the crop in this way, although it increases the volume of juice handled, increases the percentage of protein extracted. A crop that will be washed must be harvested by a reaper of the old-fashioned type with a reciprocating blade. If it is harvested by a machine with flails or a rotor, and is then blown into a trailer, it will not only be contaminated with soil sucked up by the harvester, but will also be so bruised that much of the LP will be lost during the washing. There is no need to wash the crop if the LP is intended as animal feed.

A. COMPONENTS SOLUBLE IN LIPID SOLVENTS

The DM of unfractionated LP contains 20–30% of material soluble in the usual lipid solvents. The amount of lipid is often underestimated because, although the material is largely soluble in ether or petroleum ether after it has been extracted, these solvents release only part of it from combination with other components of LP. The remainder can be extracted by a mixture of chloroform and methanol, or by a mixture of alcohol and ether in the presence of a little strong acid (Holden, 1952; Buchanan, 1969a, b; Byers, 1971b). The most noticeable, but nutritionally least important, component is the mixture of chlorophylls and their breakdown products. The importance of processing leaf extracts in such a manner that pheophorbide is not formed, has already been stressed. This hazard is easily avoided.

Nutritionally and commercially the carotenoids are the most important components of the lipid in LP. Xanthophyll is the commercially valuable component because it makes chicken's legs yellow (Colker et al., 1948) and that enhances their appeal in many countries: trivial as this may seem, it is the main reason for commercial production of LP at present (1978). The nutritionally valuable component is β-carotene (pro-vitamin A) because vitamin A deficiency is widespread in those communities that no longer eat dark green leafy vegetables regularly. There is little destruction of carotene during the separation and coagulation of leaf extracts; thereafter, especially if exposed to light, air and slightly acid conditions, it is destroyed (Walsh and Hauge, 1953; Arkcoll, 1973; Arkcoll and Holden, 1973). If protected from these deleterious agents, little carotene is lost during many months storage. Some carotene still remained in carefully stored lucerne meal after 27 years (Zscheile, 1973). The β-carotene content has not been measured on many samples of LP, but all contained 1 mg g^{-1} when freshly made and some contained 2 mg g^{-1}.

Several recent papers e.g. Lima et al. (1965); Buchanan (1969a, b); Hudson and Karis (1973), confirm the old observation that leaf lipids are rich in doubly and trebly unsaturated fatty acids. The dominant acids are palmitic (16:0), palmitoleic (16:1), stearic (18:0), oleic (18:1), linoleic (18:2) and linolenic (18:3). These unsaturated acids usually make up half the total amount of fatty acid, but there are marked apparent differences in their ratios in different species. The reality of these differences is not at present certain because the fatty acid pattern of leaves changes with age and with even brief exposure to cold (Farkas and Deri-Hadlaczky, 1975). The point deserves thorough study because of the nutritional importance of some unsaturated fatty acids (Ciba Foundation, 1972), and because their presence in LP complicates preservation and storage. Hudson and Karis (1974) point out that some leaf crops produce more lipid ha^{-1} in a shorter time than most oil-seed crops.

B. CARBOHYDRATES

The amount of starch in LP depends on the species used and the weather at the time of harvest. There is so much starch in extracts from some leaves, notably peas taken on a sunny day, that grains collect as a white sediment if the extract is allowed to stand. Unless the starch is centrifuged out of the extract before coagulation, 5% (or even more) will be present in the LP. Even when no starch grains are visible in the extract, there is usually 5–10% of carbohydrate in LP. By graded hydrolysis followed by paper chromatography, Festenstein (1976) showed that this carbohydrate differs in composition from the carbohydrate mixture in the "whey" that is filtered from the coagulum. That is to say the presence of carbohydrate is not a consequence of the LP being inadequately washed. When alkali is added during the extraction, the carbohydrates content is increased because of the presence of pectic substances. Nucleic acid supplies a little of the carbohydrate in most preparations.

C. MISCELLANEOUS COMPONENTS

If LP has been thoroughly washed and pressed it will contain less than 1% of water-soluble material. Consequently it will be nearly free from B vitamins and similar leaf components. It will however contain useful amounts of vitamins E and K.

Much of the ash in LP comes from surface dust, but some grasses contain silica that is partly extracted and coagulated along with protein. It may not therefore be possible to make from these species LP that meets the desirable standard: <3% ash and <1% acid-insoluble ash (Pirie, 1971a). Silica appears to be harmless. Nevertheless, when much ash is present, the preparative methods used should be examined carefully to see whether they, rather than the species used, are at fault.

The presence of lipid, carbohydrate and ash does not adequately account for the small N content of some LP preparations. Much of the discrepancy is due to the presence of phenolic material. Phenolics tend to increase in crops as a result of maturity or stress (e.g. Milic 1972; Wong, 1973). When studying the extent to which they impede protein extraction, and damage what protein is extracted, some of the methods that are used in the laboratory to promote the extraction of enzymes or viruses should be tried. For example: air could be excluded during extraction (Cohen *et al.*, 1956; Pirie, 1961), a reducing environment could be maintained with —SH compounds (Hageman and Waygood, 1959; Anderson and Rowan, 1967), or substances such as nicotine could be added to compete with protein for conjugation with phenolics (Thung and Want, 1951; Thresh, 1956). More recently, polyvinylpyrolidone has been used in many operations in which it is desirable to sequestrate tanning agents. When added to grass or lucerne extracts before heat coagulation the amount of phenolic material in the LP was halved (Fafunso and Byers, 1977). Methods such as these could probably not be used in large scale work, but experiments along these lines show what the potential is and which factors prevent it from being fully exploited. In large scale work, it is already possible to make quantitative and qualitative improvements by adding sulphite during the extraction; it may be possible to devise methods for removing phenolics while the crop is being washed before being pulped.

D. AMINO ACIDS

A striking feature of early amino acid analyses on LP, amply confirmed by later analyses, is the similarity of preparations from different species in spite of the well known differences in the enzyme activities of leaves of differing age and from different species. However, apart from ribulose diphosphate carboxylase, each individual enzyme probably accounts for such a small fraction of the total leaf protein that, although the enzymes differ in amino acid composition, the average composition is little affected by changes in enzyme ratios. Therefore, one of the less necessary pieces of equipment to install in an institute where work on LP is starting is an amino acid analyser. If a species should be found that extracts well and is promising from an agronomic standpoint, perhaps from a family from which LP had not hitherto been made, it is likely that some institute already equipped with an analyser will be willing to analyse one or two samples. In the unlikely event that the LP has an unusual composition, more detailed co-operation can be organized.

Byers (1971a,b) analysed many preparations; Table I summarizes her results with three types of preparation from three species. The differences hardly lie outside the range of unavoidable uncertainty in amino acid analysis. This uncertainty arises not only from uncertainty about the areas of the peaks on the elution profile given by an automatic analyser, but also from the fact that, if less than 100% of the N in the sample is accounted for in the amino acids recovered, there is no guarantee that the losses are distributed among the amino acids in the same way in all samples. Nevertheless, small differences in amino acid composition probably exist. This was demonstrated by an elaborate

TABLE I. Amino acid acid composition (expressed as g amino acid in 100 g of recovered amino acids) in fractionated and unfractionated leaf protein from three species. Ammonia, cyst(e)ine and tryptophan are excluded

Amino acid	"Chloroplast"			Unfractionated			"Cytoplasm"		
	Barley	Lupin	Chinese cabbage	Barley	Lupin	Chinese cabbage	Barley	Lupin	Chinese cabbage
Aspartic acid	9·75	10·10	9·86	9·57	10·22	10·01	9·62	10·01	10·05
Threonine	4·82	4·97	4·87	5·07	5·01	5·22	5·41	5·04	5·43
Serine	4·85	5·15	5·24	4·40	4·68	4·50	4·10	4·13	4·12
Glutamic acid	11·00	11·35	11·28	11·41	11·88	11·91	11·94	12·15	12·21
Proline	4·88	5·06	4·98	4·68	4·79	4·72	4·62	4·79	4·46
Glycine	6·12	5·97	6·53	5·64	5·69	5·35	5·38	5·32	5·29
Alanine	7·05	6·40	6·45	6·71	6·21	6·10	6·52	5·99	5·91
Valine	6·16	6·10	5·64	6·37	6·27	6·06	6·50	6·32	6·17
Methionine	2·28	1·90	2·11	2·24	1·70	1·94	2·39	1·76	2·13
Isoleucine	5·25	5·76	5·03	4·95	4·93	4·62	4·74	4·42	4·38
Leucine	10·43	10·68	10·40	9·33	9·75	9·29	8·42	9·21	8·79
Tyrosine	4·49	4·20	4·19	4·50	4·61	4·71	4·92	5·56	5·07
Phenylalanine	6·97	7·16	6·85	6·22	6·24	6·24	5·84	5·82	5·87
Lysine	5·60	4·78	5·23	6·61	6·60	7·08	7·06	7·30	7·23
Histidine	1·82	1·91	2·00	2·34	2·31	2·42	2·66	2·82	2·65
Arginine	6·29	6·13	6·33	6·89	6·35	6·46	7·01	6·67	6·89

From Byers (1971a)

statistical study (Byers, 1971b). Essentially, the differences between the largest and smallest values for each amino acid were found for 39 LP samples. Then, taking each sample in turn, the amount of each amino acid in it was compared with the amount in each of the other 39 minus 1 samples. The criterion of comparison was the extent to which each difference was less than the difference, for that amino acid, in the whole group of 39. Because cyst(e)ine and tryptophan are partly or wholly destroyed during acid hydrolysis, this was done for only 16 amino acids. It nevertheless produced a formidable collection of figures. The next process may metaphorically be described as arranging the figures in 39 minus 1 dimensional space and instructing a computer to search for the co-ordinates of the plane in that space that contained the largest differences in amino acid composition. Figure 1 shows the 39 samples plotted in accordance with these two co-ordinates. Although the three types of preparation, from three species, are not separated completely, it is clear that there is some grouping into nine categories.

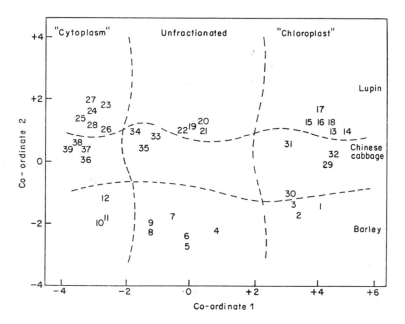

FIG. 1. Statistical analysis of the amino acid compositions of 39 preparations of leaf protein. By a technique outlined in the text, the analyses were arranged in a manner designed to bring out the differences in composition between preparations of different types. The numbers within the figure merely identify the preparations. From Byers (1971b).

Well-washed LP that has been thoroughly extracted with lipid solvents is not known to contain any sulphur in forms other than cyst(e)-ine and methionine. An upper limit for the cyst(e)ine content can therefore be deduced from the difference between the total sulphur and the sulphur contained in methionine (Subba Rau *et al.*, 1972; Byers, 1975). Byers analysed 32 preparations; by direct analysis the percentage of cyst(e)ine in the true protein component of LP from lucerne was 0·82–2·15, and by calculation 2·35–2·78. With lupin LP the correspond-ing values were "trace" to 2·79 and 2·00–2·67. Obviously, the validity of the method depends on the validity of the assumption that sulphur is never present in lipid-free LP in a third form.

VI. Preservation, Drying and Storage

Unfractionated preparations of LP have often had different nutritive values in spite of having comparable N contents. These differences are probably more often caused by differences in the ages or species of the leaves used. As all the reactions that take place during preservation are likely to be harmful, LP, like many other foods, should be used in the fresh state whenever possible. But preservation will often be necessary if LP is to be used at a distant place, or at a time when crops do not grow.

A. PRESERVATION OF MOIST LP

When LP is being washed to remove flavour, salts and carbohydrates that would damage the protein by Maillard (or "browning") reactions, it is acidified to about pH 4 to facilitate filtration. This brings it into the pH range of cheese, pickles, sauerkraut, or bottled fruit, and it has the keeping qualities of these foods. For prolonged storage, it can be canned. One attempt was made to preserve the moist cake by exposure to two megarads from a cobalt source, but the product had an unusual flavour that would probably be unacceptable.

Fully pressed material contains 60% water. If such material is mixed with one-seventh its weight of salt, rammed into a jar, and protected from access of air in the ways familiar in jam-making, it keeps well. Each gramme of LP DM is then accompanied by about 0·25 g of salt. This is an acceptable amount of salt if 5 or 10 g of LP is being eaten daily, provided the other components of the diet are not also heavily salted. The salt can, however, be partly removed before cooking by soaking the mass in water and letting the LP settle. If the final food is to be sweet, sugar can be used in the same way. The product contains approximately equal weights of LP and sugar. Subba Rao et al., (1967) preserved acidified cake for several months in the presence of 2% acetic acid and 0·2% orange peel oil. They examined the microbial population of the material in some detail. Arkcoll (1973), who preserved moist LP from seven species for six months with 1% acetic acid, found that the common soil fungus, *Mucor racemosus*, was the most common contaminant. This initial contamination is unavoidable. To avoid further contamination of the juice, the techniques of dairying are needed. The production of LP has much in common with the production of milk: there is a dirty side to the work and a clean side, and the two must be kept separate.

Fully pressed LP gives a rather hard and granular product when freeze-dried after slow freezing. The product is more attractive if the cake is moistened to 70–75% water and frozen suddenly by evaporative cooling (Pirie, 1964b). Because of its enormous surface, the unsaturated fats in it absorb oxygen rapidly; the rate depends on the extent to which tocopherol (vitamin E) (Arkcoll, 1973), and possibly other antioxidants (Hudson and Warwick, 1977), have been removed or destroyed. Consequently, freeze-dried LP should be stored in an airtight container.

When LP is dried completely in a current of air, either at room temperature or in an oven, the product is dark and gritty. If press cake is mixed with salt before drying in air at room temperature, the product is more attractive but, if salt is being added, it might as well be added as a preservative to moist cake. LP will finally be mixed with some form of flour or meal before use as human or animal food. The processes that lead to darkening and hardening are completely prevented if these substances are used as "extenders", i.e. if drying is postponed until some components of the diet have been mixed intimately with moist LP.

Many components of practical diets contain 10–12% water when in equilibrium with an atmosphere of average humidity, but can be parched in an oven without loss of nutritive value. Duckworth and Woodham (1961), and Foot (1974), improved the performance of extenders by parching them before mixing with moist LP. Dry LP without the unattractive appearance typical of material dried directly in air can also be made by drying in a current of air in a tumble drier until the water content is only 20–30% (this can be easily judged by feel); the material is then ground finely before drying is completed (Arkcoll, 1969).

The extent to which LP is damaged when dried in an oven depends not only on the temperature of the air to which it is exposed, but also on the extent to which the LP had been washed to remove sugars, and on the rate at which water is being removed. The faster the evaporation, the greater the temperature difference between LP and air, and the shorter the time for which moist LP is heated. LP containing 7% water was damaged more than LP containing 3% when heated without allowing the water to escape (Buchanan, 1969b). From this it follows that a thin layer of crumbled LP, dried quickly in a current of air, is likely to be damaged less than LP in lumps in a closed oven, even though the latter is being dried at a lower temperature.

Solvents that are miscible with water, e.g. acetone and the lower alcohols, remove chlorophyll and its breakdown products while removing lipids and water. The process is advocated by those who assume that a food should not be green. Removal of the green colour may be marginally advantageous; removal of lipids is detrimental. Nearly as much of the metabolizable energy in LP comes from the lipids as from the true protein, and the carotene would be lost. A further disadvantage of solvent extraction is that removal of the solvent at the end of the process is nearly as difficult as the direct removal of water would have been. When acetone is used, it is almost impossible to remove the smell of mesitylene and its derivatives completely.

Solvent extraction has, on the other hand, some compensating advantages. The removal of unsaturated lipids, even if it is incomplete, makes it less necessary to exclude air from material that will be stored, and thorough solvent extraction can restore digestibility to LP that has been damaged by prolonged heating when moist (Shah *et al.*, 1967; Buchanan, 1969a,b). At room temperature, the lipids become a little less easily extractable from moist LP within a few days: presumably by a process comparable to the tanning of "chamois" leather. Buchanan (1969b) measured the progress of fixation at 60°C in the presence of 1–2·5% water. Because of this fixation, and because of the risk of microbial attack, solvent extraction, if it is decided on, should start within a few days of pressing. Mokady and Zimmermann (1966) compared products made by extraction with methanol followed by chloroform; acetone followed by petrol ether; and boiling toluene, used first to distill off the water azeotropically, and then as a lipid solvent: the first system gave the best product. Some other solvent systems were compared by Bray *et al.* (1978) who concluded that polar solvents produced paler and softer products than non-polar solvents.

VII. Digestibility *in vitro*

If a protein is readily digested by several enzymes *in vitro*, it is reasonable to expect that it will be digested in the gut; if it is not digested *in vitro*, it may still be digested *in vivo* because of the simultaneous action of several proteases and of possible co-operation from the gut flora. It is obvious from the method of preparation that LP is insoluble in water. Digestion can therefore be measured in three stages: solution, loss of precipitability by trichloroacetic acid (TCA) and appearance of free amino acids. The last criterion is seldom used because it is assumed that material not precipitated by TCA will have been digested sufficiently extensively to be the nutritional equivalent of amino acids.

A. ENZYMES OF THE DIGESTIVE TRACT ON FREEZE-DRIED LP

There is unanimity (Lexander *et al.*, 1970; Bickoff *et al.*, 1975; Carlsson, 1975) that "cytoplasm" protein is more rapidly and completely digested, by pepsin followed by trypsin, than "chloroplast" protein. Digestion of the former can reach 97%, and of the latter 88%, when solubility is the criterion. About half of the soluble material remains precipitable by TCA. Considerable differences have been noticed between species, but the measurements have not been repeated on a sufficient number of different preparations for there to be any certainty that species differences are real, and do not arise from slight differences in the method used for preparing the samples. The point deserves more attention because partial digestion is one of the more likely methods for making a soluble food product economically.

B. PAPAIN ON FREEZE-DRIED LP

The digestibility of a protein by papain may have little bearing on its digestibility *in vivo*, but the enzyme is academically interesting and is widely used in the food industry. Digestion by unactivated papain is slow; even when activated by potassium cyanide, papain digests LP at only 20% the rate at which it digests casein (Byers, 1967a). This slow digestion is probably not caused by the presence of inhibitors in the LP because, in its presence, casein is digested at the normal rate. Several publications suggest the presence of anti-proteases in LP. These suggestions should be regarded sceptically until they are substantiated by experiments with well washed preparations. As in digestion with pepsin and trypsin, part of the LP is made soluble while remaining precipitable by TCA; the amount of material of this type increases as the pH of papain digests is increased (Byers, 1967a). The papain digestibility of freeze dried LP is not increased by extraction with lipid solvents at neutrality and it is diminished by extraction with solvents in the presence of strong acids. This effect is probably caused by hardening and compaction of the particles of LP so that there is less opportunity for enzyme access. Buchanan (1969a) restored digestibility by fine grinding and prolonged pre-soaking. Papain, like pepsin and trypsin, digests "chloroplast" protein more slowly than "cytoplasm" whether the fractions are separated by differential heat coagulation (Byers, 1975b) or centrifuging (Byers, 1971b). Species and age differences in the proportions of the various components of LP may explain the small differences in digestibility that Byers found when she compared preparations from 14 species harvested at different ages.

C. ENZYMES ON HEAT-DAMAGED LP

Samples of LP subjected to more prolonged heating than is necessary for coagulation, have invariably been digested more slowly than samples from the same batch not so treated. The extent of the change depends on conditions of heating. Duration and temperature, especially the duration of heating while water is still present, are important factors. The extent to which air can penetrate the mass is also a factor. Inadequately washed LP, containing components of the leaf "whey", has more opportunity for undergoing detrimental change than carefully washed material. Although hazardous, heating has compensating advantages; it is a convenient method of sterilization, and is the cheapest method for making dry products that can be easily dispensed in feeding experiments or marketed commercially. Much more research is therefore needed on the precise nature of the changes undergone by LP, from different sources and after different pre-treatments, when it is heated.

The process of making chamois leather, in which partly dried hide is beaten with unsaturated fish oil and then exposed to air to oxidize the oil, is so well known that the risk of LP becoming tanned in a similar way was obvious from the start of work on LP extraction. Shah et al., (1967; and Shah, 1971) attributed to this process the loss of digestibility when moist LP was heated. Digestibility was partly restored by solvent extraction, and the oxidation that had been associated with loss of digestibility could be inhibited by antoxidants such as amla (Emblica officinalis) powder (Shah, 1968).

Three main types of change are relevant when LP is heated during drying: effects on the protein itself, effects on the lipid, and interactions between them. Buchanan (1969a,b) dissociated the effects of temperature, time, access of oxygen and retention of water. Digestibility was lost when moist LP was heated, even in the absence of air, but solvent-extracted protein did not lose digestibility when heated in the presence of air and moisture. The digestibility of moist LP that had been heated with restricted access of air could be restored by solvent extraction. The nature of the association, or degree of entanglement, causing these changes is not known.

The behaviour of LP when heated, or during prolonged storage, differs in no essential respect from the behaviour of other proteins that contain unsaturated lipids. The behaviour of unfractionated LP when heated after solvent extraction has not been throughly investigated: there would be little reason for the investigation because the material would already be dry and sterile. Carefully made preparations of "cytoplasm" protein are nearly free from lipid. If they were being dried by heating, there could be other reactions, e.g. between the ε-NH_2 of lysine and β or γ-COOH of aspartic or glutamic acids, and various types of oxidation. Reactions of this type happen to all proteins.

VIII. Nutritive Value in Animals

Detailed experiments on animals are an essential prelude to any attempt to introduce a novel protein into human diets; they also have direct relevance when economically important animals, such as chickens and pigs, are used. Unequivocal interpretation is, however, extremely difficult. Species differ in their array of gut enzymes, in their amino acid requirements, and in their susceptibility to extraneous substances that may be present in the protein. These difficulties are inherent in the interpretation of any animal experiment. With LP there is the added difficulty that often little information is given about the antecedents of the product used. As earlier sections of this paper show, it is easy to damage a protein by inept handling; poor nutritive value is probably more often the result of technical incompetence on the part of the processor than of synthetic inconsiderateness on the part of the plant.

Experiments on pigs, chickens, and possibly fish (Cowey et al., 1971) have obvious economic importance. Although we may have little interest in the welfare of rats, there is now such a body of knowledge about their nutritional requirements that experiments on them deserve attention. The relevance of work on other mammals, and on insects, protozoa, and bacteria, is doubtful. Some of them are experimentally convenient, but these organisms are even less likely than rats to have digestive capabilities and amino acid requirements that resemble our own. In this section, results from experiments with pigs and rats only will be considered: they do not conflict with results on other organisms.

LP was marginally better than fish meal as a supplement to a predominantly cereal diet for pigs (Barber et al., 1959; Duckworth et al., 1961). Recent trials have confirmed these old results (Cheeke, 1974; Myer et al., 1975; Kanev et al., 1976; Carr and Pearson, 1976; Cheeke et al., 1977). In some of these experiments the LP was moist press-cake that had been kept frozen or had been freeze-dried in a commercial unit. It is therefore not certain that material of the same quality could be made by less expensive methods of storage or drying. Foot (1974) used the technique of Duckworth and Woodham (1961) and mixed press-cake containing 60% water with cereals containing 7–8% water. The resulting pellets contained 15–16% water and they stored satisfactorily for several months. By adding propionic acid to mixtures made with cereals of normal moisture content (10–12%), Braude *et al.* (1977) made pellets that kept well in spite of the presence of 20% water.

Almost all that is known about the digestibility of LP *in vivo* and the effects on its nutritive value of different methods of processing, and different forms of amino acid supplementation, comes from experiments on rats. There is no need to discuss here experiments showing, or purporting to show, differences between LPs made from different species. They may be real, but until comparisons are made between preparations from crops taken at several stages of growth and then separated and dried, or otherwise preserved in precisely the same way, the reality of species differences will remain uncertain. Woodham (1971) surveyed early experiments on rats comprehensively. The only experiments on rats that need be discussed here are those with a bearing on reactions between LP and phenolics and other tanning agents, and between the protein and unsaturated lipids.

A. EFFECTS OF PHENOLICS AND OTHER TANNING AGENTS

Phenolics interfere with the extraction of protein from leaf pulps. They inactivate enzymes so that elaborate precautions have to be taken if active preparations are to be made from some leaves. They tend to depress the nutritive value of fodder for ruminants (McLeod, 1974), but there is evidence that a suitable amount of tannin in fodder prevents the accumulation of foam that causes bloat. Generalizations on these subjects are inadvsiable because of the very large number of phenolics present in some leaves (Milic, 1972; Thakur *et al.*, 1974), and the changes that they undergo during harvesting and processing (Pierpoint 1971; Van Sumere *et al.*, 1975; Synge, 1975, 1976).

A reversible association between phenolics and peptide bonds, which leads to cross-linking between protein molecules, or between parts of one protein molecule, is usually invoked to explain the diminished digestibility of proteins containing phenolics. The evidence is reviewed by Van Sumere *et al.* (1975). It is usually assessed by comparing the amounts of N in the faeces of rats fed on diets containing different proteins, or no protein. The trustworthiness of this method clearly depends on the extent to which different diets abrade the intestinal mucosa, for part of the faecal N is derived from that source. However, the striking effect of small additions of tannin suggest that the method is valid.

"Chloroplast" protein is less digestible both *in vitro* and *in vivo* than "cytoplasm" protein. It is reasonable to associate this with the presence of more phenolics in the "chloroplast" protein. It would be interesting to know whether the difference arises because chloroplasts contain more phenolics, e.g. plastoquinone, or because combination with phenolics makes protein that would, in the absence of phenolics have appeared in the "cytoplasm" fraction, coagulate at 50–60°C. The component proteins in LP differ in the avidity with which they associate with phenolics (Lahiry *et al.*, 1977).

Complex formation with the ε amino group of lysine is a recognized reaction between proteins and phenolics. The comparable reaction between gossypol and the proteins of cotton seed makes the lysine in them unavailable to non-ruminants though it still appears in acid hydrolysates. Phenolics may not only make LP less digestible, but also less useful when digested. The amount of lysine that had combined with phenolics was measured by Allison (1971) and Allison *et al.* (1973) by destroying with nitrous acid the ε amino groups of those lysine molecules that were not complexed, and then hydrolysing, and measuring the lysine that had been shielded from nitrous acid.

Allison (1971) found that only 6·5% of the lysine in lucerne LP that had been protected from oxidation by processing in the presence of sulphite, was shielded from deamination, and was therefore probably unavailable to non-ruminants; 9·5% was shielded in LP made without precautions, and 18·5% when chlorogenic acid was added at the start of the extraction. The values on 15 samples from 7 species, made with no attempt to prevent oxidation or complexing, ranged from 13·3–38·2%; the larger values were given by "chloroplast" fractions. The nutritive value of these samples had been measured on rats (Henry and Ford, 1965), and it correlated reasonably well with the amount of lysine not shielded from deamination. There is so much lysine in LP that the loss in nutritive value if a little is made unavailable by complexing with phenolics is not likely to be great. This expectation was borne out experimentally (Henry and Ford, 1965; Shurpalekar *et al.*, 1969). Supplementation with lysine did not improve the nutritive value of rat diets containing LP. Woodham (1971) quotes another trial (Reddy, unpublished) with the same result, but Bickoff *et al.* (1975) found lysine supplementation advantageous.

Subba Rau *et al.* (1972) found no correlation between nutritive value and the amount of phenolics in 11 preparations from eight species, used as sole protein sources for rats. However, when the results were expressed as the ratio of phenolics to N, it was clear that the samples with greater ratios were the worse nutritionally. Rats did not grow at all when fed on samples with the largest ratios. One of them, made from unwashed carrot (*Daucus carota*) tops, contained 37·3% ash and only 3·9% of nitrogen: there may therefore have been other reasons for the rats' failure to thrive.

There will be general agreement that complex formation between tanning agents and LP is to be avoided if possible. Tanning agents exist preformed in some leaves, and in many more, phenolics oxidize to tanning agents when leaves are pulped in the presence of air. More work is needed to identify the phase of the extraction procedure at which LP is most vulnerable. It would be difficult to exclude air during bulk extraction, but the use of sulphite is conventional in the food industry, it is well known to produce pale preparations of LP, and it would be feasible economically. Such agents must however be used judiciously because they can destroy essential amino acids such as cyst(e)ine. Undoubtedly, the best policy is to work with species and varieties that are relatively free from phenolics: that would both increase the extractability of LP and prevent damage to what was extracted.

B. MODIFICATION OF CYST(E)INE AND METHIONINE

The detoxication of various aromatic substances by conjugation with cyst(e)ine to form mercapturic acids has been known since the end of the last century and may explain the protection given by a high-protein diet against some forms of poisoning, e.g. by *Senecio* (Cheeke and Garman, 1974). The gut flora of herbivores can, to a large extent, metabolize phenolics, but some phenolics are detoxicated by methylation. Mice methylate the breakdown products of lucerne tannins (Milic and Stojanovic, 1972). Several authors have made the plausible suggestion that when phenolics are present in the diet, there is an extra demand for methyl groups and therefore for methionine. The subject is discussed by Eggum and Christensen (1975); they found no evidence for this effect in rats, though it seems to exist in chickens.

Phenolics may not only increase the need for cyst(e)ine and methionine, they may also make them unavailable. Methionine can react with *o*-quinone (Vithayathil and Murthy, 1972) and *p*-quinone reacts with other thioethers (Bosshard, 1972). There is no evidence for such reactions in the conditions to which LP is exposed during extraction. Cyst(e)ine (Roberts, 1959; Pierpoint, 1969) reacts with quinones and phenolics in physiological conditions. Cyst(e)ine also reacts with plant lactones containing a :CH$_2$ group (Rodriguez *et al.*, 1977); this is unlikely to be a problem with LP because these lactones tend to cause dermatitis: plants containing them would therefore be eliminated from any crop. During the preparation and especially the drying of in-adequately washed preparations, LP is probably more susceptible to damage by conjugation with carbohydrates (cf. Pienazek *et al.*, 1975) than with phenolics.

The amount of methionine in proteins is usually measured after oxidation to the sulphone (MSO_2); any sulphoxide (MSO) present in the protein is therefore included in the value. Attempts to measure the amount of MSO precisely are frustrated because it is partly reduced to methionine during hydrolysis (Njaa, 1962; Gjøen and Njaa, 1977). But Byers (in Pirie, 1970a) found that 18% of the methionine appeared as MSO in wheat LP that had been processed quickly, and 30% in a sample made from juice that had been allowed to stand for 2 h before coagulation.

The nutritional status of oxidized methionine is not completely clear. There is agreement that MSO_2 cannot replace methionine (Miller and Samuel, 1970; Smith, 1972). Gjøen and Njaa (1977) found MSO fully equivalent to methionine in rat diets only when there was adequate cyst(e)ine, i.e. the well known partial interchangeability of the S-amino acids (e.g. Hove *et al.*, 1974) does not extend to MSO. Byers (1975) argued from measurements of total-S that LP from lucerne and lupin (*Lupinus albus*) contained 2·3–2·5% cyst(e)ine. With these proteins therefore, the replacement of 30% of the methionine by MSO should not be detrimental for rats: the value of MSO in human diets is un-known.

In the light of the argument in the preceding paragraph, it seems probable that the formation of MSO is not responsible for the apparent S-amino acid deficiency in LP. Byers (1975) points out that LP from lucerne or lupins contains more than the 3·5% of S-amino acids that is thought adequate by FAO (1973) for people. Nevertheless, the growth of rats is improved by the addition of methionine to their diets when LP is used as the protein supplement or sole protein source (Henry and Ford, 1965; Shurpalekar *et al.*, 1969; Trigg and Topps, 1971; Hove *et al.*, 1974). A partial explanation may be that people do not need as much methionine in their diets as young rats. Even so, the difference between "chloroplast" protein and "cytoplasm" protein fractions of LP remains. Subba Rau *et al.* (1972) suggested that the former contained less S-amino acid, which would agree with its smaller nutritive value, but Byers (1975) gives reasons for thinking that there is little difference. No one seems to have fed rats on "chloroplast" protein, at a level ade-quate to compensate for its relative indigestibility, supplemented with methionine. The possibility remains that, especially in "chloroplast" protein, methionine, or cyst(e)ine, undergoes some form of complexing comparable to that undergone by lysine. If so, a change in the technique of extraction might prevent it. Pulping in the presence of polyvinyl-pyrrolidone, which complexes phenolics, increased the apparent cystine content of LP (Fafunso and Byers, 1977): this procedure would scarcely be feasible in large-scale production.

C. EFFECTS OF UNSATURATED FATTY ACIDS

Although many foods are esteemed because of the flavour of oxidized fats, it is generally agreed that oxidation of fats is not nutritionally beneficial and may be harmful (Mead and Alfin-Slater, 1966). Buchanan (1969a,b) restored the nutritive value of wheat LP, that had been damaged by heat, to nearly the original value by thorough extraction with lipid solvents. Because fine grinding did not have the same restorative effect he dismissed the suggestion, made to explain heat damage to fish protein, that the lipids spread as an impermeable film over the heated particles of protein. This is not altogether convincing. He found that prolonged soaking restored digestibility to LP that had been extracted with acidified solvents: there is no reason to think that sufficiently thorough grinding would not have been efficacious. The point deserves attention because, although the advantages of working with fresh, moist, LP have been stressed, dry material will often be used. During its short sojourn in a rat's gut, hard dry material may not have time to soften to the extent necessary for enzyme action.

D. SUPPLEMENTATION OF CEREAL-BASED DIETS

The protein in interesting and palatable diets is, and should be, derived from several sources. There is therefore a lack of realism about experiments in which a concentrate such as LP is used as sole protein source. When proteins from several sources are being eaten regularly, it is the distribution of amino acids in the whole diet that is important: an essential amino acid deficiency in one component may be compensated by the abundance of that amino acid in another component of the diet. The value of LP as a supplement to barley in pig feeding has already been referred to. The following experiments were on rats.

LP supplemented a rice diet (Sur, 1961), and a simulated Ghanian diet in which rice was an important component (Miller, 1965). In Miller's experiment it was a marginally better supplement than skimmed milk. This unexpected result may have been caused by the β-carotene in the LP. An unpublished experiment by Ghosh (in an Annual Report, and in Pirie, 1970b) deserves mention because LP from water hyacinths supplemented rice when the LP supplied 30%, 40% and 50% of the protein in the diet; its value diminished when more was used. The effect of varying the ratio in which two sources of protein contribute to the total in a diet is clearly shown in experiments by Subba Rau and Singh (1971). In two experiments, the weight gain was greater when half the protein came from wheat grain and half from lucerne LP than with any other ratio. It was argued that this is what would be expected from the amino acid composition of the diets: at that ratio the relative abundance of cyst(e)ine and methionine in wheat compensates for their scarcity in LP, and the relative abundance of isoleucine, lysine, threonine and valine in LP compensates for the scarcity of these amino acids in wheat grain protein. Supplementation of wheat grain by LP from three species was also observed by Garcha et al. (1971) and Kawatra et al. (1974).

IX. Human Experiments and Trials

As soon as LP of reasonable quality was being made, the press-cake was regularly eaten as it was being removed from the filter stockings. We had by that time become accustomed to handling green material, and found the product from most species palatable. By 1957 we regularly cooked LP and during the next few years several cooks were employed for short periods so as to get as many new ideas on presentation as possible. For reasons that have already been stated, green, moist press-cake was almost always used. The initial disquiet that every cook felt at the texture and appearance of LP disappeared after one or two weeks experience of handling it.

LP from many species, e.g. cereals, cowpea and pea haulm, if properly washed, is nearly tasteless when fresh. A smell similar to that of China tea, develops on storage; the products of oxidation give dry LP a stronger flavour after a few weeks in air. Even when fresh, LP from some other leaves, e.g. clover, lucerne and potato haulm, has more flavour. It is a pity lucerne is so often used—its flavour imposes an extra barrier to acceptance.

Some forms of presentation are obviously unsuitable. Every type of baked product should be avoided because baking enhances the flavours of the breakdown products of the lipids. Furthermore, the familiar appearance of bread has so many associations that a greenish version of it is unlikely to be acceptable. LP blends well with savoury flavours, or fish, and less well with coffee, orange or lemon, but banana is an excellent flavouring agent. A mixture of LP and banana pulp has a texture that is well adapted for spreading or insertion into some type of casing.

It is reasonable to conclude from several acceptability trials (Morrison and Pirie, 1960; Byers *et al.*, 1965; Oke, 1966; Balasundaram and Samuel, 1968; Garcha *et al.*, 1971; Kamalanthan and Devadas, 1971; Toosy and Shah, 1974) that when a panel judges a familiar food that has LP added to it, the extent of acceptable divergence from the familiar standard is small. This means that extra care must be taken to ensure that the LP has been adequately washed and pressed, and that it does not have a gritty texture. These points may have been attended to more closely by Byers *et al.* (1965) than by some others who have worked on presentation: this would explain the differing degrees of success achieved. Another important factor is the duration of the trial. Many people react against every novel food on first contact but accept it when it has become familiar. Most of the people eating the dishes prepared at Rothamsted were involved in various aspects of the work on LP and had therefore already gained familiarity. This would also be the state of affairs if LP were being made in a village. I have discussed the inter-relations between factors such as these elsewhere (Pirie, 1972).

Work done on presentation in USA is directed towards producing something that could oust an existing product from the shelves of a Supermarket. Such factors as capacity for holding water or fat, emulsifying power, and the ability to make simulated whipped cream get attention (Wang and Kinsella, 1976a,b). For these purposes decolourized material is essential, and material separated from the leaf juice by acid precipitation, rather than heat coagulation, is preferable. What is made by these expensive fractionation techniques is another ingredient that can be added to a conventional food without its presence being noticed; if noticed because of mention on the label, it is assumed that it will be accepted with resignation. This approach does not exploit the basic merits of LP—that it is a human food that can be made by simple processes for local use. Several successes have been commented on, e.g. Anon. (1974). Betschart (1977) increased to 9% the protein content of biscuits, that normally contained only 7%, by adding acid precipitated protein to them. They were judged unacceptable in USA when the protein content was increased to 13%. Similarly, she could add 16% of a leaf protein fraction, but not 29%, to a split-pea soup.

Children are the group that is now most likely to be malnourished, they are therefore probable recipients of whatever novel foodstuffs are ultimately produced. Their diets in institutions are often inadequate. Consequently, trials raise no ethical problems because any form of supplementary feeding is likely to be beneficial. Their growth rate is a good index of the merits of a supplement, and they do not have such well-established food prejudices as adults.

Quantitative experiments on children (Waterlow, 1962) started ten years after LP had been eaten regularly by those working with it in Rothamsted. One infant gained 1·2 kg in the twenty days during which half his protein was LP, but the main experimental periods were too short for measurements of growth to be valid; instead, N retention was measured when dietary N came mainly from milk, and when part of it came from milk and part from LP. It was clear that there was more retention with milk when the infants were given 770 mg N per day, but no difference when they were given only 500. That result agreed with expectation. Although LP is not as good as milk, it is a useful supplement when the milk supply is inadequate.

Growth was the primary criterion used in a more prolonged trial in an institution near Mysore (Doraiswamy *et al.*, 1969). The normal diet contained ragi (*Eleusine coracana*) flour, beans, vegetables, skimmed-milk powder, oil and sugar. It supplied 39 g of protein per day and 7 MJ. Eighty boys, six to twelve years old, were divided into four matched groups. One group remained on the institutional diet; one had a daily supplement of 0·5 g of lysine (lysine deficiency is the principal defect of ragi); one group had 24 g of low-fat sesame (*Sesamum indicum*) flour; and one group 15 g of lucerne LP. The last two supplements contributed 10 g of protein to the daily diet and sugar was withdrawn from all supplemented diets to compensate for the energy in the supplement. The results after six months are summarized in Table II. They show that

TABLE II.   Mean measurements on four groups of boys, 6–12 years old, given different diets for six months

Dietary supplement	Height (cm)	Weight (kg)	Increase in Haemoglobin (g 100 ml^{-1})	Red cell count (M mm^{-3})
None (control)	2·2	0·47	0·29	0·06
0·5g lysine	4·25	1·05	0·64	0·22
10 g protein in sesame flour	3·51	0·86	0·73	0·19
10 g protein in LP	4·84	1·28	0·87	0·23

LP increased height, weight and the red cell count to a slightly greater extent that the other two supplements. There were no problems over acceptance of the supplemented diets.

In Nigeria (Olatunbosun *et al.*, 1972; Olatunbosun, 1976), the mothers of 26 children, two to six years old and suffering from kwashiorkor, were supplied with powdered dry LP made from maize and other crops. They were told to add 10 g daily to the usual food of each child. Because of the disappearance of oedema there was at first no increase in weight. After five weeks there was an increase in serum protein concentration and in appetite. The authors attached particular importance to the change from dejected apathy to cheerful alertness. Encouraged by this trial, they have installed equipment to make LP for a larger group.

Only interim reports (Kamalanathan *et al.*, 1975; Martin, 1975) have so far been published on a trial in six villages near Coimbatore (India). A nursery school (balwadi) was set up in each village; in this, on six days per week, about 60 children, two to four-and-a-half years old spend most of the day. On the six school days they have two meals which contain 80–90% of the daily energy and protein supply.

One of the balwadis is primarily educational and the food served in it is modelled, in quantity, character and quality, on food usually eaten at home. In five of the balwadis the food served contains 1·3 MJ more energy than the food served in the control balwadi. In one of these five, most of that energy comes from tapioca which supplies only 1 g of protein. The food given in the other four balwadis contains about 10 g of extra protein given in the form of horsegram, maize and Bengalgram, skimmed milk powder, or lucerne LP. The energy contents of the supplements are equalized by suitable adjustment of tapioca and sugar (jaggery). The mixture is shaped into moist balls that have the form of a familiar sweetmeat (laddu); the molasses flavour of the jaggery overpowers the flavour of the lucerne LP. There have been no medical problems: children not on the experiment gather round eagerly for any surplus remaining after the 60 have been supplied.

Table III is a summary of the results after 18 months. As was to be expected, milk is a better supplement than LP, but LP is marginally better than the other two sources of protein. Little emphasis should be put on that point. The object of the trial was not to arrange the locally available protein sources in order to merit, but to see whether LP should be classified among the acceptable and useful local sources. It is clearly established that it should be so classified. Apart from establishing the value of LP, the main point that arises from the trial is that children readily accept LP laddus, and their mothers are unperturbed by the greenish tinge of their faeces. Another point worth noting is that the group getting extra energy without extra protein shows little

TABLE III. Interim results of an 18-month comparison of different supplements to the diets of pre-school children

| | Age (months) at the start | No supplement | Diets supplemented with 1·3 MJ | | | Diets supplemented with 10 g protein + 1·3 MJ | |
			Tapioca	Horsegram	Maize + Bengalgram	Milk	Leaf protein
Increased height (cm)	24–30	9·6	10·0	10·3	10·8	12·0	10·6
	36–42	9·3	9·4	9·8	10·3	11·8	10·3
	48–54	8·8	8·3	8·9	10·1	10·8	10·1
Increased weight (kg)	34–30	2·7	2·8	3·0	3·0	3·4	3·2
	36–42	3·0	3·1	2·9	3·3	3·6	3·2
	48–54	2·9	2·9	3·0	3·0	3·4	3·0
Increased haemoglobin (g 100 ml⁻¹)	24–30	2·3	2·1	2·3	1·6	2·2	2·5
	36–42	2·4	2·9	2·4	3·1	3·2	3·5
	48–54	2·4	2·5	3·0	3·7	4·3	4·2
Serum retinol µg ml		0·2	0·23	0·34	0·39	0·38	0·41

improvement over the control. This tends to contradict the statement, that is now often made, that lack of energy is more common, in regions such as South India, than lack of protein. The results of this trial are so encouraging that a trial on 600 children is being planned.

A. β-CAROTENE

The World Health Organization (1976) estimates that 100 000 children become blind every year as a result of vitamin A deficiency. LP may be as important in human nutrition as a source of β-carotene, (which is converted in the body to vitamin A), as of protein. The technique of preparation should therefore be designed to ensure that as little of the β-carotene as possible is destroyed. When a crop is pulped the carotenoids are exposed to enzymic oxidation. Enzyme action is particularly associated with the fibre (Arkcoll and Holden, 1972); juice should therefore be separated from fibre as quickly as possible. The pH optimum for the action is on the acid side of neutrality (Walsh and Hauge, 1953; Arkcoll and Holden, 1973): carotenoids are therefore more fully preserved if the crop or pulp made from it, is made slightly alkaline by exposure to ammonia vapour at an early stage in processing. Various reasons for coagulating the extract without delay have already been outlined. The preservation of β-carotene is another: Arkcoll and Holden (1973) found that 19–59% of the carotene in extracts was lost in 24 h at 21°C. There was little loss during coagulation and pressing, but 5–15% was lost during drying. Several semi-commercial methods of drying were compared by Miller et al. (1972).

Because of these varied possibilities of loss, differences between the β-carotene contents of different LP preparations are as likely to be the result of differences in preparative technique, as of differences between the species of leaf. Preparations made in the same manner from ten species in the laboratory contained 0·8–1·7 mg β-carotene g^{-1} (Arkcoll, 1973; Connell and Foxell, 1976). LP made in semi-commercial conditions (Miller et al., 1972) from lucerne contained 0·57 mg g^{-1}. There is therefore enough β-carotene in 1 or 2 g of freshly made LP to meet the daily vitamin A needs of an infant, and enough in 3 or 4 g to meet the needs of an adult.

The LP used in the trial near Coimbatore (described above) was made without special precautions, but it was used within one or two days of being made. From time to time, a few of the children allowed a blood sample to be taken so that the amount of serum retinol (vitamin A) could be measured. Average values after about 18 months are given in Table III. The four protein supplements all seem to ensure an adequate level of serum retinol: $0.2 \mu g$ ml^{-1} is the level at which it is generally agreed that signs of deficiency may appear. The serum retinol level depends not only on the amount of β-carotene in the diet, but also on the extent to which it is absorbed and converted to retinol, and on there being sufficient retinol binding protein in the blood to mobilize retinol. The children getting no supplement, and the supplement of energy only, may have been nearing vitamin A deficiency as much because of lack of protein as lack of β-carotene or preformed vitamin A.

Though it may be easy to prevent destruction of β-carotene during the routine production of LP, it is unlikely that the LP will all be used as soon as it is made. After exposure to air for a year at 20°C, 90% of the β-carotene in dry LP was lost; with exclusion of light and air 12% was lost; there was still less loss at -20°C (Arkcoll, 1973). The extent to which losses could be diminished by working in stainless steel or non-metallic equipment has not been studied, nor has the protective role of antoxidants such as tocopherol (vitamin E) and the ferulic acid derivative that is present in lucerne (Ben Azis et al., 1968). The latter would probably be removed from LP in the "whey", but not the former. Arkcoll (1973) found 0.1 mg g^{-1}, Connell and Foxell (1976) found 0.36. Hudson and Warwick (1977) argue that three times that amount of tocopherol would have to be present if it alone were acting as the antoxidant. The behaviour of the other lipid-soluble vitamins does not seem to have been studied.

The simplest way to make use of the abundant β-carotene in dark green leafy vegetables (DGLV) is to eat more of them. As a first step, more publicity should be given to the very large yields attainable by skilled market gardening (Pirie, 1975a; 1976c). Lala and Reddy (1970) deduced that children absorbed 57–93% of the β-carotene in DGLV cooked with a little oil, adults absorbed it as well from DGLV as from carrots or papaya (Rao and Rao, 1970). Venkataswamy et al. (1976) found that 30g (wet weight) of DGLV daily was as effective as massive doses of retinol for clearing up the early signs of xerophthalmia. But there are difficulties. The small stomachs of some infants would not hold 30g of DGLV, and it will take time to restore DGLV to popularity. Separation from the cellular structure of the leaf should make the β-carotene more readily assimilable from LP than from DGLV, and the partial removal of oxalate in the "whey" would be beneficial. Ramana and Singh (1971) found LP as effective as synthetic β-carotene for replenishing retinol in the serum and liver of rats that had been on a retinol deficient diet. Even when DGLV have regained their old prestige, there will still be a place for LP in human diets.

X. The Value of the By-products

The DM of an average crop is distributed between the three products—LP, fibre and "whey"—in approximtely the ratios 1:5:1. Different crops and methods of fractionation give different ratios, but it has for long (e.g. Pirie, 1942) been obvious that, both for economy and for the sake of the amenities, all three must be used. Most of the crops that are dried commercially for winter feed contain 25–14% DM. With surface water from dew or rain the percentage of DM becomes still smaller. The fibre after LP extraction contains 30–40% DM so that only half, or less, as much water has to be evaporated from fibre as from the original crop to get the same weight of DM. In order to economize fuel when making dried fodder, several institutes have pressed out fluid equivalent to "whey" from crops heated before pressing so as to destroy their turgor (Pirie, 1966b; Damborg et al., 1976; Pirie, 1977a). The percentage of N in the "whey" from most crops is smaller than in the original crop; consequently the pressed residue usually has a greater percentage of N than the original crop. Similarly, when half the protein is extracted as LP, the percentage of N in the fibre residue is not halved. Furthermore, a larger fraction of the N in extracted residue is true protein, and its feeding value should be greater than that of an unfractionated fodder containing the same amount of N because it will have been made from younger and less lignified leaves.

Cattle eat the extracted residue readily. Greenhalgh and Reid (1975), Houseman and Connell (1976) and Connell and Houseman (1977) found that comminution had increased its palatability. In a comparison between fresh grass and the extracted fibre made from it, the daily live weight gain of cattle was 0·73 and 0·84 kg, and the weight (DM) of fodder eaten was 6·78 and 6·26 kg. That is to say, the weight of grass needed for 1 kg of live weight gain was 9·28 kg (DM), whereas the weight of fibre needed was only 7·45. Other similar comparisons have been published, but in less detailed form. The digestibility of fibre, whether in vitro or in vivo, obviously depends on the quality of the original crop, it also depends on whether the measurements are made on fresh moist fibre or on fibre that has been dried. Because of the preferential removal of the more digestible "cytoplasm" protein, there is always some loss of digestibility—about 5% with fresh material and 10% with dried.

The simplest way to use "whey" is to carry it back, as a return load, to the fields from which the crop was harvested. About half the wet weight of the crop is in the "whey", it will therefore contain about half the potassium and a smaller fraction of the phosphorus in the crop.

"Whey" from a leguminous crop may contain a quarter of the crop N, the fraction is smaller with cereals unless they are harvested soon after being fertilized. No systematic analyses for these elements have been published; their actual value as fertilizers can only be guessed. If "whey" were restored evenly to the full area from which the crop came, it would form a layer only 1 or 2 mm deep and would supply a substantial part of the potassium needed for the growth of a second harvest.

The inhibition of germination and plant growth by silage effluent is well known. This led to fear that "whey" would be similarly detrimental. If it is returned to an area very much smaller than the area from which the crop came (the conditions in the neighbourhood of a silo), it inhibits germination and may "scorch" young leaves. Experience at Rothamsted and elsewhere shows that it is harmless when returned to as little as a fifth of the area from which it came. By encouraging the growth of gas-forming bacteria such as *Clostridium butyricum* and *C. pasteurianum*, the carbohydrates in "whey" can improve the structure of intractable soils; the effect persists after the gasses escape because of soil stabilization by bacterial polysaccharides (Arkcoll, 1974).

Most of the components of "whey" are of doubtful nutritional value for non-ruminants, and "whey" is so dilute that it would be difficult to dispose of all of it in ruminant feed in its original state. "Whey" does not coagulate on heating and so can be concentrated in a multiple-effect or vapour-compression unit. In spite of the thermal economy thereby attainable, it seems unlikely that it would be worthwhile evaporating "wheys" at the more dilute end of the concentration range.

"Whey" has a very varied composition (Festenstein, 1972; Hill-Cottingham and Lloyd-Jones, 1979), but it always contains carbohydrates that are fermentable by several micro-organisms. Ideally, it would be used as the culture medium for "biomass" production, and several papers on this have been published. Systematic work will not start until a regular supply of "whey" of predictable composition is available.

XI. Prerequisites for Leaf Protein Production

There are many reasons for advocating fodder fractionation and many situations in which it could be embarked on in practice. This arouses scepticism. An advocate is often asked whether factory, farm, or family operation is envisaged. The reply that all three procedures are suitable and that choice depends entirely on the particular situation, seems to some sceptics as unconvincing as the advertisement for a panacea. Similarly, there is often argument about the relative importance of LP as a human or an animal food, and about the extent to which it is advantageous to deplete the fibrous residue of protein. Again, the answer depends on circumstances. In a poor country with poor communications, it would be advisable to extract as much LP as possible and eat it near where it is being made. In an affluent country with a long winter during which cattle need fodder, attention would be paid to the partial dewatering of the fibre, rather than to the extraction of LP, and most of what was extracted would be fed to pigs or poultry.

There will be little dispute about the value of a policy of fodder fractionation when the starting material is at present abundant and unused, e.g. a water weed or a by-product. There may be doubts about the feasibility of collecting material from water, or from the scattered sites at which by-products accumulate, but there will be no doubts about the advantage of making fodder and LP from an unexploited resource if that is feasible. But sites where a supply of weed can be regularly collected are rare, and by-products are intermittent. The main questions that arise concerning fractionation techniques are: "Should a crop that is already being used unfractioned, be fractionated; and should a crop be grown for fractionation in place of a crop grown for conventional use?"

The potential advantages of finding out how to make LP, and how to use it in suitable regions, seem so obvious that outside observers are puzzled by the slow progress of work on the subject. I have discussed elsewhere the general problem of opposition to innovation—nutritional or otherwise (Pirie, 1971b; 1972; 1975b). A specific obstacle is that thoughtful people in poor countries are understandably suspicious of the proposal that they should start using something that is not used elsewhere. The fact that climates and circumstances are different may not convince sceptics completely. Acceptance has not been helped by the tendency of various organizations, e.g. FAO (1964, 1969), US President's Science Advisory Committee (1967) UN (1968), to accompany a phrase such as ". . . the potential value of such products is unquestionable . . ." with a catalogue of all the possible difficulties that may be encountered with LP. Difficulties undoubtedly exist: it is unfortunate that it is only for LP that they are itemized, for they obtrude to a similar extent with all the other novel protein sources.

LP is now being made on a pilot-plant scale in between 20 and 30 institutes, and is being used in human feeding trials in four or five. More units will probably start working on this scale as information about the success of the human trials is published. Work such as this is of great scientific interest and demonstrates a nutritional potentiality, but it gives no information about costs. These are inflated by intermittent working, the use of unnecessarily highly qualified staff, and the lack of distinction between work essential for production, and work connected with the measurements needed in research.

Commercial production of LP started in Hungary and the USA before the recent increase in the cost of oil and other fuels. Elsewhere the idea of forage fractionation was disparaged until conventional crop drying became economically insecure. Suddenly, there is active commercial interest in many countries, this has resulted in the hasty installation of equipment designed for other operations. It is often absurdly expensive: weight for weight, industrial equipment tends to cost much more than agricultural equipment. There is a risk that the inevitable failure of some projects will be misinterpreted as a defect in the concept of fodder fractionation rather than in the manner in which it is being tackled. The prime prerequisite for success with LP production, in any circumstances, is the design of suitable equipment for the job.

Twenty years ago, rough estimates of the cost of making LP were based on the costs of grass drying. Rival gloomy estimates made the process seem uneconomic because the value of the extracted fibre was neglected. Economic analysis is now being attempted from several directions (Dumont and Boyce, 1976; Morris, 1977; Wilkins *et al.*, 1977; Slesser *et al.*, 1977). Some economists calculate the maximum cost of equipment compatible with making LP that could be sold for a somewhat arbitrarily chosen price. Others consider what that price should be if LP is to compete with established sources of carotenoids, energy and protein. Others compare several different methods of managing the integration of fodder fractionation with the other work on a farm. There are too many factors for conclusive answers to emerge from a theoretical approach; definite answers can come only from practical experience now that a *prima facie* case has been made out. The technique of fodder fractionation is in its infancy. The economics of the process, whether LP for human food or extracted fibre for ruminant feed is regarded as the primary product, will not be correctly assessed until the effects of selecting the most suitable crops, and designing suitable equipment are included in the argument.

The advisability of fractionating crops depends on the particular circumstances in a region. Where protein is scarce and it rains so frequently that it is difficult to ripen conventional seed crops, the case for LP and increased use of leaf vegetables is strong. Where fine weather can be relied on in summer, so that partial drying in the field is possible, and where LP would be used only as animal feed, there seems to be little advantage in extracting LP rather than separating the partly dried crop into protein-rich and protein-poor fractions mechanically (cf. Pirie, 1977a). The position in Britain, with unpredicable summer weather and need for conserved winter fodder, is intermediate. The case for LP will become stronger should it become necessary to be more self sufficient.

References

Allison, R. M. (1971). Factors influencing the availability of lysine in leaf protein. *In* "Leaf Protein: Its Agronomy, Preparation, Quality and Use", (Pirie, N. W., Ed.), p. 78. Blackwell, Oxford.

Allison, R. M. and Vartha, E. W. (1973). Yields of protein extracted from irrigated lucerne. *N.Z. J. Exp. Agric.*, **1**, 35.

Allison, R. M., Laird, W. M. and Synge, R. L. M. (1973). Notes on a deamination method proposed for determining "chemically available lysine" of proteins. *Brit. J. Nutr.* **29**, 51.

Anderson, J. W. and Rowan, K. S. (1967). Extraction of soluble leaf enzymes with thiols and other reducing agents. *Phytochem.* **6**, 1047.

Anonymous (1974). Alfalfa protein for human use. *Agric.Sci. Rev.* **11**, (2) 55.

Arkcoll, D. B. (1969). Preservation of leaf protein by air drying. *J. Sci. Fd Agric.* **30**, 600.

Arkcoll, D. B. (1971). Agronomic aspects of leaf protein production in Great Britain. *In* "Leaf Protein: Its Agronomy, Preparation, Quality and Use" (Pirie, N. W., Ed.), p. 9. Blackwell, Oxford.

Arkcoll, D. B. (1973). The preservation and storage of leaf protein preparations. *J. Sci. Fd Agric.* **24**, 437.

Arkcoll, D. B. (1974). The production of soil pores by bacteria. *Rev. Microbiol.* (S. Paulo). **5** (3) 63.

Arkcoll, D. B. and Festenstein, G. N. (1971). A preliminary study of the agronomic factors affecting the yield of extractable leaf protein. *J. Sci. Fd Agric.* **22**, 49.

Arkcoll, D. B. and Holden, M. (1973). Changes in chloroplast pigments during the preparation of leaf protein. *J. Sci. Fd Agric.* **24**, 1217.

Bagchi, D. K. and Matai, S. (1976). Studies on the performance of tetrakali (*Phaseolus aureus* Linn.) as a leaf protein yielding crop in West Bengal. *J. Sci. Fd Agric.* **27**, 1.

Balasundaram, C. S. and Samuel, D. M. (1968). Incorporation of different leaf proteins in South Indian dishes. *Madras Agric. J.* **55**, 540.

Balasundaram, C. S., Krishnamoorthy, K. K., Chandramani, R., Balakrishnan, T. and Ramadoss, C. (1974a). The yield of leaf protein extracted by large scale processing of various crops. *Ind. J. Home Sci.* **8**, 6.

Balasundaram, C. S., Krishnamoorthy, K. K., Balakrishnan, T., Ramadoss, C. and Chandramani, R. (1974b). Screening plant species for leaf protein extraction. *Ind. J. Home Sci.* **8**, 1.

Balasundaram, C. S., Chandramani, R., Krishnamoorthy, K. K., and Balakrishnan, T. (1975). Optimum time of cutting for maximum yield of extractable protein from some fodder grasses. *Madras Agric. J.* **62**, 431.

Barber, R. S., Braude, R. and Mitchell, K. G. (1959). Leaf protein in rations of growing pigs. *Proc. Nutr. Soc.* **18**, iii.

Batra, U. R., Deshmukh, M. G. and Joshi, R. N. (1976). Factors affecting extractability of protein from green plants. *Ind. J. Pl. Physiol.* **19**, 211.

Ben Aziz, A., Grossman, S., Budowski, P., Ascarelli, I. and Bondi, A. (1968). Antioxidant properties of lucerne extracts. *J. Sci. Fd Agric.* **19**, 605.

Betschart, A. A. (1977). The incorporation of leaf protein concentrates and isolates in human diets. *In* "Green Crop Fractionation" (Wilkins, R. J., Ed.), p. 83. Occasional Synap. No. 9, British Grassland Society.

Bickoff, E. M. and Kohler, G. O. (1974). Preparation of edible protein of leafy green crops such as alfalfa. *US Pat.* **3**, 823 128.

Bickoff, E. M., Booth, A. N., deFremery, D., Edwards, R. H., Knuckles, B. E., Miller, R. E., Saunders, R. M. and Kohler, G. O. (1975). Nutritional evaluation of alfalfa leaf protein concentrate. *In* "Protein Nutritional Quality of Foods and Feeds", (Ed. Friedman, M.), p. 319. Dekker, New York.

Bosshard, H. (1972). Uber die Anlagerung von Thioäthern an Chinone und Chinonimine in stark sauren Medien. *Helv. chim. Acta* **55**, 32.

Boyd, C. E. (1968). Fresh-water plants: a potential source of protein. *Econ. Bot.* **22**, 359.

Boyd, C. E. (1971). Leaf protein from aquatic plants. *In* "Leaf Protein: Its Agronomy Preparation, Quality and Use", (Pirie, N. W., Ed.) p. 44. Blackwell, Oxford.

Braude, R., Jones, A. S. and Houseman, R. A. (1977). The utilisation of the juice extracted from green crops. *In* "Green Crop Fractionation", (Wilkins, R. J., Ed.) p. 47. Occasional Symp. No. 9, British Grassland Society.

Bray, W. J., Humphries, C. H. and Ineritei, M. S. (1978). The use of solvents to decolourise leaf protein concentrate. *J. Sci. Fd Agric.* **29**, 165.

Brown, H. E., Stein, E. R. and Saldana, G. (1975). Evaluation of *Brassica carinata* as a source of plant protein. *J. Agric. Fd Chem.* **23**, 545.

Bruhn, H. D., Staub, R. J. and Koegel, R. G. (1977). On farm forage protein the potential and the means. Paper 3 at Annual Conference of Institute of Agricultural Engineers, London. Also *Agric. Engng.* **32**(3), 66.

Bryant, M. and Fowden, L. (1959). Protein composition in relation to age of daffodil leaves. *Ann. Bot.* **23**, 65.

Buchanan, A. R. (1969a). *In vivo* and *in vitro* methods of measuring nutritive value of leaf protein preparation. *Brit. J. Nutr.* **23**, 533.

Buchanan, A. R. (1969b). Effect of storage and lipid extraction on the properties of leaf protein. *J. Sci. Fd Agric.* **20**, 359.

Butler, J. B. and Pirie, N. W. (1978). A simple unit for extracting protein in bulk from leaves. *Proc. Nutr. Soc.* **36**, 133A.

Byers, M. (1961). The extraction of protein from leaves of some plants growing in Ghana. *J. Sci. Fd Agric.* **12**, 20.

Byers, M. (1967a). The *in vitro* hydrolysis of leaf proteins. 1. The action of papain on protein extracted from the leaves of *Zea mays. J. Sci. Fd Agric.* **18**, 28.

Byers, M. (1967b). The action of papain on protein concentrates extracted from leaves of different species. *J. Sci. Fd Agric.* **18**, 33.

Byers, M. (1971a). The amino acid composition of some leaf protein preparations. *In* "Leaf Protein: Its Agronomy, Preparation, Quality and Use", (Ed. Pirie, N. W.), p. 95. Blackwell, Oxford.

Byers, M. (1971b). The amino acid composition and *in vitro* digestibility of some protein fractions from three species of leaves of various ages. *J. Sci. Fd Agric.* **22**, 242.

Byers, M. (1975). Relationship between total N, total S and the S-containing amino acids in extracted leaf protein. *J. Sci. Fd Agric.* **27**, 135.

Byers, M. and Jenkins, G. (1961). Effect of gibberellic acid on the extraction of protein from the leaves of spring vetches (*Vicia sativa* L.) *J. Sci. Fd Agric.* **12**, 656.

Byers, M. and Sturrock, J. W. (1965). The yields of leaf protein extracted by large-scale processing of various crops. *J. Sci. Fd Agric.* **16**, 341.

Byers, M., Green, S. H. and Pirie, N. W. (1965). The presentation of leaf protein on the table II. *Nutrition* **19**, 63.

Byrom, M. H. (1956). Ramie production machinery. *US Department Agric. Inf. Bull.* **156**.

Carlsson, R. (1975). Selection of centrospermae and other species for production of leaf protein concentrates. Ph.D. Thesis, Lund.

Carr, J. R. and Pearson, G. (1976). Photosensitisation, growth performance and carcass measurements of pigs fed diets containing commercially prepared lucerne leaf-protein concentrate. *N.Z. J. Exp. Agric.* **4**, 45.

Carruthers, I. B. and Pirie, N. W. (1975). The yields of extracted protein, and of residual fibre, from potato haulm taken as a by-product. *Biotech. Bioengng* **17**, 1775.

Chan, P. H., Sakano, K., Singh, S. and Wildman, S. G. (1972). Crystalline fraction 1 protein : preparation in large yield. *Science* **176**, 1145.

Chandramani, R., Balasundaram, C. S., Krishnamoorthy, K. K. and Balakrishnan, T. (1975a). Effect of nitrogen and the frequency of cutting in guinea grass (*Panicum maximum* L.). *Madras Agric. J.* **62**, 155.

Chandramani, R., Krishnamoorthy, K. K., Balasundaram, C. S. and Balakrishnan, T. (1975b). Optimum time of cutting for obtaining maximum yield of extractable protein from fenugreek (*Trigonella foenumgraecum*) varieties. *Madras Agric. J.* **62**, 230.

Cheeke, P. R. (1974). Nutritional evaluation of alfalfa protein concentrate with rats, swine and rabbits. Proc. 12th tech. Alfalfa Conf. USDA 76.

Cheeke, P. R. and Garman, G. R. (1974). Influence of dietary protein and sulfur amino acid levels on the toxicity of *Senecio jacobaea* (Tansy ragwort) in rats. *Nutr. Reports Internat.* **9**, 193.

Cheeke, P. R., Kinzell, J. H., deFremery, D. and Kohler, G. O. (1977). Freezedried and commercially prepared alfalfa protein concentrate evaluation with rats and swine. *J. Animal Sci* **44**, 772.

Chibnall, A. C. (1939). "Protein Metabolism in the Plant" Yale University Press.

Chibnall, A. C., Rees, M. W. and Lugg, J. W. H. (1963). The amino acid composition of leaf proteins. *J. Sci. Fd Agric.* **14**, 234.

Cohen, M., Ginoza, W., Dorner, R. W., Hudson, W. R. and Wildman, S. G. (1956). Solubility and color characteristics of leaf proteins prepared in air and nitrogen. *Science* **124**, 1081.

Colker, D. A., Eskew, R. K. and Aceto, N. C. (1948). Preparation of vegetable leaf meals. *USDA Tech. Bull.* **958**, 53.

Connell, J. (1975). The prospects for green crop fractionation. *Span* **18**, 103.

Connell, J. and Foxell, P. R. (1976). Green crop fractionation, the products and their utilization by cattle, pigs and poultry. *Bienn. Rev. Natn. Inst. Res. Dairying* **21**.

Connell, J. and Houseman, R. A. (1977). The utilisation by ruminants of the pressed green crops from fractionation machinery. *In* "Green Crop Fractionation (Ed. Wilkins, R.J.), Occasional Symp. No. 9, British Grassland Society.

Cowey, C. B., Pope, J. A., Adron, J. W. and Blair, A. (1971). Studies on the nutrition of marine flatfish. Growth of the plaice (*Pleuronectes platessa*) on diets containing proteins derived from plants and other sources. *Mar. Biol.* **10**, 145.

Crook, E. M. and Holden, M. (1948). Some factors affecting the extraction of nitrogenous materials from leaves of various species. *Biochem. J.* **43**, 181.

Damborg, L., Mogensen, S. N. and Israelsen, M. (1976). Drying alfalfa with low energy consumption, less air pollution. *Feedstuffs.* **48**, 21.

Davies, M., Evans, W. C. and Parr, W. H. (1952). Biological values and digestibilities of some grasses, and protein preparations from young and mature species, by the Thomas-Mitchell method, using rats. *Biochem. J.* **52**, xxiii.

Davys, M. N. G. and Pirie, N. W. (1960). Protein from leaves by bulk extraction. *Engng* **190**, 274.

Davys, M. N. G. and Pirie, N. W. (1963). Batch production of protein from leaves. *J. Agric. Engng Res.* **8**, 70.

Davys, M. N. G. and Pirie, N. W. (1969). A laboratory-scale pulper for leafy plant material. *Biotech. Bioengng* **11**, 517.

Davys, M. N. G., Pirie, N. W. and Street, G. (1969). A laboratory-scale press for extracting juice from leaf pulp. *Biotech. Bioengng* **11**, 528.

Desmukh, M. G. and Joshi, R. N. (1973). Effect of rhizobial inoculation on the extraction of protein from the leaves of cowpea (*Vigna sinensis* L. Savi ex Hassk.). *Ind. J. Agric. Sci.* **43**, 539.

Desmukh, M. G., Gore, S. B., Mungikar, A. M. and Joshi, R. N. (1974). The yields of leaf protein from various short-duration crops. *J. Sci. Fd Agric.* **25**, 717.

Dev, D. V. and Joshi, R. N. (1969). Extraction of protein from some plants of Aurangabad, *J. Biol. Sci*, **12**, 15.

Dev, D. V., Batra, U. R. and Joshi, R. N. (1974). The yields of extracted leaf protein from lucerne (*Medicago sativa* L.). *J. Sci. Fd Agric.* **25**, 725.

Doraiswamy, T. R., Singh, N. and Daniel, V. A. (1969). Effects of supplementing ragi (*Eleusine coracana*) diets with lysine or leaf protein on the growth and nitrogen metabolism of children. *Brit. J. Nutr.* **23**, 737.

Duckworth, J. and Woodham, A. A. (1961). Leaf protein concentrates. I. Effect of source of raw material and method of drying on protein value for chicks and rats. *J. Sci. Fd Agric.* **12**, 5.

Duckworth, J., Hepburn, W. R. and Woodham, A. A. (1961). Leaf protein concentrates II. The value of a commercially dried product for newly-weaned pigs. *J. Sci. Fd Agric.* **12**, 16.

Dumont, A. G. and Boyce, D. S. (1976). Leaf protein production and use on the farm: an economic study. *J. Brit. Grassland Soc.* **31**, 153.

Dykyjova, D. (1971). Productivity and solar energy conversion in reedswamp stands in comparison with outdoor mass cultures of algae in the temperate climate of central Europe. *Photosynthetica* **5**, 329.

Eggum, B. O. and Christensen, K. D. (1975). Influence of tannin on protein utilization in feedstuffs with special reference to barley. *In* "Breeding for seed protein improvement" Internat. Atomic Energy Agency p. 135.

Elliott, K. and Knight J., Eds (1972). "Lipids, Malnutrition and the Developing Brain." Ciba Foundation Symposium. Elsevier, Amsterdam.

Fafunso, M. and Bassir, O. (1976). Effects of age and season on yield of crude and extractable proteins from some edible plants. *Expl Agric.* **12**, 249.

Fafunso, M. and Byers, M. (1977). Effect of pre-press treatments of vegetation on the quality of the extracted leaf protein. *J. Sci. Fd Agric.* **28**, 375.

Fafunso, M. A. and Oke, O. L. (1977). Leaf protein from different cassava varieties. *Nutr. Rep. Internat.* **14**, 629.

Farkas, T. and Deri-Hadlaczky, E. (1975). Effect of temperature on the linolenic acid level in wheat and rye seedlings. *Lipids* **10**, 331.

Festenstein, G. N. (1972). Water-soluble carbohydrates in extracts from large-scale preparations of leaf protein. *J. Sci. Fd Agric.* **23**, 1409.

Festenstein, G. N. (1976). Carbohydrates associated with leaf protein. *J. Sci. Fd Agric.* **27**, 849.

Food and Agriculture Organisation (1964). "The state of food and agriculture." FAO, Rome.

Food and Agriculture Organisation (1969). "Provisional indicative world plan for agricultural development." FAO, Rome.

Food and Agricultural Organisation (1971). "Production yearbook." FAO, Rome.

Food and Agricultural Organisation (1973). Energy and protein requirements. *Tech. Report. Ser.* **522.**

Foot, A. S. (1974). Lucerne juice for pigs. *Pig Farming* **22** (9) 71.

Garcha, J. S., Kawatra, B. L. and Wagle, D. S. (1971). Nutritional evaluation of leaf proteins and the effect of their supplementation to wheat flour by rat feeding. *J. Fd Sci. Tech.* **8,** 23.

Ghosh, J. J. (1967). Leaf protein concentrates: problems and prospects in the control of protein malnutrition. *Trans. Bose Res. Inst. (Calcutta)* **30,** 215.

Gjøen, A. U. and Njaa, L. R. (1977). Methionine sulphoxide as a source of sulphur-containing amino acids for the young rat. *Brit. J. Nutr.* **37,** 93.

Goel, U., Kawatra, B. L. and Bajaj, S. (1977). Nutritional evaluation of califlower leaf protein concentrate by rat feeding. *J. Sci. Fd Agric.* **28,** 786.

Gore, S. B. and Joshi, R. N. (1976a). Effect of fertiliser and frequency of cutting on the extraction of protein from *Sesbania. Ind. J. Agron.* **21,** 39.

Gore, S. B. and Joshi, R. N. (1976b). A note on the effect of simazine on the yields of dry matter and crude protein, and on the extractability of protein from hybrid napier grass. *Ind. J. Agron.* **21,** 491.

Gore, S. B., Mungikar, A. M. and Joshi, R. N. (1974). The yields of extracted protein from hybrid napier grass. *J. Sci. Fd Agric.* **25,** 1149.

Greenhalgh, J. F. D. and Reid, G. W. (1975). Mechanical processing of wet roughage. *Proc. Nutr. Soc.* **34,** 74A.

Hageman, R. H. and Waygood, E. R. (1959). Methods for the extraction of enzymes from cereal leaves with especial reference to the triosephosphate dehydrogenases. *Plant Physiol.* **34,** 396.

Hanczakowski, P. (1974). Wplyw dodatku syntetycznej metioniny i lizyny na wartosc pokarmowa bialka koncentratow z zielonki. *Rocz. nauk. Zoot.* **1,** 139.

Heath, S. B. (1978). The production of leaf protein concentrates from forage crops. *In* "Plant proteins" (Norton, G., Ed.). Butterworth, London.

Heath, S. B. and King, M. W. (1977). The production of crops for green crop fractionation. *In* "Green Crop Fractionation" (Wilkins, R. J., Ed.). Occasional Symp. No. 9, British Grassland Society.

Henry, K. M. and Ford, J. E. (1965). The nutritive value of leaf protein concentrates determined in biological tests with rats and by microbiological methods. *J. Sci. Fd Agric.* **16,** 425.

Hill-Cottingham, D. G. and Lloyd-Jones, C. P. (1979). Translocation of nitrogenous compounds in plants. *In* "Nitrogen Assimilation of Plants", (Hewitt, E. J. and Cutting, C. V., Eds.) Academic Press, London and New York. 397.

Holden, M. (1952). The fractionation and enzymic breakdown of some phosphorus compounds in leaf tissue. *Biochem. J.* **51,** 433.

Holden, M. (1974). Chlorophyll degradation products in leaf protein preparations. *J. Sci. Fd Agric.* **25,** 1427.

Houseman, R. A. and Connell, J. (1976). The utilization of the products of green-crop fractionation by pigs and ruminants. *Proc. Nutr. Soc.* **35,** 213.

Hove, E. L. and Bailey, R. W. (1975). Towards a leaf protein concentrate industry in New Zealand. *N.Z. J. Exp. Agric.* **3,** 193.

Hove, E. L., Lohrey, E., Urs, M. K. and Allison, R. M. (1974). The effect of lucerne-protein concentrate in the diet on growth, reproduction and body composition of rats. *Brit. J. Nutr.* **31,** 147.

Hudson, B. J. F. and Karis, I. G. (1973). Aspects of vegetable structural lipids: I. The lipids of leaf protein concentrate. *J. Sci. Fd Agric.* **24,** 1541.

Hudson, B. J. F. and Karis, I. G. (1974). Aspects of vegetable structural lipids: II. The effect of crop maturity on leaf lipids. *J. Sci. Fd Agric.* **25,** 1491.

Hudson, B. J. F. and Warwick, M. J. (1977). Lipid stabilisation in leaf protein concentrates from ryegrass. *J. Sci. Fd Agric.* **28,** 259.

Hudson, J. P. (1975). Weeds as crops. Proc. 12th Brit. Weed Control Conf. 333.

Hudson, J. P. (1976). Food crops for the future. *J. Roy. Soc. Arts.* **124,** 572.

Hussain, A., Ullah, M. and Ahmad, B. (1968). Studies on the potentials of leaf proteins for the preparation of concentrates from various leaf-wastes in West Pakistan. *Pak. J. Agric. Res.* **6,** 110.

Jamaica, Scientific Sci. Res. Council Tech. Rep. (1965). Investigations into the production of high protein concentrate from leaves for inclusion in the diet of infants and children.

Kamalanathan, G. and Devadas, R. P. (1971). Acceptability of food preparations containing leaf protein concentrates. *In* "Leaf Protein: Its Agronomy, Preparation, Quality and Use", (Pirie, N. W., Ed.), p. 145. Blackwell, Oxford.

Kamalanathan, G., Karuppiah, P. and Devadas, R. P. (1975). Supplementary value of leaf protein and groundnut meal in the diets of preschool children. *Ind. J. Nutr. Dietet.* **12,** 203.

Kanev, S., Boncheva, I., Georgieva, L. and Iovchev, N. (1976). Tests of a protein concentrate from lucerne for fattening pigs and poultry. Quoted from *Nutr. Abs. Rev.* **46,** 282.

Kawatra, B. L., Garcha, J. S. and Wagle, D. S. (1974). Effect of supplementation of leaf protein extracted from berseem (*Trifolium alexandrinum*) to wheat flour diet. *J. Fd Sci. Tech.* **11,** 241.

Knuckles, B. E., de Fremery, D., Bickoff, E. M. and Kohler, G. O. (1975). Soluble protein from alfalfa juice by membrane filtration. *J. Agric. Fd Chem.* **23,** 209.

Lahiry, N. L., Satterlee, L. D., Hsu, H. W. and Wallace, G. W. (1977). Characterization of the chlorogenic acid binding fraction in leaf protein concentration. *J. Fd Sci.* **42,** 83.

Lala, V. R. and Reddy, V. (1970). Absorption of β carotene from green leafy vegetables in undernourished children. *Am. J. Clin. Med.* **23,** 110.

Lexander, K., Carlsson, R., Schalen, V., Simonsson, A. and Lundborg, T. (1970). Quantities and qualities of leaf protein concentrates from wild species and crop species grown under controlled conditions. *Ann. Appl. Biol.* **66,** 193.

Lima, I. H., Richardson, T. and Stahmann, M. A. (1965). Fatty acids in some leaf protein concentrates. *J. Agric. Fd Chem.* **13,** 143.

Lohrey, E., Tapper, B. and Hove, E. L. (1974). Photosensitization of albino rats fed on lucerne-protein concentrates. *Brit. J. Nutr.* **31,** 159.

Lugg, J. W. H. (1939). The representativeness of extracted samples and the efficiency of extraction of protein from the fresh leaves of plants; and some partial analyses of the whole proteins of leaves. *Biochem. J.* **33,** 110.

Mahadeviah, S. and Singh, N. (1968). Leaf protein from the green tops of *Cichorium intybus* L. (chicory). *Ind. J. Exp. Biol.* **6,** 193.

Martin, C. (1975). Leaf protein child feeding trial. *League Internat. Fd Educ. Newsletter* March.

Matai, S. (1976). Protein from water weeds. *In* "Aquatic weeds in S.E. Asia", (Varshney, C. K. and Rzoska, J., Eds.), p. 369. Junk, The Hague.

Matai, S., Bagchi, D. K. and Roy Chowdhury, S. (1971). Leaf protein from some plants in West Bengal. *Sci. Engng.* **24**, 102.

Matai, S., Bagchi, D. K. and Chanda, S. (1973). Optimal seed rate and fertilizer dose for maximum yield of extracted protein from the leaves of mustard (*Brassica nigra* Koch) and turnip (*Brassica rapa* L.). *Ind. J. Agric. Sci.* **43**, 165.

Matai, S., Bagchi, D. K. and Chanda, S. (1976). Effects of seed rate, nitrogen level and leaf age on the yield of extracted protein from five different crops in West Bengal. *J. Sci. Fd Agric.* **27**, 736.

McLeod, M. N. (1974). Plant tannins—their role in forage quality. *Nutr. Abs. Rev.* **44**, 804.

Mead, J. F. and Alfin-Slater, R. B. (1966). Toxic substances present in food fats. Nat. Acad. Sci./Nat. Res. Council Publ. 1354, p. 238.

Milic, B. L. (1972). Lucerne tannins. I. Content and composition during growth. *J. Sci. Fd Agric.* **23**, 1151.

Milic, B. L. and Stojanovic, S. (1972). Lucerne tannins. III. Metabolic fate of lucerne tannins in mice. *J. Sci. Fd Agric.* **23**, 1163.

Miller, D. S. (1965). Some nutritional problems in the utilization of non-conventional proteins for human feeding. *Rec. Adv. Fd Sci.* **3**, 125.

Miller, D. S. and Samuel, P. D. (1970). Effects of addition of sulphur compounds to diet on utilisation of protein in young growing rats. *J. Sci. Fd Agric.* **21**, 616.

Miller, R. E., Edwards, R. H., Lazar, M. E., Bickoff, E. M. and Kohler, G. O. (1972). PRO-XAN process: air drying alfalfa leaf protein concentrate. *J. agric. Fd. Chem.* **20**, 1151.

Mokady, S. and Zimmermann, G. (1966). The effect of different liquid extractants used with impulse-rendered lucerne paste on the nutritional and calorigenic properties of the proteins. *Proc. 7th Internat. Cong. Nutr.* **5**, 279.

Monsod, G. G. (1976). The versatility and economics of water hyacinth. Phillipine Council agric. Resources Res., Fisheries Forum, Manila.

Monteith, J. L. (1977). Climate and efficiency of crop production in Britain. *Phil. Trans. R. Soc.* (B) **281**, 277.

Morris, T. R. (1977). Leaf protein concentrate for non-ruminant farm animals. *In* "Green Crop Fractionation", (Wilkins, R. J., Ed.), p. 67. Occasional Symp. No. 9, British Grassland Society.

Morrison, J. E. and Pirie, N. W. (1960). The presentation of leaf protein on the table. *Nutrition* **14**, 7.

Morrison, J. E. and Pirie, N. W. (1961). The large scale production of protein from leaf extracts. *J. Sci. Fd Agric.* **12**, 1.

Mungikar, A. M., Tekale, N. S. and Joshi, R. N. (1976a). The yields of leaf protein and fibre that can be obtained from fractionation of berseem (*Trifolium alexandrinum* L.). *Ind. J. Nutr. Dietet.* **13**, 114.

Mungikar, A. M., Batra, U. R., Tekale, N. S. and Joshi, R. N. (1976b). Effects of nitrogen fertilisation on the yield of extracted protein from some crops. *Exp. Agric.* **12**, 353.

Myer, R. O., Cheeke, P. R. and Kennick, W. H. (1975). Utilization of alfalfa protein concentrate by swine. *J. Animal Sci.* **40**, 885.

Njaa, L. R. (1962). Some problems related to detection of methionine sulfoxide in protein hydrolysates. *Acta Chem. Scand.* **16**, 1359.

Oke, O. L. (1966). The introduction of leaf protein into the Nigerian diet. *Nutrition* **20**, 18.

Olatunbosun, D. A. (1976). Leaf protein for human use in Africa. *Ind. J. Nutr. Dietet.* **13**, 168.

Olatunbosun, D. A., Adadevoh, B. K. and Oke, O. L. (1972). Leaf protein: a new protein source for the management of protein calorie malnutrition in Nigeria. *Nigerian med. J.* **2**, 195.

Patriquin, D. G. and Knowles, R. (1972). Nitrogen fixation in the rhizosphere of marine angiosperms. *Mar. Biol.* **16**, 49.

Pienazek, D., Rakowska, M. and Kunachowicz, H. (1975). The participation of methionine and cysteine in the formation of bonds resistant to the action of proteolytic enzymes in heated casein. *Brit. J. Nutr.* **34**, 163.

Pierpoint, W. S. (1969). o-Quinones formed in plant extracts. Their reactions with amino acids and peptides. *Biochem. J.* **112**, 609.

Pierpoint, W. S. (1971). Formation and behaviour of o-quinones in some processes of agricultural importance. *Ann. Rep. Roth. Exp. Sta.* **1970**, 199.

Pieterse, A. H. (1974). The water hyacinth. *Trop. Abs.* **29**, 77.

Pirie, N. W. (1942). Direct use of leaf protein in human nutrition. *Chemy Ind.* **61**, 45.

Pirie, N. W. (1959). Large-scale production of leaf protein. *Ann. Rep. Roth. exp. Sta.* **1958**, 93.

Pirie, N. W. (1961). The disintegration of soft tissues in the absence of air. *J. agric. Engng Res.* **6**, 142.

Pirie, N. W. (1964a). Large-scale production of leaf protein. *Ann. Rep. Roth exp. Sta.* **1963**, 96.

Pirie, N. W. (1964b). Freeze-drying, or drying by sublimation. *In* "Instrumental methods of experimental biology", (Newman, D. W., Ed.), p. 89. Macmillan, New York.

Pirie, N. W. (1966a). Improvements to machinery. *Ann. Rep. Roth. exp. Sta.* **1965**, 106.

Pirie, N. W. (1966b). Fodder fractionation: an aspect of conservation. *Fertil. Feeding Stuffs J.* **63**, 119.

Pirie, N. W. (1970a). Large-scale protein preparations. *Ann. Rep. Roth. exp. Sta.* **1969**, 132.

Pirie, N. W. (1970b). Weeds are not all bad. *Ceres* **3**(4) 31.

Pirie, N. W., Ed. (1971a). "Leaf Protein: Its Agronomy, Preparation, Quality and Use." Blackwell, Oxford.

Pirie, N. W. (1971b). Some obstacles to innovation. *Pugwash Newsletter* **9**, 16.

Pirie, N. W. (1972). The direction of beneficial nutritional change. *Ecol. Fd Nutr.* **1**, 279.

Pirie, N. W. (1974). Fixation of nucleic acid by leaf fibre and calcium phosphate. *Proc. R. Soc.* (B) **185**, 343.

Pirie, N. W. (1975a). The potentialities of leafy vegetables and forages as food protein sources. *Baroda J. Nutr.* **2**, 43.

Pirie, N. W. (1975b). Some obstacles to eliminating famine. *Proc. Nutr. Soc.* **34**, 181.

Pirie, N. W. (1976a). "Food Resources: Conventional and Novel", Penguin Books, Harmondsworth, Middx.

Pirie, N. W. (1976b). Food protein sources. *Phil. Trans. R. Soc.* (*B*) **274**, 489.

Pirie, N. W. (1976c). Restoring esteem for leafy vegetables. *Appropriate Technology* **3**(3) 24.

Pirie, N. W. (1977a). The extended use of fractionation processes. *Phil. Trans. R. Soc.* (*B*) **281**, 139.

Pirie, N. W. (1977b). A simple unit for extracting leaf protein in bulk. *Exp. Agric.* **13**, 113.

Pirie, N. W. (1978). "Leaf Protein and Other Aspects of Fodder Fractionation." Cambridge University Press, Cambridge.

Powling, W. T. (1953). Protein extraction from green crops. *World Crops* **5**, 63.

Ramana, K. V. R. and Singh, N. (1971). Nutritional efficiency of lucerne leaf protein as a source of β carotene in rat diets. *Ind. J. exp. Biol.* **9**, 378.

Rao, C. N. and Rao, B. S. (1970). Absorption of dietary carotenes in human subjects. *Am. J. Clin. Nutr.* **23**, 105.

Raymond, W. F. (1977). Farm wastes. *Biologist* **24**, 80.

Roberts, E. A. H. (1959). The interaction of flavonol orthoquinones with cysteine and glutathione. *Chemy Ind.* **995**.

Rodriguez, E., Towers, G. H. N. and Mitchell, J. C. (1977). Allergic contact dermatitis and sesquiterpene lactones. *Compositae Newsletter* **4**, 4.

Rouelle, H. M. (1773). Observations sur les fécules ou parties vertes des plantes, et sur la matière glutineuse ou végétoanimale. *J. Med. Chir. Pharm.* **40**, 59.

Savangikar, V. A. and Joshi, R. N. (1976). Influence of irrigation and fertiliser on the yields of extracted protein from lucerne. *Forage Res.* **2**, 125.

Savangikar, V. A. and Joshi, R. N. (1978). Edible protein from *Parthenium hysterophorus* L. *Expl. Agric.* **14**, 93.

Schubert, K. R. and Evans, H. J. (1976). Hydrogen evolution: a major factor affecting the efficiency of nitrogen fixation in nodulated symbionts. *Proc. Nat. Acad. Sci.* USA **73**, 1207.

Shah, F. H. (1968). Changes in leaf protein lipids *in vitro*. *J. Sci. Fd Agric.* **19**, 199.

Shah, F. H. (1971). Effect of heat on the extractability of lipids from leaf protein meal. *Pak. J. Sci. Ind. Res.* **14**, 492.

Shah, F. H., Riaz-ud-Din and Salam, A. (1967). Effect of heat on the digestibility of leaf proteins. I. Toxicity of the lipids and their oxidation products. *Pak. J. Sci. Ind. Res.* **10**, 39.

Shah, F. H., Zia-ur-Rehman, and Mahmud, B. A. (1976). Effect of extraction techniques on the extraction of protein from *Trifolium alexandrinum*. *Pak. J. Sci. Ind. Res.* **19**, 39.

Shurpalekar, K. S., Singh, N. and Sundarvalli, O. E. (1969). Nutritive value of leaf protein from lucerne (*Medicago sativa*): growth responses in rats at different protein levels and to supplementation with lysine and/or methionine. *Ind. J. Exp. Biol.* **7**, 279.

Singh, N. (1962). Proteolytic activity of leaf extracts. *J. Sci. Fd. Agric.* **13**, 325.

Singh, N. (1964). Leaf protein extraction from some plants of northern India. *J. Fd Sci. Tech.* **1**, 37.

Siren, G. (1973). Protein ur skogsträd. *Svensk Naturv.* p. 41.

Siren, B., Blombäck, B. and Alden, T. (1970). Proteins in forest tree leaves. Royal Coll. Forestry (Sweden) Res. Note **28**.

Slade, R. E., Branscombe, D. J. and McGowan, J. C. (1945). Protein extraction. *Chemy Ind.* **23**, 194.

Slesser, M., Lewis, C. and Edwardson, W. (1977). Energy systems analysis for food policy. *Fd Policy* **2**, 123.

Smith, R. C. (1972). Acetylation of methionine sulfoxide and methionine sulfone by the rat. *Biochim. Biophys. Acta* **261**, 304.

Subba Rao, M. S., Singh, N. and Prasanappa, G. (1967). Preservation of wet leaf protein concentrates. *J. Sci. Fd Agric.* **18**, 295.

Subba Rau, B. H. and Singh, N. (1971). Studies of nutritive value of leaf protein from lucerne (*Medicago sativa*): III. Supplementation of rat diets based on wheat. *J. Sci. Fd Agric.* **22,** 569.

Subba Rau, B. H., Ramana, K. V. R. and Singh, N. (1972). Studies on nutritive value of leaf proteins and some factors affecting their quality. *J. Sci. Fd Agric.* **23,** 233.

Sur, B. K. (1961). Nutritive value of lucerne-leaf proteins. Biological value of lucerne proteins and the supplementary relations to rice proteins measured by balance and rat growth methods. *Brit. J. Nutr.* **15,** 419.

Synge, R. L. M. (1975). Interactions of polyphenols with proteins in plants and plant products. *Qual. plantarum* **24,** 337.

Synge, R. L. M. (1976). Damage to nutritional value of plant proteins by chemical reactions during storage and processing. *Qual. plantarum* **26,** 9.

Tapper, B. A., Lohrey, E., Hove, E. L. and Allison, R. M. (1975). Photosensitivity from chlorophyll-derived pigments. *J. Sci. Fd Agric.* **26,** 277.

Taylor, K. G., Bates, R. P. and Robbins, R. C. (1971). Extraction of protein from water hyacinth. *Hyacinth Control J.* **9,** 20.

Tekale, N. S. and Joshi, R. N. (1976). Extractable protein from by-product vegetation of some cole and root crops. *Ann. Appl. Biol.* **82,** 155.

Thakur, M. L., Somaroo, B. H. and Grant, W. F. (1974). The phenolic constituents from leaves of *Manihot esculenta*. *Can. J. Bot.* **52,** 2381.

Thresh, J. M. (1956). Some effects of tannic acid and of leaf extracts which contain tannins on the infectivity of tobacco mosaic and tobacco necrosis viruses. *Ann. appl. Biol.* **44,** 608.

Thung, T. H. and van der Want, J. P. H. (1951). Viruses and tannins. *Tids. Pl. Ziekt.* **57,** 72.

Toosy, R. Z. and Shah, F. H. (1974). Leaf protein concentrate in human diet. *Pak. J. Sci. Ind. Res.* **17,** 40.

Tracey, M. V. (1948). Leaf protease of tobacco and other plants. *Biochem. J.* **42,** 281.

Tragardh, C. (1974). Production of leaf protein concentrate for human consumption by isopropanol treatment. A comparison between untreated raw juice and raw juice concentrated by evaporation and ultra-filtration. *Lebensmitt. Wiss. Technol.* **7,** 199.

Trigg, T. E. and Topps, J. H. (1971). The effects of additional methionine on the quality of leaf protein concentrates differing in nutritive value. *Proc. Nutr. Soc.* **31,** 45A.

United Nations (1968). "International Action to Avert the Impending Protein Crisis." U.N., New York.

United States President's Science Advisory Committee. (1967). The world food problem. Govt. Printing Off., Washington.

Van Sumere, C. F., Albrecht, J., Dedonder, A., de Pooter, H. and Pe I. (1975). Plant proteins and phenolics. *In* "The Chemistry and Biochemistry of Plant Proteins." (Harborne, J. and Van Sumere, C. F., Eds.), p. 211. Academic Press, London and New York.

Vartha, E. W. and Allison, R. M. (1973). Extractable protein from "Grassland Tama" Westerwolds ryegrass. *N.Z. J. Exp. Agric.* **1,** 239.

Venkataswamy, G., Krishnamurthy, K. A., Chandra, P. and Pirie, A. (1976i). A nutrition rehabilitation centre for children with xerophthalmia. *Lancet* 1120.

Vithayathil, P. J. and Murthy, G. S. (1972). New reactions of o-benzoquinone at the thioether group of methionine. *Nature New Biol.* **236,** 101.

Walsh, K. A. and Hauge, S. M. (1953). Carotene: factors affecting destruction in alfalfa. *J. Agric. Fd Chem.* **1**, 1001.

Wang, J. C. and Kinsella, J. E. (1976a). Functional properties of novel proteins: alfalfa leaf protein. *J. Fd Sci.* **41**, 286.

Wang, J. C. and Kinsella, J. E. (1976b). Functional properties of alfalfa leaf protein: foaming. *J. Fd Sci.* **41**, 488.

Wareing, P. F. and Allen, E. J. (1977). Physiological aspects of crop choice. *Phil. Trans. R. Soc.* (*B*) **281**, 107.

Waterlow, J. C. (1962). The absorption and retention of nitrogen from leaf protein by infants recovering from malnutrition. *Brit. J. Nutr.* **16**, 531.

Wilkins, R. J. Ed. (1977). "Green Crop Fractionation." Occasional Symp. No. 9, British Grassland Society.

Wilkins, R. J., Heath, S. B., Roberts, W. P. and Foxell, P. R. (1977). A theoretical economic analysis of systems of green crop fractionation. *In* "Green Crop Fractionation", (Wilkins, R. J., Ed.), p. 131. Occasional Symp. No. 9, British Grassland Society.

Wong, E. (1973). Plant phenolics. *In* "Chemistry and Biochemistry of Herbage", (Butler, G. W. and Bailey, R. W., Eds.), Vol. 1, p. 263. Academic Press, London and New York.

Woodham, A. A. (1971). The use of animal tests for the evaluation of leaf protein concentrates. In Pirie (1971a) p. 115.

World Health Organisation/U.S.A.I.D. (1976). Vitamin A deficiency and xerophthalmia. *Tech. Rep. Ser.* **590**. WHO, Geneva.

Yemm, E. W. and Folkes, B. F. (1953). The amino acids of cytoplasmic and chloroplastic proteins of barley. *Biochem. J.* **55**, 700.

Yokoyama, H., Hayman, E. P., Hsu, W. J., Poling, S. M. and Bauman, A. J. (1977). Chemical bioinduction of rubber in guayule plant. *Science* **197**, 1076.

Zscheile, F. P. (1973). Long-term preservation of carotene in alfalfa meal. *J. agric. Fd Chem.* **21**, 1117.

Game Ranching in Africa

C. R. FIELD

UNESCO Arid Lands Project,
P.O. Box 30592, *Nairobi, Kenya*

I. INTRODUCTION

A. SCOPE AND LIMITATIONS

I know of no review of Game Ranching which covers the whole of Africa. This review is an attempt at being as comprehensive as possible but has East Africa as the central theme since it is the area in which I have greatest experience.

Before proceeding further it is necessary to define the term Game Ranching as used in this paper and to state how broadly it will be used.

The term "Game" has become rather loosely used to refer to all those species of wild animals which are hunted and, it normally follows, used by man. Thus game refers to mammals, birds and fish. Another term "Big Game" is loosely used in Africa to refer to large ungulates and carnivores. There is no diminutive and I will avoid using this term

63

where possible as it is open to misinterpretation. Emphasis in this review will be placed on those species of wild hoofed mammal which can be and are utilized by man. Thus the terms "Game" and "Wildlife" are synonymous and will refer largely to these species.

There are three terms which appear widely in this review namely Wildlife or Game Farming, Ranching, and Cropping. Game Farming is considered to be the intensive utilization and the domestication of wild animals on fenced farmland; while Game Ranching is the extensive utilization particularly of wild animals on often unfenced ranchland of low potential. Game cropping is the procedure by which wildlife is removed from any kind of land whether it be farmland, ranchland, game reserve or National Park.

This review covers game farming and ranching and considers case histories of game cropping operations before assessing the relative merits of the different forms of land use.

It should be noted that the scope of this review is limited to the use of wildlife for meat and does not include the other very important aspects of tourism and sport hunting.

B. PREHISTORY AND HISTORY

Hunting for food is a human way of life and undoubtedly preceded all other forms of human nutrition except gathering. It still continues among the Bushmen of Botswana, the Hadza of Central Tanzania and to varying degrees of importance among many tribes, e.g. the Zaghawa of Sudan (Tubiana and Tubiana, 1975) and Wandorobo of Kenya, (Spencer, 1973). Graham (1973) discusses the motivations, history and ethics of hunters in a rather novel manner. Among the Valley Bisa of Zambia it has been shown that certain individuals are significantly more efficient than others at hunting and rely for their nutrition on this source (Marks, 1973). The Hadza have a nutritionally adequate diet and spend less time obtaining their food than agricultural tribes (Woodburn 1968). The average diet of the Kung bushmen exceeds minimum energy requirements by 165 calories per day and 33 g protein and involves only 2–3 days work per week (Lee, 1968 cited in Parker and Graham, 1971). Some tribes have recently been deprived of major hunting areas by the creation of National Parks and ranches e.g. the Waliangulu (Holman, 1967). Small mammals are still hunted on a large scale in some areas. Thus, Butynski (1973) states that over 2·5 million spring hare (*Pedetes capensis* Forster) are killed in Botswana annually. This represents about four per person yielding a total of 3·4 Mkg of meat per annum worth M1·4$.

In Zambia a study of the red lechwe (*Kobus leche leche* Gray) in the Busanga plains of Kafue National Park (Grimsdell and Bell, 1972) has shown that since traditional hunting by fishermen was stopped in 1948 the population has increased exponentially at 14% per annum. A lag occurred in the response from 1950 to 1958 and this may be explained either by traditional hunting with dogs, leading to a differential mortality of females, or possibly by an overgrowth of vegetation during periods of low grazing pressure which would be unfavourable to lechwe (Grimsdell and Bell, 1972). At all events a considerable offtake by hunting is implied. Similarly in the Kafue flats area traditional lechwe drives or "chilas" were common and may have taken up to 3000 lechwe in three days (Michell and Uys, 1961). Chilas were finally outlawed in 1957 although illegal hunting continues. It is now thought that nutritional stress is a major factor limiting lechwe populations (Bell *et al.*, 1973).

Poaching where it involves non-trophy animals, is still an important and unquantifiable food resource for the people of the undeveloped countries in East Africa. Unfortunately the law has driven the practice underground where it has become commercialized.

C. RATIONALE AND PRINCIPLES

1. *The area*

Estimates by Thornthwaite (1933) and others have indicated that 31% of the earth's surface is arid or semi-arid and these areas occur in approximately equal proportions. These regions are found mostly in the sub-tropics with the Sahara and Danakil to the north and the Kalahari and Namib to the south. A few deserts occur within the tropics such as the Chalbi in north Kenya and the Somali deserts. Bordering these deserts are regions of sub-desert with rainfall usually below 250 mm and rather unpredictable. Semi-arid areas have a rainfall up to twice this, but owing to poor seasonal distribution or high evaporation rates or a combination of these, crops cannot be grown and the availability of drinking water is scarce or highly seasonal. The natural vegetation is of a type that has become adapted over long periods to tolerate heat stress, evaporative loads well in excess of annual rainfall, very low soil moisture and often high salt concentrations. Strong winds exacerbate the situation as does the highly eroded, rocky rugged terrain. The area is not, however, unproductive for man as the vegetation can be made available by conversion to meat and milk by certain herbivores (Ledger *et al.*, 1967).

These herbivores include insects and birds as well as large and small

Table I. Some animal densities per km² in wildlife reserves in Africa

Species	1. Garamba NP, Zaire	2. Kabalega Falls NP, Uganda	3. Ruwenzori NP, Uganda	4. Lake Manyara NP, Tanzania	5. Serengeti NP, Tanzania	6. Nairobi NP, Kenya	7. Tarangire GR, Tanzania	8. Kidepo Valley NP, Uganda	9. Mkomasi GR, Tanzania	10. Ruaha NP, Tanzania	11. Tsavo NP, Kenya	12. Lake Nakuru NP, Kenya
Hippopotamus	0·4	17·3*	9·1	—	—	—	—	—	—	—	—	0·4
Elephant	5·1	1·9-3·8	1·7	5·4	0·2	—	1·6	0·4	0·2-0·9	1·7	1·7	—
Buffalo	11·8	2·5-7·8	15·6	19·4	2·6	0·1	5·8	0·9	0·2	1·5	1·0	0·9
Giraffe	—	—	—	0·4	0·5	0·7	1·1	0·2-0·3	0·1	0·4	0·03-0·2	—
Zebra	—	—	—	1·5	6·4	4·3	8·5	0·4	0·03-0·1	0·6	0·3-2·3	—
Eland	—	—	—	—	0·2	0·3	0·2	0·2	0·2	—	0·1-0·2	—
Wildebeest	—	—	—	0·1	12·4	5·5	3·5	—	—	—	—	—
Hartebeest	1·7	0·9-2·4	—	—	1·3	7·4	0·6	1·4	0·3	—	0·3-1·5	—
Topi	—	—	11·4	—	—	—	—	—	—	—	—	—
Waterbuck	0·8	0·2-3·4	2·9	—	—	—	—	—	—	—	—	31·1
Kob	1·6	2·2-7·8	22·2	—	—	—	—	—	—	—	—	—
Oryx	—	—	—	—	—	—	—	—	0·03-0·1	—	0·3-0·7	—
Impala	—	—	—	3·7	5·0	5·9	21·0	—	0·2	1·3	1·1-1·2	9·0
Grants gazelle	—	—	—	—	0·2	3·6	0·3	0·3	0·1-0·2	—	0·5-0·8	—
Thomson's gazelle	—	—	—	—	32·7	2·9	—	—	—	—	—	8·9
	21·4	25·0-42·5	62·9	30·5	61·5	30·7	42·6	3·9	1·4-2·3	5·5	5·3-9·6	50·3

1. Savidge, et al. (1976) 2. Laws et al. (1970, 1975) 3. Field and Laws (1970) 4. Leuthold and Leuthold (1976) 5. Leuthold and Leuthold (1976) 6. Leuthold and Leuthold (1976) 7. Lamprey (1964) 8. Ross et al. (1976) 9. Harris (1972) 10. Norton-Griffiths (1975) 11. Leuthold and Leuthold (1976) 12. Kutilek (1974)

*mean density in limited area of distribution.

mammals, but in general those which can be utilized most efficiently by man are the large herbivores. This is of course because the effort required to obtain a given amount of meat is greatly reduced the larger the animal to be hunted or cropped. In the past there has been much discussion of the potential use of wildlife for meat (Talbot et al., 1965; Ledger et al., 1967; Crawford, 1968) but there has been very little active utilization based on scientific evidence. Only since the work of Dasmann (1964) has rational utilization been obtained and this has not gathered force until the last decade. Possible reasons for the increased use of wildlife in this manner are the rapid growth of human populations (Kenya's population is increasing at 3·5% per annum (Myers, 1973)), with a corresponding decline in the standard of human nutrition and an increasingly sophisticated agriculture in which wildlife must be seen to pay its way or go. Another reason (also a function of increased human population) is the increase in National Parks of certain large herbivores, in particular elephants (*Loxodonta africana* Blumenbach), in response to human pressure. What then is the rationale for using wildlife instead of or in addition to domestic stock?

2. *Numbers, densities, biomass*

Large numbers of wild ungulates occur in National Parks, Game Reserves, in controlled hunting areas and on ranches and farms in East Africa and southern Africa. Thus Skinner (1973) estimates present populations of five species of antelope in south and south-west Africa as follows:

Springbok (*Antidorcas marsupialis* Zimmerman)	369 100
Impala (*Aepyceros melampus* Lichtenstein)	350 300
Blesbok (*Damaliscus dorcas* Pallas)	96 800
Greater Kudu (*Tragelaphus strepsiceros* Pallas)	>97 550
Eland (*Taurotragus oryx* Pallas)	6 810

The current estimate for wildebeest (*Connochaetes taurinus* Burchell) in the Serengeti National Park (NP) in Tanzania is 754 028 ± 8·5% (Norton-Griffiths, 1973).

However, these figures do not take into account the densities involved, which are clearly of importance to all persons planning to ranch or farm wildlife. Leuthold and Leuthold (1976) have recently summarized existing data for nine areas in East Africa. In Table I I have presented information from twelve wildlife reserves (Fig. 1), six quoted by Leuthold and Leuthold (1976) and another six from the literature.

FIG. 1. Africa showing place names mentioned in the text. Numbers in East Africa are as follows:

Kenya

1. Nairobi National Park (N.P.)   2. Kajiado District   3. Amboseli N.P.   4. Tsavo N.P.   5. Galana ranch   6. Mara-Loita   7. Akira ranch   8. Olmorogi and Kekopey ranches   9. Lake Nakuru N.P.   10. Suguroi ranch and Aberdares Mts. 11. Isiolo   12. Baragoi plains

Rwanda

1. Akagera N.P.

Tanzania

1. Serengeti N.P. and Ngorongoro Crater   2. Manyara N.P.   3. Taragnire Game Reserve (G.R.)   4. Loliondo G.R.   5. Mkomasi G.R.   6. Ruaha N.P.   7. Lake Rukwa G.R.   8. Shinyanga

Uganda

1. Rwenzori N.P.   2. Semliki G.R.   3. Kabalega Falls N.P.   4. W. Acholi and Aswa Lolim G.R.   5. Kidepo Valley N.P.

These show that highest recorded animal densities occur in the Serengeti where the dominant species are plains ungulates, gazelle (*Gazella granti* Brooke and *G. thomsoni* Günther) and wildebeest. Other plains areas also have high animal densities such as Tarangire NP, the Mara-Loita adjacent to Serengeti and Nairobi NP. Five areas, namely Kabalega NP, Garamba NP, Rwenzori NP, Lake Manyara NP and Lake Nakuru NP carry high numerical densities because of abundant ground water and non-migratory year round grazing. The drier areas (with annual rainfall of 60 cm or less) show densities less than 10 km^{-2}. These occur in the Tsavo-Mkomazi ecological unit, central Tanzania and northern Kenya and Uganda.

Table I shows that different species contribute differently to overall densities in each area. Thus in the plains areas (areas 5–6 in Table 1), gazelle, larger antelope and zebra (*Equus burchelli* Gray) are important, whereas in the year round grazing areas (1–4) where species are non-migratory, buffalo (*Syncerus caffer* Sparrman), elephant, hippopotamus (*Hippotamus amphinbiush*) and certain water-dependant antelope such as waterbuck (*Kobus defassa* Rüppell) and Uganda kob (*Adenota kob thomasi* Erxleben) are important. Lake Nakuru (12) is a possible exception to this because the lake is saline and it should probably be regarded as a plains area. In the drier areas (9–11) where woody vegetation is dominant owing to its deeper roots and ability to reach moisture in the soil at greater depth than grasses, browsing herbivores, principally elephant, buffalo and impala comprise the greatest proportion of the overall densities. Two areas, Tarangire Games Reserve (7) and Kidepo Valley (8) have both plains and dry areas with corresponding fauna.

Another consideration of some importance to the potential game rancher or to any cropping operation is the standing crop biomass of the wildlife populations available. This indicates what the potential offtake of meat may be, although there are a number of limitations, as will be seen later.

Total wildlife biomass figures per unit area are shown for 31 different areas in Africa in Table II. This information is based on the revised figures of Leuthold and Leuthold (1976) for ten of the areas, but does not allow for the fact that the unit mass used by Bourlière and Verschuren (1960) for elephant is twice that used by Leuthold *et al.* (1976). From Table II it is apparent that, whereas plains grassland areas (P) may contain the greatest numerical densities they are only half or a third the biomass of wetter year-round grazing areas in Uganda and Zaire (Y). When biomass densities are plotted against rainfall for 18 of the 27 areas for which rainfall data are available, there

TABLE II. Biomass densities of wildlife and rainfall in Africa

Locality (see Fig. 1)	Biomass density kg/km²	Presence of domestic stock % if known	Annual rainfall cm	References
Spanish Sahara	0·3	*		Cloudsley-Thompson (1969)
Taro Nimri Forest Reserve, Ghana	5–6	0		Cloudsley-Thompson (1969)
W. of Oum-Cha-Louba, Tchad	80	*		Cloudsley-Thompson (1969)
Aberdare Mountains, Kenya	420	0		Cloudsley-Thompson (1969)
Borgu Game Reserve, Nigeria	703	0	100–125	Child (1974)
Baragoi plains, Kenya	895	*		Harris (1970)
Wajir District, Kenya (D.)	1 151	100	22	Watson (1972)
Mkomasi Game Reserve, Tanzania	1 200	*	40–60	Harris (1970)
Mandera District, Kenya (D.)	1 901	100	23	Watson (1972)
Isiolo, Kenya	2 000	*	30–60	Leuthold and Leuthold (1976)
Akagera NP, Rwanda	2 140	0		Spinage (1969)
Turkana District, Kenya (D.)	2 406	100	33	Watson (1972)
Mara-Loita, Kenya (P.)	2 470	*	70	Leuthold and Leuthold (1976)
Shinyanga, Tanzania	2 810	*		Harris (1970)
Garissa District, Kenya (D.)	3 818	100	40	Watson (1972)
Tsavo NP N; Kenya	4 116	0	30–60	Leuthold and Leuthold (1976)
Nairobi NP, Kenya (P.)	4 150	0	90	Leuthold and Leuthold (1976)
Tsavo NP S, Kenya	4 454	0	30–60	Leuthold and Leuthold (1976)
Ruaha NP, Tanzania	4 570	0	10–30	Norton-Griffiths (1975)
Ngorongoro Crater, Tanzania (P.)	6 100	*	80–120	Lamprey (1964)
L. Nakuru NP, Kenya (P.)	6 298	0		Kutilek (1974)
Samburu District, Kenya (D.)	6 514	72	50	Watson (1972)
Amboseli NP, Kenya (P.)	7 800	*	40	Western (1973)
Kaputei District, Kenya (D.)	7 883	86	71	Watson (1972)
Achwa, Uganda	7 971	*	75–88	Leuthold and Leuthold (1976)
Tarangire GR, Tanzania	10 170	*	60	Leuthold and Leuthold (1976)
Kabalega Falls NP, Uganda (Y.)	13 100	0	110–140	Laws et al. (1975)
L. Manyara NP, Tanzania (Y.)	19 259	0	75	Leuthold and Leuthold (1976)
P.N. de la Garamba, Zaire (Y.)	20 100	0	140–170	Savidge et al. (1976)
P.N. de la Virunga, Zaire (Y.)	20 485	0		Bourlière and Verschuren (1960)
Ruwenzori NP, Uganda (Y.)	21 373	0	60–120	Field and Laws (1970)

GR = Game Reserve   PN/NP = National Park   P. = Plains grassland areas   D. = Domestic stock   Y. = Year round grazing is a good correlation for all but five of these areas. Four of them: Tarangire, Amboseli, Manyara and Rwenzori all have ground water equivalent to rainfall much greater than that measured. The remaining area, Borgu Game Reserve in Nigeria occurs in an area of high population and heavy use, which probably explains the exceptionally low biomass figures. The relationship of biomass densities to rainfall has been expressed by Coe *et al.* (1976). This may be a useful indication of maximum stocking rates for the ranches. Comparisons with domestic stock show that stocking rates or standing crop biomasses of wildlife are sometimes higher than that of domestic stock on similar range. This will be discussed in more detail later. The point to be emphasized is that the wildlife resource is not inconsiderable. A further consideration for a potential game farmer will be the sustained offtake. Clearly this favours the smaller ungulates, gazelle and other antelope which breed faster and have a more rapid turnover than larger ungulates. It should be remembered, however, that smaller animals have a higher food intake per unit weight than larger animals and also there is a greater financial outlay in cropping small animals per unit weight gained.

A better guide to the total biological effect of animals in their environment is their expenditure of metabolic energy (Lamprey, 1964). Thus, although elephants contributed more than zebras to biomass in the Tarangire they used less metabolic energy (Lamprey, 1964). Another way of looking at the system is to record energy flowing through animals (Macfadyen, 1964). Thus, it has been shown that when a large herbivore, the elephant, became dominant over a smaller herbivore, the buffalo, the overall utilization of the vegetation fell from 6·1% to 3·9% per annum (Field, 1971). It seems likely that in ranch land there would be a greater energy flow through wild ungulates which use a wider range of food plants than through the domestic cow [*Bos indicus/ B. taurus*] with its limited food habits. I shall turn now to the explanations for the sometimes greater biomass of wild ungulates compared with domestic stock, which come under the categories of nutrition, physiology and disease.

3. *Nutrition*

It is well known that different species of herbivores occupy different food niches (Fraser-Darling, 1960; Field, 1968). Although there may be considerable overlap of feeding habits when food is abundant, during droughts or periods of over-utilization of the range, herbivores tend to resort to certain food plants to which they are particularly well adapted, either through habitat selection, mouth shape, grazing level, tolerance of otherwise unpalatable compounds (Field, 1976a) or ruminal physiology (Hofmann, 1973). Almost all wild herbivores in Africa have evolved alongside their food plants. Among the domestic species in Africa, possibly only the camel (*Camelus dromedarius* L.) is comparable as it was originally domesticated in Arabia, where the vegetation was similar to that of north and east Africa. The process of evolution is seen in the case of browsers such as giraffe (*Giraffa camelopardalis* L.) which are able to eat *Acacia* thorns, and others such as eland which depend on plant species without thorns. The Acacias of Australia have not evolved thorns because there are no large marsupial herbivores and hence the selection pressure for protective thorns is weak.

Thus it can be seen that the diverse African vegetation types can be better utilized by a wide range of wild ungulates with differing food habits, than by cattle alone. There is also evidence that springbok feed on a wider range of plants than sheep (*Ovis aries*) (Liversidge, 1975). The inclusion of sheep and more particularly goats (*Capra hircus*) on cattle ranches, goes some way to compensating for this lack of diversity, but there are nevertheless plant species which are beyond the reach of, or remain poisonous to stock but are utilized by wildlife (Verdcourt and Trump, 1969; Skinner, 1975). Sometimes wildlife can avoid poisonous plants in pastures which are otherwise closed to domestic stock (Skinner, 1975). Comparisons of oryx (*Oryx belisa callotis* Rüppell), eland, buffalo and cattle (Field, 1975) show that the latter two species are bulk feeders and require large quantities of food, whereas oryx, with smaller mouths, are selective of protein and energy rich parts of plants, and require less bulk. This may explain why experimentally paddocked oryx and cattle performed equally well but the oryx did much less damage to the vegetation, leaving twice the amount of herbage at the end of the trial (Field and Lewis unpubl. data). Roth and Osterberg (1971) conclude that eland feeding behaviour is directed towards optimum nutrition without intoxication (euphagia) while domestic stock have to some extent lost this ability (Arnold, 1964). Field (1975) suggests that eland move over large distances in order to optimize protein and energy intake and that this may be a disadvantage on small ranches, or with domestic eland on game farms.

Daily food intake of wild and domestic herbivores decreases with size when expressed as a percentage of body weight, but for a given diet appears to be a function of $\log_{10}$ body weight. Regressions have been developed by Field (1976b) of the order: dry matter intake (DMI) in kg $= 4 -$ log body wt for eland, hartebeest, sheep, goats and cattle. DMI as a percentage of metabolic weight (kg $^{0.73}$) is similar for most ruminants. Eland however, showed lower digestibilities than other species in 17 different comparison; they were particularly poor at digesting fibre (Field, 1976b). These findings agree in general with studies on these species using artificial diets (Arman and Hopcraft, 1975). On the other hand, oryx show similar dry matter digestibilities to sheep and cattle (Stanley Price, 1976). The evidence suggests that eland, at least, are not as efficient as cattle or sheep at utilizing energy. Skinner (1967) gives food conversion efficiencies of 5·0 for cattle and 6·8 for eland. Taylor and Lyman (1967) found eland inferior to Hereford steers in terms of productivity. Much of these disadvantages attributed to eland may however be a function of diet. Eland are concentrate feeders while cattle are bulk feeders. The comparison is unfavourable to eland when made on grass; when a browse diet is presented, the opposite is likely. The poor performance of eland in digesting fibre is possibly due to the absence of certain cellulolytic bacteria and suitable delaying mechanisms in the rumeno-reticulum (Hofmann, 1973). Since fibre may influence the digestion of certain other components, eland are often less efficient at digesting the latter in high fibre grass diets. Cattle, hartebeest (*Alcelaphus buselaphus cokii* Pallas) and sheep being roughage feeders, were all able to digest fibre more efficiently than eland (Field, 1976). Eland also overcome the disadvantage of being unable to digest fibre by having a higher passage rate and selecting less lignified plants or plant parts. A small rumen aids mobility and escape from predators as has been suggested by Hoppe *et al.* (1977). However, an animal requiring a continuous flow of digesta through the rumen is less suited to the restricted grazing regime imposed by domestication. Evidence from Lewis (1975) shows that eland subjected to a typical pastoral regime spend more time feeding and are therefore exposed to heat stress for longer than other ruminant species.

4. *Physiology*
There is considerable evidence to suggest that certain wildlife species are better adapted to arid conditions than domestic species (with the exception of the camel). Man can make best use of wildlife by exploiting their inherent physiological adaptations in their natural habitats. The main drawback to the camel in this respect is that it succumbs easily to trypanosomiasis and is intolerant of tsetse (*Glossina* sp.) infested areas. Eland, oryx (Taylor, 1971), gerenuk (*Litocranius walleri* Brooke), dik-dik (*Rhynchotragus guentheri* Thomas), Grevy's zebra (*Equus grevyi* Oustalet), and Grant's gazelle (Hofmann, 1973; Dorst and Dandelot, 1970; Lamprey, 1963) all sustain themselves for long periods without water. Taylor(1971) has estimated that pre-formed and metabolic water yield from Acacia leaves ingested by eland can amount to 5·3 litres/ 100 kg⁻¹ per day. Although the leaves of *Duosperma* are known to be

hygroscopic at night, there is insufficient evidence that these are a major item of diet in the oryx (Taylor, 1968). King *et al.* (1975) have shown that during daylight grazing, the water turnover of oryx ranged from 24–98 ml kg^{-1} day^{-1} while eland was 42–121 ml kg^{-1} day^{-1}. There were significant correlations between water turnover and heat load but whereas Lewis (1975) found positive correlations between heat load and shade seeking in eland, this was not so in oryx. Other workers (Mac-Farlane and Howard, 1972) group eland and cattle together as animals with high water turnover, which is correlated with higher metabolic rate and oxygen turnover. Oryx and camels have low rates of water turnover and lower metabolic rates. Low rates of movement of water and energy through animals allow them longer survival in, and better adaptation to, desert conditions. Coat colour and structure is also important in the environmental adaptability of animals. Finch (1972) showed that the light coat of a hartebeest reflects 42% of incident short-wave radiation, while that of an eland reflects only 22%. The dense hair of a hartebeest permits little penetrance of radiation while that of an eland, which is sparse, permits high penetration. Evaporative heat loss from an eland is cutaneous (78%), while 62% of heat loss from hartebeest is respiratory. Furthermore Bligh (1972) assesses the advantages of different methods of evaporative heat loss and concludes that panting has advantages over sweating. The camel, however, which sweats, only does so when its body temperature has reached 41°C (Schmidt-Nielsen, 1959). Its thermol ability is a great advantage in conservation of water and this characteristic is shared by other desert adapted species, such as the oryx.

5. *Reproduction*

Rates of reproduction vary widely in both wild and domestic species. In general, large animals take longer to reach maturity and have longer gestation and lactation periods. Thus, of the species in Table III only springbok start to breed in their first year. Most of the smaller antelopes, sheep and goats start breeding in their second year as do a few fast growing eland and cattle. Most eland and cattle breed in their third year while the slow growing zebu cow, camel and giraffe all start in their fourth year. Gestation periods range from 110–150 days in the Thomson's gazelle, sheep and goats, to 370 days in the camel and 450 in the giraffe. Birth weights tend to be correlated with gestation periods although that of the eland and improved Afrikander cow (*Bos taurus*) is more, and that of the camel, less than expected.

The annual calving percentage is low in camels and giraffe, owing to their long gestation period and lactational anoestrus. The highest

TABLE III. Some reproductive parameters of wild and domestic herbivores

	Age at first conception months	Gestation period days	Birth weight kg		Annual calving %	Calving interval in days	Reference
			♂	♀			
Springbok	7	168	3·2	3·4	46–100	—	Cited in Skinner (1973)
Thomson's gazelle	15	110–112	—	—	100	170	Hopcraft and Arman (1971)
Thomson's gazelle	13	150	2·7	2·7	98	—	Field and Blankenship (1973a)
Grant's gazelle	14	195	5·2	5·2	98	—	Field and Blankenship (1973a)
Impala	18	196	5·0	5·0	90	365	Cited in Skinner (1973)
Blesbok	18–29	±225	7·0	7·0	84·5	365	Rowe-Rowe and Bigalke (1972) Cited in Skinner (1973)
Coke's hartebeest	24	240	12·5	12·5	97	—	Field and Blankenship (1973a)
Greater Kudu	17	210–214	—	—	100	365	Cited in Skinner (1973)
Eland	28·7 ± 2	271 ± 3	30·0	25·5	83	354 ± 20	Cited in Skinner (1973)
(range for five authors)			±1·3	±0·7			
Giraffe	36	450	54·5	54·5	91	—	Field and Blankenship (1973a)
Sheep and goats (in N. Kenya)	10–15	150	2·0	2·0	170–210	200	A. C. Field (pers. comm.)
Afrikander cow	18–30	296 ± 1	32·7	30·9	78·5	591–759	Cited in Roth et al. (1972)
Zebu cow	38	295	25·5	22·7	—	—	
Camel	36–48	370	23·5	—	41	700–800	Bremaud (1969), C. R. Field (unpubl. data), Watson (1972)

calving percentages occur among the small gazelle, sheep and goats, but that of the eland is high for its size owing to a short *post partum* anoestrus and a short gestation period. Thus its calving interval was significantly less than that of the Afrikander cow while that of the camel can exceed two years under drought conditions.

6. *Growth rate and meat production*

According to Skinner (1973) springbok females may reach 83% of adult weight at seven months and males reach 57% at the same age; growth is then retarded by the South African winter. Growth *curves* are also published for eland (in Russia and Rhodesia), and also for blesbok and impala (Skinner, 1973). At three years Russian eland bulls are 68% of their adult weight (700 kg) which is reached at seven years, while females are 75% of the adult weight (500 kg) which is reached at about four-and-a-half years; Rhodesian female eland are 88% of their adult weight (425 kg) at three years. Blesbok males attain 63% of their adult weight (80 kg) in one year while females reach 69% of their adult weight (65 kg) over the same period. Impala females, however, reach 71% of their adult weight (42 kg) in the first year and males about 63%. For comparison, at the other extreme, female camels in northern Kenya reach 25–40% of their adult weight (400 kg) in their first year of growth (Field, unpubl. data).

In contrast to domestic stock, springbok show a continuous increase in the proportion of carcass lean up to a peak of about 48% of the carcass at maturity. The mean carcass fat does not exceed 4% of the carcass (Skinner, 1973). Ledger *et al.* (1961) and Ledger (1968) give the following carcass lean percentages: European cattle: 31·7, African cattle 31·6–39·8, goats, 31·3, hippopotamus 32·3 at the low end of the scale and Thomson's and Grant's gazelle 48%; lesser kudu (*Tragelaphus imberbis* Blyth) 50% and gerenuk 52·4% at the upper end. High lean percentages are desirable for western markets but Africans seem to prefer a higher proportion of fat. Skinner (1973) also shows that in wild animals in southern Africa there is a seasonal influence on fat reserves which peak in May.

The dressing percentage for some wild animals also tends to be higher than some range cattle, e.g. thin zebu cows are 46·8% compared with gerenuk, lesser kudu and Grant's gazelle which are all over 60%. Improved cattle, however, may be similar to wildlife in this respect.

Very little work has been carried out on meat quality, but a study by Von la Chevallerie (1972) of four species of wild animal showed that eland meat contained significantly more fat and had a larger fibre diameter than the other species, resulting in tougher meat, while springbok meat was the least tough. A taste panel scored blesbok meat as significantly more intense (strong tasting) than springbok and impala, while springbok was significantly more acceptable than the rest. It was concluded that springbok meat fared best although the tests did not disqualify any of the meat on trial (Skinner, 1973). A number of factors were not, however, considered in the study. Although not a study of African wildlife, the work of Ables *et al.* (1973) deserves mention here. In their studies on the nilgai antelope, a species of Indian wild ungulate introduced to Texas, sensory evaluation panels rated round steaks and lion steaks below beef steaks in flavour and juiciness, but similar in tenderness. When mixed with beef in varying proportions they were indistinguishable from beef.

7. *Milk production*

Although no wild animal can compete with cattle in milk yield, the productivity of the eland is worth mention here. In the USSR, Treus and Kravchenko (1968) report lactation periods of 200–300 days, a mean milk production of about 340 kg per lactation and a maximum daily production of about 3·3 kg. Eland milk had approximately twice as much protein and fat as milk from cattle on the same range. The milk is considered valuable in the treatment of ulcers and related illnesses in humans. For comparison female Rendille camels of the Tupcha clan average 1·33 kg milk day^{-1} (Sato, 1976) while Torry (1973) estimates one litre per day during drought conditions. It is not clear how much is available for the calf, but twice this figure might be considered reasonable as total production (Field, unpubl. data). In the USSR, however, total camel milk production was about 8 litres day^{-1} (Heraskov, 1953, 1965; Kuliev, 1959) and in Somalia mean yield was 6 litres day^{-1} (Rossetti and Congiu, 1955). Although these figures suggest eland milk production to be of a similar order to camels, the latter will continue to produce milk under semi-desert conditions which eland are unable to survive. At the other end of the size spectrum, springbok have yielded up to 170 g of milk day^{-1} but "let down" may not have been complete (van Zyl and Wehmeyer, 1970), while Somali goats produced an average of 325 g day^{-1} (Rossetti and Congiu, 1955).

8. *Animal behaviour*

This will be discussed at length in the section on domestication. Lewis (1975) studied the activity patterns of eland, oryx and cattle under semi-arid conditions on a ranch in Kenya. The animals were semi-domesticated and he concluded that this puts eland at a disadvantage. Their poor adaptation to heat stress necessitates their feeding at night and this was not possible where predators occur. (Cattle, and in particular oryx, were unaffected by the diurnal regime.) Furthermore their need for moisture and a high protein diet makes them dependant on browse under dry conditions (Field, 1975). This means that eland have large inter-individual distances and a loose herd structure unsuited to herding by man (Lewis, 1975). These problems are also encountered with camels (Torry, 1977) but this is offset by the camels' adaption to desert conditions. Difficulties such as these are occasionally glossed over by some authors, such as Kyle (1972), in their endeavour to promote eland.

9. *Disease*

It is perhaps in disease tolerance that wildlife scores over domestic stock. Although wildlife is susceptible to certain diseases, in particular rinderpest, some of the major scourges of domestic stock which inhibit their large scale development (such as trypanosomiasis) are tolerated by wild animals because of the adaptation during their long evolution in Africa.

However, Fay (1972) states that wildlife in Kenya is subject to a wide variety of infectious and parasitic diseases as well as nutritional deficiencies. The prevalence of serum antibodies to certain viral and blood protozoal agents indicates that the incidence of exposure to diseases caused by these agents is very high. While it is often thought that wild animals are highly resistant to the indigenous or long-established pathogens through many generations of exposure, there is little reliable information at hand to prove that such beliefs are necessarily always true. Wild animals are rarely under close enough surveillance to enable sporadic losses to be noted, particularly among infants. It is probable that the ability of wildlife to thrive under adverse conditions is as much related to their mobility as to special inherent physiological adaptations. Parasitic and nutritional diseases may become more problematic for some wild species as their movements are restricted by fences and Park boundaries. Also, the reduction of predators will reduce the offtake of sick and weak animals, and accentuate disease problems (Fay, 1972). Fay commonly found the following diseases or their antibodies in different wildlife in Kenya: malignant catarrh in wildebeest, African horse sickness in zebra, foot and mouth, blue tongue, Nairobi sheep disease and Rift Valley fever which are diseases caused by viruses, and anaplasmosis, babesiosis, theileriosis, helminthosis, sarcosporidiosis and cysticercosis. Wildlife was free from or rarely had rinderpest, pleuropneumonia, Johne's disease, brucellosis, leptospirosis, salmonellosis and trypanosomiasis. Hammond and Branagan (1973) sound a similar warning with regard to premature large scale domestication of wildlife.

10. *Conclusions*

To summarize this section, it appears that the wildlife resource is real and involves substantial numbers, although the higher densities are in National Parks where game utilization is usually incompatible with tourist viewing. Wildlife has diversified in relation to the food resource and is able to utilize it more fully than domestic stock. It also has greater diversity in strategies of digestion although the efficiency of domestic species in digesting high-fibre grass diets is equal if not better than that of most wild species. There are many wildlife species which are physiologically adapted to arid conditions while among domestic stock only camels fall into this category. The oryx in particular is worthy of mention as it is a desert adapted grazer which could well fill an empty niche among domestic species.

With regard to rates of reproduction and growth of wildlife, a number of antelope and gazelle species equal if not surpass sheep and goats. The eland is also faster breeding than domestic animals of similar size.

In general, wildlife has a significantly higher lean carcass and also many has higher carcass percentages than domestic stock under arid conditions. The low fat content in wildlife meat tends to make it less easy to cook and less palatable to traditional tastes. However, in advanced cultures where cattle feedlots lead to an excessively fatty carcass, meat from wildlife is considered a delicacy.

It seems from this discussion that wildlife should not be considered as a replacement for domestic stock or vice versa. Each has its own advantages and disadvantages and the role of wildlife in ranching should be seen as complementary to conventional stock raising to a varying degree, depending on the suitability of the environment for raising exotic or indigenous species. This differs from Kyle (1972) who promotes wildlife at the expense of domestic stock. Thus it seems likely that wildlife will gradually be squeezed out of high rainfall areas with improved pastures but could become of considerable importance in semi-arid areas. Some species however, may find an intermediate niche as will be described for the eland in the next section.

II. Game Farming

A. INTRODUCTION AND METHODS

As mentioned earlier, game farming is the intensive use of wild and domesticated wild animals on fenced farmland.

Farmers in South Africa have for decades shot and marketed game, and trophy hunting has been a feature of the South African way of life since the time of the first settlers. Not until recently, however, have sound principles for animal exploitation been applied (Skinner, 1975). On the one hand, profit from marketing game has never reached a level comparable with conventional animal husbandry and on the other, trophy hunting is directed at mature or old male animals which are not the best to eat (Skinner 1975).

Farmers have exercised lawful ownership and enclosed both the springbok and blesbok in paddocks so that they are no longer truly feral. Game farming is expanding in South Africa; for example in north-west Transvaal there were four farms fenced with game-proof fencing in 1965. Eight years later there were 39. The Natal Parks Board employs a full time officer to advise game farmers and to approve land for re-stocking.

Some useful bonuses have been revealed with game farming. Old males are not wasted, but sold as trophies and if springbok calves are cropped when young the inhibition imposed on the mother by lactation is removed and the reproductive rate increases (Skinner, Von la Chevallerie and van Zyl, 1971).

Domestication is a more labour and land intensive form of farming. The species is brought into subjection to, or dependence upon, man. Breeding, care and feeding are subject to continuous control by man, which is not the case in taming (Hale, 1962). The essence of domestication is a disappearance of the prey reaction to a predator (man) on the part of the domesticant. In the absence of pain or other alarm stimuli emanating from man, animals soon relax their fleeing or aggressive response and become habituated or tame.

Animals in the National Parks in Uganda and elsewhere have become habituated to tourists and their vehicles. The next stage, actual handling by man—in this case of buffaloes—has been described by Parker and Graham (1971). Provided the procedure is not too traumatic for the animal, man can then start to impose control over feeding and breeding of the animal. Ultimately the species undergoes a physical, physiological and temperamental change through selection by man. Such a change may not necessarily be for the good of the species although it invariably enhances man's relationship with it. Parker (1975) describes two routes to tameness and hence to domestication. One involves the use of the critical period of imprinting in an infant and man as the foster parent. Problems arise at maturity as the animal which has been imprinted does not recognize its own kind and shows little fear of its foster parent. This leads to complications with breeding and herding. It is also expensive and often retarding to feed on a milk substitute. The preferred route to tameness and domestication is through habituation of a young animal which is caught in the wild soon after being weaned. The method, as used on Galana ranch, Kenya, is described by Field (1974). Since then it has been shown that the use of a trap (Oelofse, 1970; Densham, 1974) is a far less traumatic method of capture and also less expensive than chasing by vehicle (Field, 1974). Further details on the care and capture of wild animals are given by Young (1973) and Field gives a scoring of behavioural characteristics of various ungulates with regard to their suitability for taming (1970 after Hale 1962).

Apart from the ostrich (*Struthio camelus* L.) there is no other species of animal which has been domesticated in Africa until recent times. Available evidence (Buillet, 1975) suggests that the camel was domesticated in the Arabian Peninsular between 3000 and 2500 B.C. and did not reach Africa until about 2000 B.C. in the Horn and 50 B.C. in the north. Although Egyptian reliefs of about 2500 B.C. show five species of ungulate in captivity, they were almost certainly not domesticated, but used for fattening and religious purposes (Smith, 1969). It has been suggested by Short (1976) that rather than domesticate wild animals, which in the case of today's livestock has taken 10 000 years of selection by man for domesticity, attempts should be made to graft "wild genes" onto stock of proven domestic temperament by interspecific hybridization.

B. RESULTS

Recently there have been attempts to domesticate five species of wild ungulate in East Africa: Thomson's gazelle, wildebeest, oryx, eland and buffalo (Field, 1974). All are herd species but they vary greatly in temperament; the wildebeest, buffalo and Thomson's gazelle adult males being highly dangerous to man. Thus male buffaloes at Galana ranch were aggressive and had to be slaughtered, although females were docile. They were not penned at night and were allowed to be mated by wild bulls, then returned after service and calved in captivity (King and Heath, 1975). Little trouble has been experienced from adult male eland and oryx. At Galana ranch both species are nomadic and several animals have left the herds in search of better feed or apparently to avoid being worried by biting flies. About 75% return, often fatter than their coevals and sometimes pregnant. The animals are all herded by men by day and kept in portable pens at night. There are now about 100 oryx and 20 eland at the ranch. The results are presented in King and Heath (1975) for water requirements and productivity, Field (1975) for climate and food habits and Lewis (1975) for behaviour and activity patterns. Reference has already been made to the latter two papers. The productivity data are summarized as follows. When on trial at similar stocking rates, oryx grew faster than eland and cattle under dry conditions; under wetter conditions there was no significant difference between the species. Oryx have 25%, sheep 45%, goats 50% and eland 60% of the drinking water requirements of cattle when equated on the basis of metabolic weight. With regard to breeding, sheep and goats had their first offspring at about 15 months, oryx at 30 months and eland and cattle at 38–43 months. Oryx sustained a calving interval of 10 months compared with 15 months for cattle and 21 months for eland. The latter were less able to cope with droughts. Calving rates ranged from 57% per annum in the eland to 102% in the oryx and 108% in goats. Slaughter age ranged from one year in goats to two years in oryx and 32–38 months in eland and cattle. Dressing percentages ranged from 45 in sheep and goats to 52 in cattle, 55 in eland and 57 in oryx (King and Heath, 1975).

The value of cattle, oryx and sheep sold to a tourist resort at the Kenya Coast has also been compared. Total value per beast was in the ratio $10:7\cdot5:1$ respectively. However, for each ranch unit (area required to raise one cow) the number of stock was in the ratio $1:2:5$ respectively. Thus the value per ranch unit was in the ratio $2:3:1$. Apart from growth rate, therefore (oryx grow at $0\cdot18$ kg day^{-1} compared with cattle at $0\cdot3$ kg day^{-1}), oryx outscore cattle and eland from the point of view of water consumption, maturation, calving rate, age at slaughter, dressing percentage and value to the ranch. Eland are relatively non-productive in the hot semi-arid environment of Galana under a day grazing regime. In the Kenya Rift Valley at 01 Morogi ranch Gilgil, where the rainfall to potential evaporation ratio is twice as high as in Galana, feeding activity is less restricted and eland perform better. They breed 8 months earlier, have a 100% effective calving rate and are ready for slaughter at 30 months (King and Heath, 1975).

Other studies of domestication centre almost entirely on eland, although Jewell (1969) makes a plea for a wider range of species. Unfortunately eland studies in southern Africa are of less value since they do not include conventional domestic stock for comparison (Stainthorpe, 1972; Keep, 1972 in Natal; Posselt, 1963; Roth and Osterberg, 1971; Roth et al., 1972, in Rhodesia). Table IV shows the results derived from these studies and includes data from the USSR for comparison.

Supplementary food was given to the Loteni and Askanya Nova herds. At Loteni, age at first conception was reduced from 28 months to 17 months when animals were fed on concentrates. Dry conditions on both Galana ranch and at Manyoli probably explain the greater age at

TABLE IV

Place	Age at first conception (months)	Gestation period (days)	Birth weight ♂ Kg ♀		Annual calving %	Calving interval (days)
Manyoli, Rhodesia	26–43	280	36·4	28·6	100	337
Loteni, Natal South Africa	17–28	273	28·4	23·9	—	370
Galana, Kenya	35	—	—	—	57	630
Ol Morogi, Kenya	27	—	—	—	100	310 (Field n = 9 unpubl. data)
Askanya Nova, USSR	c. 27	255	35·0	28·0	—	—

first conception. Birth weights of Loteni eland were below average which reflects the smaller body size of adult Drakensburg eland. Both calving percentages and intervals were low on Galana because of the dry conditions prevailing there.

C. CONCLUSION

In conclusion it is apparent that both oryx and eland are useful domesticants. The former has great potential to complement camel browsing in very arid areas, while eland, owing to its poorer performance in arid areas, is likely to be limited to medium potential small scale ranch or farmland, where overgrazing had led to a proliferation of bush upon which eland are known to thrive. Again a monoculture is not recommended because the greatest productivity per unit area is likely to come from a combination of conventional domestic grazers with eland. The possibility of domesticating other species and of hybridization between wild and domestic species should not be overlooked.

III. GAME RANCHING

A. INTRODUCTION

As mentioned in the Introduction to this review Game Ranching is the extensive utilization of wild and domesticated wild animals on unfenced low potential ranchland. The difference between Game Ranching and Game Farming is often unclear and the borderline is a matter for debate and individual opinion. Many would say that the work described at Galana is game ranching rather than farming. An important difference, however, is that originally there was no attempt to use the wild ungulate population in their wild state on a sustained yield basis except for one intensive elephant "cropping" operation. After an initial research phase of intensive game farming which lasted for about five years, the Directors of Galana ranch have taken over the operation and are now using their capital to make the oryx operation extensive and a profitable commercial enterprise. Thus it is developing from an intensive game farming to an extensive game ranching operation.

On many ranches in eastern and southern Africa in marginal or semi-arid land, wildlife is still abundant. Fencing is a doubtful undertaking since the fences quickly become damaged by wildlife. Furthermore, predators and stock theft quickly discourage night time grazing, the major bonus accruing from fencing. Thus many ranches remain unfenced and wildlife moves on and off the land at will, depending on the availability of food and water, protection etc. In times of drought a well managed ranch may be invaded by thousands of wild herbivores which quickly destroy any reserve grazing. They are also capable of drinking prodigious quantities of water, damaging installations and in many cases have been accused of transmitting disease to the domestic animals. In order to compensate for the inconvenience of wildlife, they are utilized by ranchers to varying degrees. At first there were few legal restrictions and many ranchers eliminated their unwanted wildlife. Later it was possible in Kenya, for example, to obtain a licence for the sale of a limited number of skins per annum, while none of the meat could be marketed. In certain cases wildlife populations have now grown so large that special permits have been issued to enable their management and utilization.

In the Cape and Transvaal Provinces of South Africa the game ordinances have recently been adjusted to accommodate the land owner on whom is conferred virtual ownership of the game on the land, provided it is suitably fenced (Skinner, 1975). In Natal Province the Parks Board actively encourage ranchers to restock their land with wildlife, such as blesbok and impala, from their Parks (Mentis, 1972). The animals are caught, sold and transported by the Parks Board to the ranches provided these are adequately fenced (Mentis, pers. comm.).

Game ranching was pioneered by Dasmann and Mossman in 1960 in Rhodesia (Dasmann, 1964). According to Savory (1969) this practice had spread to over 50 ranches by 1964 producing in the region of 1 M kg of game meat. One ranch, Buffalo Range, sustained an average offtake of about 750 animals over the thirteen year period, 1961–1973.

In some cases (Field and Blankenship, 1973b) alternative uses of wildlife make game ranching incompatible. For example, on Akira ranch, Kenya, after a lengthy study it was concluded that the sport hunting operations were probably adequate in keeping the stocking rate at a tolerable level.

One interesting difference between game farming and ranching is that the scientific groundwork necessary for the latter is basically ecological —concerned with establishing inventories and optimum stocking rates and combinations, while the farmer takes a more narrow view, involves the individual animal and emphasizes ethology rather than ecology.

B. RESULTS

In this section I propose to take studies in Rhodesia and Kenya as examples. In Rhodesia, Cobban (1965) analysed returns from seven game ranches in 1964. Five of them were cattle ranches where game was utilized and two were purely game ranches. The ranches varied in size from 8094 ha to 477 951 ha. Major species were impala, duiker (*Sylvicapra grimmia* L.), zebra, kudu and eland in decreasing numerical order of quotas set. The highest proportion of the quotas taken were for the largest animals, eland (65·1%) and zebra (49·5%). Duiker and kudu are more elusive and so only 20·3% and 38·7% of the quotas were shot, respectively. A little over 5000 animals were taken or 38·4% of the total quota. More than half the animals were impala. It was estimated (Cobban, 1965) that a little over 2 M kg of meat were available on quota on all game ranches in 1964. Only 51% of the overall quota of meat was taken. Cropped meat sold at about 0·41$ 1977 per kilogram, hence the total value of the cropped meat was just under 500 000$ 1977. Reasons for the discrepancy between the quota and the actual yield are as follows. Game cropping is still a subsidiary to cattle ranching, so most time and capital are spent on the latter. There is no central marketing organization and the rancher has to find his own outlets for cropped meat. Foot and mouth restrictions have been a handicap. Cropping methods, in particular accuracy of shooting, have often been below standard.

In Kenya the reduction of woody vegetation by charcoal burners on two ranches, Kekopey and Suguroi led to an increase in grassland. There was a corresponding increase in Thomson's gazelle and impala and their reduction proved necessary (Blankenship and Qvortrup, 1974). The ensuing management was a form of reduction cropping to be discussed later. There was no intention to eliminate the animals and further cropping has been carried out to obtain a sustained yield. Combined quotas of animals for the two ranches were 2600 animals. In 60 working nights 91% of this quota was taken. This included an eight-day experimental phase in which not more than 15 animals were taken each night. The Government Veterinary and Game Departments laid down a stringent list of 11 conditions. Animals were shot during dark phases of the moon using spotlights and silenced 0·22 rifles. A processing line with an overhead rail was set up, in an open area, to enable compliance with the conditions. Average time from slaughter to processing was 47 min while it took a further 12·5 min for impala and 9·5 min for gazelle to be weighed, skinned, eviscerated and inspected. Between 3·3% and 4% of animals shot on the two ranches were condemned for poor bleeding, disease, contamination, because they were shot through the body or were unweaned immatures. A total of 25 162 kg of carcasses were produced by the two ranches (Parker and Graham, 1973).

On marketing the meat there was, contrary to expectations, poor demand and little interest from tourists in game meat. This contrasts with southern Africa where there is a tradition of utilizing wildlife. The meat in Kenya was sold for an average of 0·43 $ kg^{-1}. Currently, veterinary regulations preclude export of fresh meat to Europe. Skins were sold for 4·4–5 $ and some horns were sold. A 45% profit over cost for the combined operations was realized. A high degree of skill is required in the hunting and processing. The production of carcasses and skins to acceptable standards set by the Kenya Government is, weight for weight, more difficult and expensive than it is for domestic stock (Parker and Graham, 1973). The ranches hired Wildlife Services Ltd. PO Box 30678, Nairobi, to do the cropping and thereby accepted a loss in income. Subsequently, a further crop was carried out on Kekopey ranch and this time no meat was marketed, only the hides and horns were sold. This reflects the problems involved with meat inspection and the poor response to marketing.

C. CONCLUSION

Clearly it is possible to ranch wildlife alongside cattle and to utilize the former to augment the income from the cattle ranching operation. This, in turn, will help pay for the inconvenience of having wildlife on a ranch. However, unless a flourishing and viable market exists for fresh game meat or for biltong, it seems likely that problems will arise from trying to sell the meat products. Production of meat meal may be a way round the many restrictions which occur at present. It would be unwise therefore to recommend game ranching in the absence of a more reliable form of income such as raising domestic stock. Nevertheless, there is likely to be an increasing world demand for meat which could lead to a substantial increase in its price. Under these circumstances, game ranching would have the opportunity to contribute to the needs of meat-hungry countries, which in general do not have stringent import restrictions on meat.

IV. GAME CROPPING IN PARKS AND RESERVES

A. INTRODUCTION

Game cropping is the procedure by which wildlife is removed from farmland, ranchland, Game Reserve or National Park. It has been used with particular reference to the use of wildlife in the latter two areas. However, as we have seen in the previous section, cropping is also the method by which animals are removed on a game ranch. Game cropping may be necessary in order to reduce a heavily overstocked area in which wildlife is out of balance with its range. Such reduction cropping, when repeated on an annual or regular basis, can lead to the restoration of equilibrium. The offtake required to maintain the level is called a sustained yield crop.

With the establishment of National Parks and Games Reserves in eastern and southern Africa, many wildlife populations became subject to a novel form of management. On one side of a line on a map, frequently not apparent on the ground by natural markers, protection was afforded, but on the other there was no or limited protection. Some species, in particular the elephant, quickly learned to move into the protected areas. Such immigration (Laws *et al.*, 1970) led to a gross imbalance and inevitable destruction of the vegetation. Other large species such as the hippopotamus and buffalo also began to increase once human predation, which was not inconsiderable (Temple-Perkins, pers. comm.) ceased inside the Parks. Thus it has happened that in almost all National Parks and some Game Reserves in eastern and southern Africa where elephants occur, there has been an increase in their density, with corresponding destruction of the vegetation (Buechner and Dawkins, 1961; Laws, 1969; Field, 1971; Ross *et al.*, 1976; Leuthold, 1977; Watson and Bell, 1969; Savidge, 1968; van Wyk and Fairall, 1969). There are many alternative theories put forward to explain the destruction of the vegetation (Glover, 1970; Harthoorn, 1966; Lawton and Gough, 1970), but none have stood the test of scientific scrutiny. As a result of the serious damage to woody vegetation, it was decided to crop elephants. To date, reduction crops of elephants have taken place in Kabalega Falls (formerly Murchison Falls) NP, Uganda (Laws *et al.*, 1970), in the Luangwa Valley, Zambia (Steel, 1968; Astle, 1971) and in the Kruger NP, South Africa. Sample crops of elephants have also been taken from Tsavo NP (Laws, 1969) and Mkomasi Game Reserve (Parker and Archer, 1969).

In the Rwenzori NP (formerly Queen Elizabeth) it was decided to crop hippopotamus because of serious overgrazing (Field, 1969, Thornton, 1971) and the effects this had on other grazing herbivores. For similar reasons cropping of hippopotamus has taken place at Kabalega Falls NP, the Luangwa Valley (Astle 1971) and the Kruger NP (Joubert, 1977).

Although sample crops of buffalo were taken in the Rwenzori NP (Grimsdell, 1969) they have not been reduced in East African National Parks on a large scale. Cropping of buffalo has occurred in the Aswa Lolim Game Reserve, Uganda (Bindernagel, 1968), the Luangwa Valley and Kruger NP.

B. RESULTS

It is worth analysing some of the results from reduction cropping of large herbivores in detail. Firstly special methods were needed to crop these animals. Initially in Uganda hippopotamus were shot when they were on land at night. This was unsatisfactory because the buyers did not arrive until dawn by which time the meat may have been spoiled by lion or hyena. To avoid this the hippopotamus were shot soon after dawn when they had returned to water. Targets were small and as cropping proceeded the remaining animals became exceedingly shy necessitating very skilled marksmanship (Field, 1974). They were usually shot in the brain, sank immediately and floated 30–60 minutes later after the accumulation of fermentation products buoyed them to the surface. A launch brought the carcasses to a point where they were dragged ashore by a tractor.

In the case of elephant it has been important to avoid undue disturbance of the herds during cropping in a National Park. Therefore complete herds comprising one or more family units were taken. In Kabalega Falls Park herds were shot by marksmen on foot. Frequently when the leading female was shot the remainder of the group became disorientated and could be shot easily. Later in Tsavo, Mkomasi and Kruger National Parks, a helicopter has been used to herd any elephant that escapes the marksmen back to them. The standard 0·762 NATO rifle with a self loading magazine of 20 rounds had proved quicker than the conventional bolt-action rifles. As a result elephant which have survived the cropping operations have not proved to be any more wild than before (Laws *et al.*, 1975).

In the Rwenzori Park all hippopotamus carcasses 315 cm long or more were sold for US$43·5 by an agent to buyers. Cropping usually took place on market day or the day preceding it. The meat was eventually transported over an area of 40 000 km^2 to neighbouring towns and villages. A similar procedure was followed for the disposal of hippopotamus and elephant carcasses in Kabalega Falls Park. In Tsavo Park and Mkomasi Game Reserve a specially trained team of butchers were used. They were selected mainly from the Waliangulu tribe who are traditional elephant hunters. Unfortunately much of the meat from Tsavo was wasted because the Kenya Game Department, who had agreed to take it, were unable to handle it properly.

In the Luangwa Valley and Kruger NP darting with the tranquillizer succinyl choline chloride has been used on elephant, hippopotamus and buffalo (Steel, 1968). The animals were taken to an abattoir for meat processing. This consisted of a main hall for skinning and dismembering, a washing room, boning room and a cold room (Steel, 1968).

Some information on the yield from reduction crops of elephant, hippopotamus and buffalo is shown in Table V. The most sustained operations have been in the Rwenzori National Park, Luangwa Valley, and the Kruger National Park. Hippopotamus densities in the Rwenzori Park reached 28 km^{-2} and cropping was designed to create two hippopotamus free areas while others were reduced to a range of densities. Attempts to tan hides failed owing to their thickness and their arrangement of collagen fibres. Later however, Wildlife Services Ltd. in Kabalega Falls NP developed a technique of planing down the thicker parts of both elephant and hippopotamus skins so that all the body skin could be used. In 1962–63 the total running cost of the Rwenzori National Park was 60 070$ (1977) (Reinwald and Hemingway, 1968). Hence, at that time the mean revenue from cropping would account for more than 50% of the running costs of the Park. Furthermore, studies by Field (1969) and Thornton (1971) in two areas where hippopotamus were eliminated showed that there was a recovery of the grasses from poor quality annuals to palatable perennials.

In Kabalega Falls NP revenue from the sale of hides of elephant exceeded the combined value of meat and ivory. The mean combined weight of ivory was only 10 kg per animal valued at 55$ (1977). There is evidence that shrub regeneration in the *Hyparrhenia* and *Sporobolus-Setaria* grasslands only occurs with the reduction of grazing. In *Combretum-Terminalia* woodland the evidence is less clear, it being necessary

TABLE V Estimated numbers and yield of selected cropping operations in Africa

Place	Date	Crop	Species	Numbers	Dressed kg	Revenue[a] Meat(Shs)	Revenue[a] Ivory, hides(Shs)	Reference
Rwenzori NP, Uganda	1958–1967	R	Hippopotamus	c8 000	4 702 400	2.4 m	Tusks only	Field (1974)
Kabalega Falls NP, Uganda	1965–1970	R	Elephant	2000	1 700 000	748 000	Tusks	Field (1974)
			Hippopotamus	4000	2 351 200	1 034 528	880 000	
Tsavo East NP, Kenya	1967	S	Elephant	300		Not sold	Tusks + 3760 m^2 hides	Parker, (pers. comm.)
Luangwa Valley GR, Zambia	1965–1969	R	Elephant	1453	645 429	1 774 930	—	Steel (1968)
		R	Hippopotamus	595	225 307	619 596	—	
		R	Buffalo	231	60 823	200 717	—	
Semliki GR, Uganda	1963–1970	SY	Uganda Kob	6964	320 344	452 660	Hides 34 820	Kyeyune (pers. comm.)
W. Acholi District, Uganda	1965–1967	SY	Uganda Kob	475	25 884	30 373	Hides only	Bindernagel (1968)
		SY	Buffalo	368	92 365	104 548		
		SY	Hartebeest	116	9 735	11 817		
		SY	Others	82	2 806	3 278		
Kajiado District, Kenya	1972–1974	SY	Wildebeest	566	22 649	53 223	21 150	Swank et al. (1974)
NDC Ranch, W Kilimanjaro, Tanzania	1970?	R	Thomson's gazelle	300	2 708	⎱ 21 554	⎱ 14 000	Field (1974)
			Grants gazelle	100	3 040	⎰	⎰	
Loliondo, Tanzania	1969–1971	SY	Zebra	775	—	15 166	384 161	Gogan (1972)
KeKopey Ranch, Kenya	1971–1972	R	Thompson's gazelle	820	⎱ 22 000	⎱ 120 672	87 165 Skins	Parker and Graham (1973)
			Impala	638	⎰	⎰		
Suguroi Ranch, Kenya	1972	R	Thomson's gazelle	500	⎱ 13 162		2 755 Horns	Parker and Graham (1973)
			Impala	401	⎰			

R = Reduction S = Sample SY = Sustained yield
[a] NB: Revenue is given in EA Shillings 1$ = 8 EA Shillings (1975–1977)

to reduce both burning and grazing for recovery (Spence and Angus, 1970).

In Tsavo East NP the sample cropping has been inadequate to effect a vegetation change and widespread damage to trees has been attributed almost entirely to utilization by elephants (Leuthold, 1977). It remains to be seen whether the subsequent reduction of elephant through starvation will enable the vegetation to recover (Corfield, 1973).

Sustained yield cropping of wildlife has been carried out in several Game Reserves, some of which are listed in Table V. In the Semliki Valley, Uganda, a mean annual crop of 774 Uganda kob was taken over a nine-year period. The annual quota was not more than 1000 animals (Buechner, 1974). Carcasses of females sold for 7·5$ (1977) while males were 8·75$ (1977). Untreated hides sold for 0·63$ (1977) only (Kyeyune, pers. comm.).

In the West Acholi District of Uganda a total of 1041 animals were cropped over a two-and-a-half year period (Bindernagel, 1968). These involved 46% Uganda kob, 35% buffalo, 11% Jackson's hartebeest, and the remainder a variety of species. These animals yielded a total of 130 790 kg of dressed carcasses valued at 18 572$ (1977) buffalo were about 70% of the total revenue and Uganda kob about 20%. Meat was sold to schools, hospitals and local contractors. Cropping was hampered by flooding rivers and poor transport. The area has now been opened for settlement.

At Loliondo in northern Tanzania a pilot cropping of several species of wildlife by Wildlife Services Ltd. experienced difficulty in selling meat when markets were boycotted. Subsequently, however, Gogan (1972) reported that in 1969–71 775 zebra carcasses were inspected. Four marketing possibilities were explored, namely freezing for sale in Arusha, or for sale overseas or sun drying for sale in Arusha. The sale of fresh meat encountered objections from beef producers and a threatened boycott of shops. Dried meat was sold rapidly however. Data from Balson (pers. comm.) for 1970 showed that after tanning, zebra hides realized rather more than 81·25$ (1977) each. A total of 570 hides yielded 48 020$ (1977) but the meat realized only 1896$ (1977). Costs of this operation were 14 375$ (1977) with an additional 14 217$ (1977) for tanning; hence the net yield was 160 988 Sh.

In southern Tanzania at Lake Rukwa cropping was begun in 1966 as a single action scheme with the intention of continuing it as an annual crop if it was profitable (Reinwald and Hemingway, 1968). Fixed costs of cropping 160 zebra were 333–375$ (1977) and variable costs were 414$ (1977). Carcasses were sold initially for 5$ (1977) each and would have covered the cost of the operation. Skins realized 37·5$

(1977) each or a total profit of 6000$ (1977). However, by 1971, 300 zebra and 500 topi were being cropped but carcasses were being sold for only 2·5$ (1977) each. (Balson pers. comm.)

Finally it is important to mention a recent programme in Kajiado District of Kenya. (Swank *et al.*, 1974). This cropping operation was intended to lead to sustained yield offtake. In the event, however, it lasted for only two years owing to opposition by preservationists and the view that the project UNDP/FAO Kenya Wildlife Management Project, had taken the wrong course of action. Early phases were devoted to developing techniques and equipment. At first animals were driven into a large trap with a helicopter using a technique developed in South Africa by Oelofse (1970). This was only partially successful and it was found that daytime shooting of most species on the range was practical. Up to 50 animals were processed on a normal day. About 60% of wildebeest carcasses had to be retained (i.e. frozen for 14 days) because of muscular cysts. A large sample of cysts were subsequently examined and found to be larval stages of the tapeworms of lion and hyena which are harmless to man. As a result the Veterinary Services Division altered the meat inspection standards for wildebeest. This will increase the value of such meat when cropped in future. Marketing was restricted to the Nairobi fresh meat outlets and these presented some development problems in particular their inability to store large quantities of frozen meat. In the event 751 animals were processed. A sample of 77% of these yielded 22 649 kg of dressed carcasses valued at 6653$ (1977). Hides were worth 2644$ (1977), but the net revenue was only 1632$ (1977).

C. CONCLUSION

Reduction cropping in National Parks has been necessary where there is excessive destruction of the vegetation by over-grazing. This presupposes a Park policy to conserve as great a variety of habitats and associated flora and fauna as the environment will permit. Under such conditions the dominance of a species leading towards a monoculture is intolerable. Population reduction has proved to be a most successful kind of operation since the crop is abundant and costs are minimized. This also permits experimentation with cropping techniques without undue risk to the programme.

Reduction cropping has also served its purpose in enabling the recovery of the vegetation. In the long term, however, it is hoped that small-scale sustained yield cropping will prevent the need for large-scale reduction crops. Large-scale reductions of wildlife populations over short periods may even permit the overgrowth of vegetation, before other herbivorous populations can recover from their suppressed state (Field, 1969). Wildlife cropping may cause a sudden drain of nutrients from the ecosystem. Field (1968) estimated that hippopotamus cropping with the removal of carcasses from the ecosystem resulted in the loss of 48 864 kg of ash per annum in the Rwenzori NP. Since hippopotamus graze on land and excrete some 75% of their faeces in the water (Field, 1968) they constitute a natural energy sink (Laws, 1968) and in areas of poor soil additional losses from cropping losses probably can not be sustained. Immigrant animals such as elephants have the reverse effect.

Sustained yield crops are desirable from the point of view of sound land management. They have also been most successful where there are large concentrations of game. The cost of obtaining animals is usually higher since the animals are less abundant than in National Parks and more wild having been hunted over a prolonged period.

Many cropping problems have arisen which are often unrelated to the culling procedure. Emotional feelings run high among those who wish to preserve rather than manage, and the preservationists have often lobbyed successfully against cropping. Competition with butchers, poor transport and corruption are among the factors which have reduced the success of cropping.

V. General Conclusions

In this review an attempt has been made firstly, to determine whether an unexploited and potential resource still exists, and secondly, to determine whether and how it can be utilized.

From the brief discussion of the history of wildlife utilization it is clear that hunting, which is traditional to man, is still important to some people especially in underdeveloped countries and evidence indicates that resources are still large and in many areas are mainly untapped.

The complex spectrum of herbivorous wildlife scores over domestic stock through a more comprehensive utilization of the wide range of food resources. Actual amounts eaten when compared on the same basis do not differ between wildlife and domestic stock. Some wildlife species e.g. eland, are not as efficient as domestic stock at digesting high fibre diets, which may normally be outside their food range. With the exception of the camel, many wildlife species are better adapted to arid conditions than domestic stock.

Rates of reproduction are generally related to size although the Suiformes are exceptions to this rule. Growth rates of wild ungulates tend to be faster than equivalent domestic animals under similar range conditions. They have a higher dressing percentage and a higher proportion of carcass lean. Meat quality of wildlife tends to be poorer than domestic animals, but difficult to distinguish on panel tests.

Milk production of wild animals tends to be lower than domestic animals with the possible exception of the eland.

Loose herding of some wild animals, such as the eland, renders them less suitable for domestication.

Wild animals are more tolerant of endemic diseases than domestic stock and it is probably in this, and in their wider range of food habits that they justify their utilization as a source of meat, alongside domestic stock on farms and ranches.

The domestication of new ungulate species is an under-developed technique. A major disadvantage is the large capital outlay necessary to obtain and tame a herd of wild animals, with no guaranteed return for a prolonged period while the herd reaches exploitable numbers. In general, people who can afford to do this can also afford the luxury of game viewing or hunting. There is for them little incentive to domesticate, and perhaps the opposite as a species under the control of man no longer provides a challenge to the hunter (Field, 1974).

It has been pointed out, however, that above all domestication fulfills a basic requirement of man, i.e. insurance for the future through ownership of animals (Parker and Graham, 1971). Ownership of land in semi-arid areas is impractical since rainfall is so scattered and unreliable that people are obliged to concentrate their stock wherever it falls (Dyson-Hudson and Dyson-Hudson, 1969). As human populations increase in Africa there is a gradual expansion into semi-arid areas where conventional domestic stock often die. It is here that wild animals, in particular the oryx, show the greatest potential for use through domestication.

Game cropping, whether on ranches, Game Reserves or National Parks has met with moderate success. In southern Africa where there is a long tradition of wildlife utilization for meat, objections and barriers to cropping have been overcome with the minimum of difficulty. There is now a full time wildlife processing factory in the Kruger National Park where meat is canned and sold at the gate. In eastern Africa, however, a number of problems have had to be overcome. These range from the development of techniques for obtaining wildlife, and complying with the high standards of meat hygiene set by Veterinary Departments, to problems with a poor response to marketing, and boycotting. In some cases however, wildlife cropping has made a significant contribution to the diet of people. For example, in Uganda's Western

Province, Burgess (1962) estimated that only 5·8 g of animal protein was available per human daily, compared with 61·1 g in the USA. Since then the animals cropped in the Rwenzori Park and Semiliki Valley have yielded an estimated 558 082 kg of carcasses per annum over nine years. This would support an additional 263 448 persons at the original rate of 25 000 at the rate of the US citizen.

There is no longer any need for reduction of elephants in most East African National Parks as the increase in the price of ivory had lead to commercialized poaching.

Sustained wildlife utilization is, therefore a sophsticated science for which emergent African nations have neither the expertise nor the time. It is to be hoped that the work being carried out in southern Africa will survive any political changes. This knowledge could then be used in eastern Africa if the pressure of human population does not force a decline in the numbers of wildlife.

Acknowledgements

I am most grateful to Professor John Skinner of the University of Pretoria, Dr H. Jahnke of ILCA Addis Ababa and my wife Alison, for bringing to my attention information of value in compiling this review. I wish to thank Dr R. M. Laws for his criticism of this manuscript.

I would also like to thank Mrs Heather Dainty for typing the manuscript.

Bibliography

Ables, E. D., Carpenter, Z. L., Quarrier, L. and Sheffield, L. J. (1973). "Carcass and Meat Characteristics of Nilgai antelope." Texas A and M University. B1130 8pp.

Arman, P. and Hopcraft, D. (1975). Nutritional studies on East African herbivores: 1. Digestibilities of dry matter crude fibre and crude protein in antelope, cattle and sheep. *Brit. J. Nutr.* **33**, 255–264.

Arnold, G. W. (1964). Some principles in the investigation of selective grazing. *Proc. Aust. Soc. Anim. Prod.* 5: 258.

Astle, W. L. (1971). Management in the Luanwa Valley, *Oryx* **11**, 135–139.

Bell, R. H. V., Grimsdell, J. J. R., van Levieren, L. P. and Sayer, J. A. (1973). Census of Kafue lechwe by aerial stratified sampling. *E. Afr. Wild. J.* **11**, 55–74.

Blankenship, L. H. and Qvortrup, S. A. (1974). Resource management on a Kenya Ranch. *J. Sth. Af. Wildlife Management Ass.* **4**, 177–183.

Bligh, J. (1972). Evaporative heat loss in hot arid environments. *In* "Comparative Physiology of Desert Animals," (Maloiy, G. M. O., Ed.), pp. 357–369. Academic Press, London and New York.

Bindernagel, J. A. (1968). "Game cropping in Uganda." Report to Uganda Game Dept., Entebbe. 200 pp. Mimeo.

Bourlière, F. and Verschuren, J. (1960). "Introduction à Lécologie des Ongulés du Parc National Albert." Inst. des Parcs Nationaux du Congo, Brussels.

Bremaud, O. (1969). "Notes on Camel Production in the Northern Districts of the Republic of Kenya." I.L.C.A., Addis Ababa, 119 pp. Mimeo.

Buechner, H. K. (1974). Implications of social behaviour in the management of Uganda Kob. In "The Behaviour of Ungulates and its Relation to Management." I.U.C.N., Morges.

Buechner, H. K. and Dawkins, H. C. (1961). Vegetation change induced by elephants and fire in Murchison Falls National Park. Uganda Ecology 42, 752–766.

Buillet, R. W. (1975). "The Camel and the Wheel." Harvard University Press, Cambridge, Mass. pp. 327.

Burgess, A. P. (1962). Untitled. E. African Med. J. 39, 449.

Butynski, T. M. (1973). Life history and Economic Value of the spring hare Pedetes capensis Forster in Botswana. Botswana Notes and Records 5, 209–213.

Child, G. S. (1974). "Kainji Lake Research Project, Nigeria: An Ecological Survey of the Borgu Game Reserve." FAO SF/NIR 24 Tech. Rep. 130 pp. Mimeo.

Cloudsley-Thomspon, J. L. (1969). "The Zoology of Tropical Africa." (Ed. Carrington, R.). Weidenfeld and Nicolson, London.

Cobban, E. W. (1965). The productivity of the lowveld in Rhodesia when game animals are cropped on the basis of sustained yield. B.Sc. Thesis, University of Rhodesia 58 pp.

Coe, M. J., Cumming, D. H. and Phillipson, J. (1976). Biomass and production of large african herbivores in relation to rainfall and primary production. Oecologia 22, 341–354.

Corfield, T. F. (1973). Elephant mortality in Tsavo National Park, Kenya. E. Afr. Wild. J. 11, 339–368.

Crawford, M. A. (1968). Possible use of wild animals as future sources of food in Africa. Vet. Rec. Mar. 16, 305–314.

Darling, F. F. (1960). "Wildlife in an African Territory." O.U.P., London 160 pp.

Dasmann, R. F. (1964). "African Game Ranching." Pergamon, Oxford. 75 pp.

Densham, W. D. (1974). A method of capture and translocation of wild herbivores: using opaque plastic material and a helicopter. Lammergeyer 21, 1–25.

Dorst, J. and Dandelot, P. (1970). "A Field Guide to The Larger Mammals of Africa." Collins, London.

Dyson-Hudson, R. and Dyson-Hudson, N. (1969). Subsistence herding in Uganda. Sci. Amer. 222, 76–88.

Fay, L. D. (1972). Report to the Government of Kenya on Wildlife Disease Research. U.N.D.P. TA. 3049. 42pp. Rome.

Field, C. R. (1968). The food habits of wild ungulates in Uganda. PhD Thesis, Univ. of Cambridge.

Field, C. R. (1969). A study of the feeding habits of the hippopotamus (Hippopotamus amphibius Linn.) in the Queen Elizabeth National Park, Uganda, with some management implications. Zool. Africana. 5(1), 71–86.

Field, C. R. (1970). Observations on the food habits of tame warthog and antelope in Uganda. E. Afr. Wildl. J. 8, 1–18.

Field, C. R. (1971). Elephant ecology in the Queen Elizabeth National Park, Uganda. E. Afr. Wildl. J. 9, 99–124.

Field, C. R. (1974). Scientific Utilization of Wildlife for meat in East Africa: a Review. J. Sth. Afr. Wildl. Mgmt. Ass. 4, 177–183.

Field, C. R. (1975). Climate and the food habits of ungulates on Galana Ranch. E. Afr. Wildl. J. 13, 203–220.

Field, C. R. (1976a). Palatability factors and nutritive value of the food of buffaloes (*Syncerus caffer*) in Uganda. *E. Afr. Wildl. J.* **14**, 181–201.

Field, C. R. (1976b). Feeding trials to determine intake and digestibility of the diets of five herbivore species. FAO KEN/71/526 Project working Document No. 11.

Field, C. R. and Blankenship. L. H. (1973a). Nutrition and Reproduction of Grant's and Thomson's gazelles, Coke's hartebeest and giraffe in Kenya. *J. Reprod. Fert.*, suppl. **19**, 287–301.

Field, C. R. and Blankenship, L. H. (1973b). On making the game pay. *Africana* **5**, 22–23.

Field, C. R. and Laws, R. M. (1970). The distribution of the larger herbivores in the Queen Elizabeth National Park, Uganda. *J. Appl. Ecol.* **7**, 273–294.

Finch, V. A. (1972). Energy exchange with the environment of two East African antelopes, the eland and the hartebeest. *In* "Comparative Physiology of Desert Animals", (Maloiy, G. M. O., Ed.), pp. 315–326. Academic Press, London and New York.

Glover, P. E. (1970). The Tsavo and the elephants. *Oryx* **10**, 323–325.

Gogan, J. P. (1972). The Loliondo zebra cropping scheme. Biologists' report to the Game Division, Arusha. 22pp. Mimeo.

Graham, A. D. (1973). "The Gardeners of Eden." Allen & Unwin, London 246pp.

Grimsdell, J. J. R. (1969). Ecology of the buffalo, *Syncerus caffer* in Western Uganda. PhD Thesis, Cambridge University.

Grimsdell, J. J. R. and Bell, R. H. V. (1972). Population growth of red lechwe, *Kobus leche leche* Gray, in the Busanga Plain, Zambia. *E. Afr. Wildl. J.* **10**, 117–122.

Hale, E. B. (1962). Domestication and the evolution of behaviour. Pp. 21–53. *In* "The Behaviour of Domestic Animals." (Hafez, E. S. E., Ed.), pp. 619. Bailliere, Tindall and Cox, London.

Hammond, J. A. and Branagan, D. (1973). The disease factor in plans for the domestication of wild ruminants. *Africa. Vet. Rec.* **92**, 367–369.

Harris, L. D. (1970). Some structural and functional attributes of a semi arid East African ecosystem. PhD Thesis Michigan State University.

Harris, L. D. (1972). An ecological description of a semi-arid East African Ecosystem. Colorado State University Range Science Department Science Series **11**.

Harthoorn, A. M. (1966). The Tsavo Elephants. *Oryx* **8**, 233–236.

Heraskov, S. G. (1953). Camel's milk and its products. *Konevodstvo* **23**(11), 35–37.

Heraskov, S. G. (1965). Camel milk a valuable food product. *Konevod. Konnyǐ Sport.* **35**, 14–15.

Hofmann, R. R. (1973). The Ruminant Stomach. East African Literature Bureau, Nairobi. 354 pp.

Holman, D. (1967). "The Elephant People." John Murray, London.

Hopcraft, D. and Arman, P. (1971). Preliminary report on comparative productivity of wild and domestic animals. 8 pp. mimeo.

Hoppe, P. P., Qvortrup, S. A. and Woodford, M. H. (1977). Rumen fermentation and food selection in East African sheep, goats, Thomson's gazelle, Grant's gazelle and impala. *J. Agric. Sci.*, Camb. **89**, 129–135.

Jewell, P. A. (1969). Wild mammals and their potential for new domestication. *In* "The Domestication and Exploitation of Plants and Animals." (Ucko, P. J. and Dimbleby, G. W., Eds.). Duckworth, London.

Joubert, S. (1977). South African elephants. Pattern for the future. In WWF/IUCN Elephant Survey and Cons. Progr. News 2:3.

Keep, M. E. (1972). The Meat Yield and pathology of eland in Natal. *Lammergeyer* **17**, 1–9.

King, J. M. and Heath, B. R. (1975). Game domestication for animal production in Africa. *World Anim. Rev.* **16**, 23–30.

King, J. M., Kingaby, G. P., Colvin, J. C. and Heath, B. R. (1975). Seasonal variation in water turnover by oryx and eland on the Galana Game Ranch Research Project. *E. Afr. Wildl. J.* **13**, 287–296.

Kuliev, K. (1959). The utilization of camel's milk. *Mol. Promyslenn* **20**(2), 28.

Kutilek, M. J. (1974). The density and biomass of large mammals in Lake Nakuru National Park. *E. Afr. Wildl. J.* **12**, 201–212.

Kyle, R. S. (1972). Meat production in Africa. The case for new domestic species. Bristol Vet. School. 62 pp. Mimeo.

Lamprey, H. F. (1963). Ecological separation of large mammal species in the Tarangire Game Reserve. Tanganyika. *E. Afr. Wildl. J.* **1**, 63–92.

Lamprey, H. F. (1964). Estimation of large mammal densities, biomass and energy exchange in the Tarangire Game Reserve and the Masai Steppe in Tanganyika. *E. Afr. Wildl. J.* **2**, 1–46.

Laws, R. M. (1968). Interactions between elephant and hippopotamus populations and their environment. *E. Afr. agric. For. J.* special issue **33**, 140–147.

Laws, R. M. (1969). The Tsavo Research Project. *J. Reprod. Fert. Suppl.* **6**, 495–531.

Laws, R. M., Parker, I. S. C. and Johnston, R. C. B. (1970). Elephants and habitats in North Bunyoro, Uganda. *E. Afr. Wildl. J.* **8**, 163–180.

Laws, R. M., Parker, I. S. C. and Johnstone, R. C. B. (1975). Elephants and Their Habitats. Oxford University Press, London.

Lawton, R. M. and Gough, M. (1970). Elephants or fire—which to blame? *Oryx* **10**, 244–248.

Ledger, H. P. (1968). Body composition as a basis for a comparative study of some East African mammals. *In* "Comparative Nutrition of Wild Animals" (Crawford, N. A., Ed.), pp. 289–310. Academic Press, London and New York.

Ledger, H. P., Sachs, R. and Smith, N. S. (1967). Wildlife and food production. *World Rev. Anim. Prod.* **3**, 13–37.

Lee, R. B. (1968). What hunters do for a living, or, how to make out on scarce resources. *In* "Man the Hunter." (Lee, R. B. and De Vore, I., Eds.). Aldine Publ. Co., Chicago.

Leuthold, W. (1977). Changes in tree populations of Tsavo East National Park, Kenya. *E. Afr. Wildl. J.* **15**, 61–69.

Leuthold, W. and Leuthold, B. M. (1976). Density and Biomass of ungulates in Tsavo National Park, Kenya. *E. Afr. Wild. J.* **14**, 49–58.

Lewis, J. G. (1975). A comparative study of the activity of some indigenous African ungulates and conventional stock under domestication. PhD Thesis, London University.

Liversidge, R. (1975). Productivity and management of game. Game Farm Owners. Conf., Kimberly. 12 Aug. pp. 14–19.

Macfadyen, A. (1964). Energy flow in Ecosystems and its exploitation by grazing. *In* "Grazing in Terrestrial & Marine Environments." Blackwells, Oxford pp. 3–20.

Macfarlane, W. V. and Howard, B. (1972). Comparative water and energy economy of wild domestic mammals. *In* "Comparative Physiology of Desert Animals" (Maloiy, G. M. O., Ed.), pp. 261–296. Academic Press, London and New York.

Marks, S. A. (1973). Prey selection and annual harvest of game in a rural Zambian community. *E. Afr. Wildl. J.* **11**(2) 113–128.

Mentis, M. T. (1972). Game on the farm. *Natal Farmers Weekly* May/June Parts 1 and 2.

Michell, B. L. and Uys, J. M. C. (1961). The problem of the lechwe (*Kobus lechwe*) on the Kafue Flats. *Oryx* **6**, 171–183.

Myers, N. (1973). The people crunch comes to East Africa. *Nat. Hist.* **82**, 10.

Norton-Griffiths, M. (1973). Counting the Serengeti migratory weildbeest using two-stage sampling. *E. Afr. Wildl. J.* **11**, 135–150.

Norton-Griffiths, M. (1975). The numbers and distribution of large mammals in Ruaha National Park Tanzania. *E. Afr. Wildl. J.* **13**, 121–140.

Oelofse, J. (1970). Plastic for Game Catching. *Oryx* **10**, 306–308.

Parker, I. S. C. (1975). "Two routes to tameness." Mimeo.

Parker, I. S. C. and Archer, A. L. (1969). Elephant cropping in Mkomazi Game Reserve, Tanzania. Unpubl. report to Tanzanian Government.

Parker, I. S. C. and Graham, A. D. (1971). The ecological & economic basis for game ranching in Africa. 11th *Symp. Brit. Ecol. Soc.* 393–404.

Parker, I. S. C. and Graham, A. D. (1973). Game use on two Kenya ranches. Report to the Government of Kenya. 24 pp. Mimeo.

Posselt, J. (1963). The domestication of the eland. *Rhod. J. Agric. Res.* **1**, 81–87.

Reinwald, H. and Hemingway, P. (1968). Some economic considerations of game cropping for export. *E. Afr. Agric. For. J.* Special Issue **33**, 104–109.

Ross, I. C., Field, C. R. and Harrington, G. N. (1976). The savanna ecology of Kidepo Valley National Park, Uganda. III Animal populations and park management recommendations. *E. Afr. Wildl. J.* **14**, 35–48.

Rossetti, G. and Congiu, S. (1955). Zootechnical and Veterinary Investigations on the domestic animals of Somalia. Ispellorato Veterinario. Admin. Fiduciaria Italiana della Somalia 207 pp.

Roth, H. H., Kerr, M. A. and Posselt, J. (1972). Studies on the utilization of semi-domesticated Eland (*Taurotragus Oryx*) in Rhodesia. *Z. Tierzücht. ZüchtBiol.* **89**, 69–83.

Roth, H. H. and Osterberg, R. (1971). Studies on the Agricultural utilization of semi-domesticated eland (*Taurotragus oryx*) in Rhodesia. 4. Chemical composition of eland browse. *Rhod. J. Agric. Res.* **9**, 45–51.

Rowe-Rowe, D. T. and Bigalke, R. C. (1972). Observations on the breeding and behaviour of Blesbok. *Lammergeyer* **15**, 1–14.

Sato, S. (1976). Preliminary report of camel ecology among the Rendille in the Northern Kenya. Kyoto University. 8 pp. Mimeo.

Savidge, J. M. (1968). Elephants in the Ruaha National Park, Tanzania-Management Problem. *E. Afr. Agric. For. J.* Special Issue **33**, 191–196.

Savidge, J. M., Woodford, M. H. and Croze, H. (1976). Report on a Mission to Zaire FAO W/K1593, Rome 34 pp. Mimeo.

Savory, C. A. R. (1969). Crisis in Rhodesia. *Oryx* **10**, 25–30.

Schmidt-Nielsen, K. (1959). The physiology of the camel. *Sci Amer.* **201**, 140–151.

Short, R. V. (1976). The introduction of new species of animals for the purpose of domestication. *In* "The Zoological Society of London 1826–1976 and Beyond", (Professor Lord Zuckerman, Ed.), pp. 1–13. Academic Press, London and New York.

Skinner, J. D. (1967). An appraisal of the eland as a farm animal in Africa. *Anim. Breed. Abstr.* **35**, 177–186.

Skinner, J. D. (1973). An appraisal of the status of certain antelope for game farming in South Africa. *Z. Tierzücht. ZüchtBiol.* **90**, 263–277.

Skinner, J. D. (1975). Game farming in South Africa, *Jl. S. Afr. Biol. Soc.* **16,** 8–15.

Skinner, J. D. and Van Zyl, J. H. M. (1969). Reproductive performance of the common eland *Taurotragus oryx* in two environments. *J. Reprod. Fert. Suppl.* **6,** 319–322.

Skinner, J. D., Von La Chevallerie, M. and Van Zyl, J. H. M. (1971). An appraisal of the springbok for diversifying animal production in Africa. *Anim. Breed. Abstr.* **39,** 215–224.

Smith, H. S. (1969). Animal domestication and animal cult in predynastic Egypt. In "The Domestication and Exploitation of Plants and Animals." (Ucko, P. J. and Dimbleby, G. W., Eds.), pp. 581. Duckworth, London.

Spence, D. H. N. and Angus, A. (1970). African grassland management—burning and grazing in Murchison Falls National Park, Uganda. *Symp. Brit. Ecol. Soc.* **11,** 319–332.

Spencer, P. (1973). "Nomads in Alliance." Oxford University Press, London. 230 pp.

Spinage, C. A. (1969). Report of the ecologist to the Rwanda National Parks Ministry of Overseas Development, London.

Stainthorpe, H. L. (1972). Observations on captive eland in the Loteni Nature Reserve. *Lammergeyer* **15,** 27–38.

Stanley Price, M. (1976). Feeding studies of Oryx on the Galana Ranch. *A.W.L.F. News* **11,** 7–11.

Steel, W. S. (1968). The technology of wildlife management, game cropping in the Luangwa Valley, Zambia. *E. Afr. Agric. For. J.* Special issue **33,** 266–270.

Swank, W. G., Casebeer, R. L., Thresher, P. B. and Woodford, M. H. (1974). Cropping, processing and marketing of wildlife in Kajiado District, Kenya. FAO KEN/71/526 Proj, Working Document **6,** 120 pp. Mimeo.

Talbot, L. M., Payne, W. J. A., Ledger, H. P., Verdcourt, L. D. and Tablot, M. H. (1965). The meat production potential of wild animals in Africa. Commonw. Agric. Bur. Tech. Comm. **15,** 1–42.

Taylor, C. R. (1968). Hygroscopic food: a source of water for desert antelopes? *Nature, (London)* **219,** 181–182.

Taylor, C. R. (1972). The desert gazelle: a paradox resolved *In* "Comparative Physiology of Desert Animals" (Maloiy, G. M. O., Ed.), pp. 215–227. Academic Press, London and New York.

Taylor, C. R. and Lyman, C. P. (1967). A comparative study of the environmental physiology of an East African antelope, the eland and the Hereford steer. *Physiol. zool.* **40,** 280–295.

Thornthwaite, C. W. (1933). *Geogr. Rev.* **23,** 453.

Thornton, D. D. (1971). The effect of complete removal of hippopotamus on grassland in the Queen Elizabeth National Park, Uganda. *E. Afr. Wildl. J.* **9,** 47–56.

Torry, W. I. (1973). Subsistence ecology among the Gabra: Nomads of the Kenya/Ethiopia frontier. PhD Thesis, Columbia University.

Torry, W. I. (1977). Life in the camels shadow. *Nat. Hist., N.Y.* pp. 64–68.

Treus, D. B. and Kravchenko, D. (1968). Methods of rearing and economic utilization of the eland in Askanya-Nova Zoological Park. *In* "Comparative Nutrition of Wild Animals" (Crawford M.A., Ed.), pp. 395–411. Academic, Press, London and New York.

Tubiana, M. and Tubiana, J. (1975). Tradition et dévelopment au Soudan oriental: l'exemple zaghava *In* "Pastoralism in Tropical Africa". (Monod, T., Ed.). I.A.I. Oxford.

Van Wyk, P. L. and Fairall, N. (1969). The influence of the African elephant on the vegetation of the Kruger National Park. *Koedoe* **12,** 57–89.

Van Zyl, J. H. M. and Wehmeyer, A. S. (1970). The composition of the milk of springbok (*Antidorcas marsupialis*), eland (*Taurotragus oryx*) and Wildebeest (*Connochaetes gnou*) *Zoolgica Afr.* **5,** 131–133.

Verdcourt, B. and Trump, E. C. (1969). "Common Poisonous Plants of East Africa." Collins, London pp. 254.

Von la Chevallerie (1972). Meat quality in seven wild ungulate species. *S. Afri. J. Anim. Sci.* **2,** 101–104.

Watson, R. M. (1972). Results of aerial livestock surveys of Kaputei division, Samburu district and North-eastern Province. Statistics Division. Min. of Finance and Planning, Republic of Kenya.

Watson, R. M. and Bell, R. H. V. (1969). The distribution, abundance and status of the elephant in the Serengeti region of Northern Tanzania. *J. Appl. Ecol.* **6,** 115–132.

Western, D. (1973). The structure, dynamics and changes of the Amboseli ecosystem, Univ. of Nairobi, PhD Thesis.

Woodburn, (1968). In Parker I. S. C. and Graham, A. D. 11th *Symp. Brit. Ecol. Soc.* 393.

Young, E. (1973). "The capture and care of wild animals." Ed. Human and Rousseau, Cape Town, 224 pp.

Some Problems in the Management of Marine Resources

JOHN H. STEELE

*Woods Hole Oceanographic Institution,
Woods Hole, Massachusetts, USA*

I. Introduction

There appears to be a developing dichotomy between the applied manager concerned with one stock of a species and those who attempt the general study of ecosystems. Caughley (1976), discussing the management of ungulates, states that we are almost totally ignorant of the process by which the two components, ungulates and vegetation, interact to achieve an equilibrium.

Similarly, those concerned with fish stock management consider, in practice, only the interactions between the stock and one predator, man. If the implications of a limiting food supply are introduced, then the competitors for this food cannot be neglected. Once this process is started, it is very difficult to close the system before the whole food web in a particular area, such as the North Sea, becomes the necessary object of study. In this process of expansion, the original remit—to improve the management of North Sea fish stocks—may be submerged in the proliferation of interactions, each of which may need to be specified in some individual manner.

The other object of management is protection from environmental changes induced by man's activities. There is now considerable knowledge of the distribution of certain chemicals, and some information on their effect at lower trophic levels or on individual organ isms These effects, in a natural community, may be moderated or enhanced by the interactions within the system and must be considered interms. of the resilience (Holling, 1973) to existing stresses. This is especially the case for commercially exploited species which are already subject to significant stress.

The semantic conciseness of the ecosystem concept can provide a framework for general theories but these are not intended to deal with specific management problems (Maynard Smith, 1974). The alternative is the simulation model. In ecology there are no effective limits on assimilation within a computer and very large programmes can be constructed to simulate major ecosystems or biomes. The limitations are conceptual and relate in part to our abilities to interpret the outputs from such large models. They also depend for their usefulness on the nature of the inputs. If there is a large number of components (such as species), and for each component (and each interaction) the parameters have to be determined independently, then, as these parameters are varied, there is a huge number of possible outputs. If, as in meterological models, the number of basic parameters is relatively small, even though the computer model is very large, then the range of possible interpretations may be manageable.

For these reasons we cannot escape the need to have adequate and fairly general hypotheses as a basis for theoretical work whether it is mathematical or numerical. Thus a discussion of management, as it involves several species, is essentially a consideration of the scope of present concepts about interactions between ecosystem components. Apart from the nature of the concepts, there is a further limitation on theoretical development. Both at the beginning and more especially at the end, there is a need for comparison with field observations. In this respect, the quality of the data is a critical factor. If the available data are highly variable in space and time, then almost any theory may give values within the limits of such data. In many cases the "bulk" parameters such as total numbers of a species, or biomass of a trophic level, may display very large variations. On the other hand, "internal" features such as percentage size or age distribution may show less variation or more regular changes with space or time. Also, statistical properties of the distribution in space or time may have consistent properties; the spectral distribution of variance as a function of scale has been used in this way (Platt and Denman, 1975). If such regularities exist, then theories may need to be developed in a form which will permit direct comparison with data presented in the same way.

I shall attempt to illustrate these problems from work in marine ecology with special reference to fishery applications. There is some measure of agreement that future fisheries management in the open seas must be carried out on a multi-species basis. There is less agreement on the critical factors for such larger scale assessments. It is necessary, however, to narrow the field of study from the whole ecosystem to certain aspects if the required intensity of research is to be achieved. This essay will suggest certain hypotheses rather than reach definite conclusions.

I wish to express my thanks to Rodney Jones and others at the Marine Laboratory, Aberdeen, Scotland, for valuable discussions of these problems.

II. Single Species Models

Management models of single-species fish stocks are the main features found in the wide-ranging literature on this aspect. The changes in population are shown either as biomass variations, or through numbers in different age classes.

The biomass model used by Schaefer (1954) took

$$\frac{1}{B}\frac{dt}{dB} = a(b - B) - F \tag{1}$$

where B is the biomass of the stock and F is the fishing mortality. The natural rate of increase of the stock follows a logistic curve and at steady state the yield, Y, is given by

$$Y = FB = ab(b - B)$$

There is then a maximum yield at $B = b/2$. More complicated functional forms than the logistic can be used (see Schaefer and Beverton, 1963) giving other positions for the maximum, but the essential dependence on total biomass remains. The use of the logistic growth curve for the population implies some factors limiting the total biomass of the population, but the general form provides no indication whether these limitations occur through changes in growth rate or recruitment.

For higher animals, especially fish, the stages through which they pass—egg, larva, juvenile and reproducing adult—make the use of a biomass term particularly inappropriate. Further, the commercial harvesting of fish is usually restricted to individuals of a species above a certain size and the choice of this size is an important factor in management. For these reasons, Beverton and Holt (1957) considered the development of a particular cohort of a species with increasing weight $W(t)$ and decreasing numbers $N(t)$ so that

$$\frac{1}{B}\frac{dB}{dt} = \frac{1}{W}\frac{dW}{dt} + \frac{1}{N}\frac{dN}{dt} \tag{2}$$

It can be shown experimentally (e.g. Edwards et al., 1970a) that for a particular species at a given weight, dW/dt can vary considerably. For the natural populations, however, variations in dW/dt are very much less than those observed experimentally and to a first approximation appear to follow a fairly constant pattern so that a relation such as the Bertalanffy equation

$$\frac{dW}{dt} = aW^{2/3} - bW \tag{3}$$

is adequate for a particular species with a and b as defined constants for a particular stock. For this reason variations in population biomass, and so in commercial yield, depend on changes in numbers

$$\frac{dN}{dt} = -(F + M)N \tag{4}$$

where N is the natural mortality and F is that due to fishing activity. The natural mortality during the egg and larval phase is known to be high, usually of the order of 5–10% per day. During the juvenile and adult phase the rate is taken to be much lower, possibly about 20% per year for demersal species like haddock (*Melanogrammus aeglefinus* (L.)), whiting (*Merlangius merlangus* (L.)) and cod (*Gadus morhua* L.). In heavily fished areas such as the North Sea, the fishing mortality is of the order of 50% per year. Given values for F and N, then from (2), (3) and (4), total yield as biomass from a cohort can be calculated if the number of recruits N_0 is assumed. This is usually expressed as Y/N_0 the yield per recruit, where the recruits are defined as the number of juveniles before they reach the size when they begin to be caught in the commercial fishery. In this form an optimum fishing effort F can be calculated for which yield will be maximum. If the fishing is managed, not by effort control but in terms of quotas, then for each year, an estimate must be made of N_0 from which the absolute value of Y is calculated.

Because of the relative constancy of growth rates, the variations in stock appear as year-to-year differences in N_0 which can be very large. This, in turn, requires extensive efforts to monitor the pre-recruit populations of each stock subject to exploitation. Such a procedure causes a significant limitation on longer-term management since control can only be exerted on a year-to-year basis. With effective pre-recruit assessment, it has the advantage of requiring very little dependence on tenuous ecological assumptions about the general factors limiting stock size which are inherent in the Schaefer model.

Longer-term assessments for each stock can only be made if, based on previous years' data, one assumes an average recruitment which will not change with alterations in fishing effort. This forms the basis for proposals to decrease fishing effort from present high rates in certain stocks so that yield may be increased. However, as Jones R. (1976) has pointed out, decreased fishing effort implies increased biomass of the stock and therefore increased food requirement. If food for a particular stock is limiting to some extent, then the predicted increase in yield may not be attainable and the maximum yield may occur at a higher level of fishing effort than that predicted by the model where there is no food limitation.

Implicit in this argument is the assumption that each stock occupies a niche sufficiently separate from other species. If this is so, its abundance can be considered independently of other species, with changes in mortality rates being balanced by alterations in recruitment to maintain an effective utilization of its own food supplies. In other words, recruitment, N_0, becomes a function of food requirement of the total stock at any time. A modification of this kind was envisaged by Beverton and Holt (1957) and would extend the management models, to allow longer-term assessments, but these would still be carried out for each species independently of the others.

If, however, we introduce the concepts of food limitation and of the natural mortality of early stages related to this food limitation, then it is necessary to consider at least some of the ecological problems concerning the sources of this food and of the predators responsible for the mortality. Further, it becomes difficult to avoid questions about the interactions between species whose food requirements may overlap at some stages in their life.

III. Multi-species Assemblages

Because of the number of species, any structuring of the system requires some preconceptions. The two methods commonly used can be defined roughly as considering interactions between trophic levels in terms of energy flow; or else within a trophic level in relation to competition for a common resource; both have an extensive literature. The aim here is to illustrate both and then to emphasize the need to combine these aspects for an adequate picture not only for the ecological problems but also of the management consequences of interference with a system.

A. ENERGY FLOW IN THE NORTH SEA

A synthesis of earlier studies in the North Sea (Steele, 1965, 1974) provided a picture of energy flow through the food web from primary production to man (Fig. 1). In this presentation the benthic components

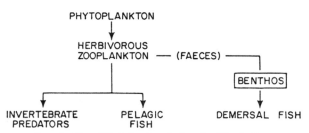

FIG. 1. Simplified food web for the North Sea.

have been simplified to one block. There were three major conclusions.

1. The available energy was being fully utilized in the commercial harvest. Thus there was no spare capacity which would permit large increases in total sustainable yield of the exploited stocks.

2. Significant changes are most likely to arise from the alterations in the relative quantities of flow in different parts of the food web.

3. The herbivorous zooplankton form a critical point in the web where energy is split between the pelagic and demersal components.

In any such representation there have to be aggregations of species or groups into compartments and this is particularly the case with such a simple picture as Fig. 1. Developments from this arise from recent data which permit the subdivision of categories in Fig. 1.

In the period between 1960–70, there were major changes in the North Sea fisheries with a marked decline in the main pelagic species, herring (*Clupea harengus* L.) and mackerel (*Scomber scombrus* L.), due to over-fishing (Burd, in press). There was also an increase in demersal fish such as haddock, whiting and cod, due to increased recruitment (Jones and Hislop, in press). Changes in physical environment and in plankton were also observed. The observations were given in a symposium held by the International Council for the Exploration of the Sea (Hempel, in press).

Jones and Richards (1976) have used the recent fish stock data to quantify the biomass changes between 1960–70. Simplified pictures of their main conclusions are given in Fig. 2, where the decimation of the large pelagic species, herring and mackerel, has, possibly, resulted in the transfer of predation on the copepods to smaller pelagic fish such

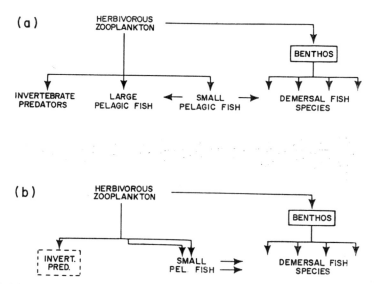

FIG. 2. Simplified description of fish stock interaction: (a) about 1960; (b) about 1970.

as sand eels (*Ammodytes* spp.) and Norway pout (*Trispoterus luscus* (L.)) and to juvenile stages of demersal fish. More important it is assumed that all the main demersal species now have a greater component of pelagic species (such as sand eels) in their diet, compared with the situation in 1960. Jones and Richards are able to show that, with the more detailed representation of the fish species, the energy "book" balances both before and after the major North Sea changes; and in both cases there is still no surplus energy.

This new evaluation raises three particular environmental questions.

1. When large pelagic fish were removed, why did the energy go to smaller fish and not flow into invertebrate predators? The implicit assumption in Fig. 2b is that this is a relatively self-contained box with its own ecological constraints on population expansion. The justification for this hypothesis is highly relevant to any future attempts to return the stocks to the 1960 picture.

2. The food requirements of the benthos are met by detrital material from the pelagic region, mainly faecal pellets of the herbivores (Steele, 1974). Thus the assumption is that this aspect of the system did not change. In turn, this implies that the primary production and its partitioning by the herbivores was unaltered even though there were significant changes in the species composition (Colebrook, in press; Reid, in press). This postulate of the relative lack of change in the benthos requires further study.

3. What effect will changes in the composition of plankton have on fish stocks or conversely, will fishery changes affect the plankton? These questions are raised by recent work on plankton dynamics and there are three relevant developments:

(i) During the 1960s there have been significant changes in plankton population structure in the North Sea (Colebrook, in press; Reid, in press).

(ii) Experiments in Canada and the UK with plankton ecosystems in large enclosures show that, under stress, these systems do not necessarily alter the total energy flow through the main trophic levels but do change the size structure of the populations within a trophic level (Menzel, 1977; Gamble et al., 1977).

(iii) Theoretical studies of multi-species plankton systems (Steele and Frost, 1977) show that such changes in population structure are as likely to occur by changes in higher trophic level (e.g. predators on the herbivores) as by changes in the physical or chemical environment (e.g. nutrients, mixing). This is discussed in more detail in a later section.

B. COMPETITION WITHIN A TROPHIC LEVEL

These energy flow diagrams, Figs 1 and 2, began as relatively simple chains dividing the production into a pelagic and demersal component. The analysis of the recent North Sea changes has emphasized the importance of the horizontal links and has led to the hypothesis that energy can be diverted not merely between neighbouring components but across apparently major divisions in the web. This, in turn, emphasizes the need to consider the interactions between species or groups apparently feeding from the same general resource.

Again there is a well-developed theory concerning competition between species and this has been quantified in terms of the permissible degree of overlap in relation to a common resource. Recently, May (1976) has quantified this overlap in terms of two parameters the width w of the niche and the distance d between two competing species expressed in the form $S = \exp\left(-d^2/4w^2\right)$. Theoretical studies by

May suggest that d/w should not be significantly less than unity, and further work by Roughgarden (see May, 1976) has proposed that as a result of evolutionary adaptation $d/w \to 1$. These concepts can be illustrated from the plankton communities in northern latitudes. Estimates of size selection of phytoplankton food by herbivorous copepods led Steele and Frost (1977) to use the selection function

$$S = \exp(-[\log \ \lambda]^2/\mu) \tag{5}$$

where $\mu = 2 \cdot 5$ and λ is proportional to (copepod weight)$^{1/3}$. The major copepod species in the North Sea have adult weights (in carbon units) of approximately 100 μgC for *Calanus* spp. and 10 μgG for such as *Pseudocalanus* and *Acartia*. Thus the ratio of equivalent lengths is approximately $2 \cdot 2$ and so $d = \log_e \ 2 \cdot 2 = 0 \cdot 79$ In May's notation $w = \sqrt{2 \cdot 5/4} = 0 \cdot 79$. The exact relation $d/w = 1$ is obviously fortuitous but indicates some measure of agreement with theory. Also, the other major copepod group in the North Sea, *Oithona* spp., is a further order of magnitude smaller in weight.

Size of organism in relation to food selection can provide a first approximation for division within the marine herbivore population, but within each of these copepod groups there are, of course, several species and these must be separated into niches by other definitions besides food. Thus, of the two main *Calanus* spp. one, *Calanus finmarchicus* (Gunnerus), occurs mainly in the spring and early summer whereas the other, *Calanus helgolandicus* (Claus), is most abundant later in the year.

For the pelagic carnivorous fish, a similar division may be possible. It is interesting to note that two of the main pelagic fish feeding on the herbivorous plankton, the sprat (*Sprattus sprattus* (L.)) and the herring, also have a final adult weight difference of approximately ten (Beverton, 1963). Further, although details of their food selection is not well known, herring show some decrease in growth rate when there is a shift in dominance in their food from the larger *Calanus* to the smaller *Pseudocalanus* (see Steele, 1965). It is possible that other planktonic fish such as Norway pout and mackerel might, to some extent, be fitted into the same small and large categories. Further, for the larger planktonic fish there are temporal separations. The two main stocks of herring are spring and autumn spawners and the mackerel occupy an intermediate position, spawning in the summer. For the early stages this can produce some size separation in relation to feeding. For the mature fish, feeding is related to the maturation cycle producing some temporal separation in feeding behaviour. Further, each of these stocks may follow a different migration pattern within the North Sea providing spatial separation.

For the demersal fish, there is a much greater available variety in mode of feeding but, again, two of the main species, cod and haddock, have final lengths in the ratio 2:5, whereas haddock and whiting are very similar in size.

In this way there is an emerging pattern of partitioning within groups which are usually placed together in the broader energy flow diagrams. Such subdivisions will be based firstly on weight categories in relation to feeding behaviour. Within these weight categories there are further subdivisions to species or stocks where the niche factor may be temporal or spatial separation.

In this simple application of theory to the main size groups there is the necessary assumption that the resource spectrum, in this case size of food particles, is invariant. In particular, it is assumed that it is not altered by the grazing. On the other hand, the food concentration must have some limiting effect in each population, usually assumed to operate through a logistic growth relation. These highly specific assumptions are unlikely to hold in many natural environments; and in the sea, in relation to pelagic herbivores and carnivores, we normally assume that grazing does alter the population density of the prey. Thus the competitive aspect cannot be considered separately from the food chain dynamics.

IV. Examples of Multi-species Models

Given these general comments, some examples of fishery and plankton models will be considered. I do not intend to give details of the internal structure of these models for which reference should be made to the original papers. The aim will be to consider the ecological boundaries set for each model. Any theory must choose some region of a much larger, effectively infinite, ecosystem, and so close off a certain portion of the system for detailed study. It must also limit the degree of detail which is given for each group or species. These closure decisions are critical features which may be as important in determining the response of the model as the "internal" features.

A. HERRING IN THE GULF OF ST LAWRENCE

As described in the preceding section, competition can be considered to occur between similarly sized species separated by a temporal developmental cycle. Lett and Kohler (1976) have studied this aspect for the spring and autumn spawned herring in the Gulf of St Lawrence. The third comparable sized component, mackerel, are included only as a predetermined population which prey on the larval and early juvenile stages of the herring. There is also cannibalism by the older herring on the younger stages.

As stressed earlier, a critical factor is how the recruitment of juvenile herring is determined. Lett and Kohler use a relation of the form

$$\log R = a \log P - b (\log P)^2 \tag{6}$$

where R is numbers recruiting in any year and P is the yearly production resulting from growth of the combined spring and autumn stocks. The coefficients a and b depend on maximum yearly temperature and total (herring plus mackerel) biomass respectively. The values of a and b were determined by multivariate analysis of ten years of data. The spring and autumn spawning recruits are then divided in proportion to the adult stocks.

In the first simulation with a constant mackerel stock, the spring herring stock gradually declined to zero but, when the mackerel stock was made to oscillate, both herring stocks survived. The authors claim "the oscillating mackerel biomass added robustness to the model" since periods of low mackerel predation kept the spring stock viable. Further, the total biomass of the pelagic fish remained relatively constant, indicating that the management of the mackerel may be as important as the direct manipulation of the herring stock in determining the available biomass of herring for exploitation.

These factors, associated with the total biomass of the various pelagic stocks, suggest to the authors that the determination of maximum sustainable yield is better represented by the Schaefer type model, where overall biomass limitations are included, than by the Beverton and Holt approach based on yield per recruit. This results from the essential role in the model of the relation (6) between recruitment and production. Relations of this type were first postulated by Ricker (1954) using the formulation

$$R = aBe^{-bB}$$

which, as with (6) gives a maximum recruitment at intermediate stock densities with low or zero recruitment at smaller and larger populations. Ricker suggested that the density dependent mortality was generated by aggregation of predators, including adults of the same species, on the fish larvae. Lett and Kohler use predation by the parent stock as the main source of this mortality. Such cannibalism is well known to provide a stabilizing effect. It has the further advantage of being an internal control so that the system is closed without reference to other trophic levels. In this case some statistical evidence is available for the relation. Normally, however, the scatter in stock-recruitment relations is so great (Cushing, 1976) that it is difficult to specify the mathematical form and, in consequence, to propose ecological factors underlying the relation.

B. THE CALIFORNIAN SARDINE

The Lett and Kohler model deals with that fairly restricted part of the total ecosystem where species are of approximately the same size and

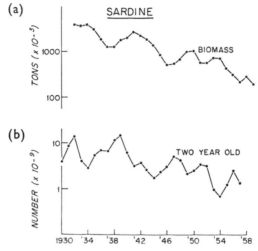

FIG. 3. (a) Population of 2-year old and older Californian sardines; (b) numbers of recruits determined from 2-year-old fish (from Murphy, 1966).

might be expected to have similar food requirements. It attempts to show how a balance between the stocks may be maintained. A major feature of other fisheries, however, is the relatively rapid switching which can occur when a species is replaced by another over a period of a relatively few years. The change from herring to pilchard (*Sardina pilchardus*) in the English Channel in the 1930s has been well documented (see Cushing, 1976), and is attributed largely if not entirely to changes in the natural environment rather than to the effects of fishing. In the western Pacific the decline in sardines appears to follow from changes in the mean level of recruitment rather than from any change in the log-normal variance. The recruitment to the sardine fishery is indicated by the numbers of two-year-old fish (Fig. 3b) and it can be seen that this is closely related to the total biomass (Fig. 3a) through the predominance of two-year and three-year-old fish in the commercially available stock (Murphy, 1966). The change from sardine (*Sardinops caerulea*) to anchovy (*Engraulis mordax*) occurred within the years 1950–58. Riffenburgh (1969) developed a Markov chain model to simulate this period. The food web (Fig. 4) requires, as input, the

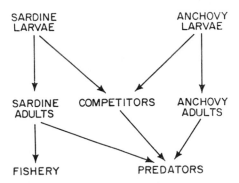

FIG. 4. A diagram of prey–predator relations used in the model of the Californian sardine fishery.

larval densities, and these were obtained from field data. Thus the model tests firstly, the ability of the interactions within the system to produce the observed yields or abundance of the two stocks—and does this reasonably well. Secondly, it can also be used to determine how far

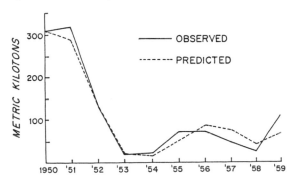

FIG. 5. Sardine catches as recorded (—) and as predicted (- - -) by the model (Riffenburgh, 1969).

fishing would be considered responsible for the observed changes and concludes that the population abundances were not completely controlled by fishing. Given the very large decline in sardine recruitment (Fig. 5), this is not surprising. Thus models of this kind can test our assumptions about prey–predator interactions within the higher trophic levels but do not explore the reasons for the observed changes in recruitment.

C. CHANGES IN NORTH SEA STOCK

The Lett and Kohler and the Riffenburgh models consider interactions between stocks which are, ecologically, closely related. The problem for the North Sea stocks described earlier, is that changes occurred over a wide range of ecological groups including both pelagic and demersal fish species. This requires consideration not only of species with similar feeding habits which may be separated temporally, but also the interactions of groups with very different feeding patterns.

Andersen and Ursin (1977) have developed a simulation model which, in its full form, takes the North Sea as a single system from the uptake of nutrients (phosphate) to the yield of 11 commercial fish species. Because of the complexity of the whole system, however, the published results deal only with the higher trophic levels having as the effective base of the food web three zooplankters and three benthic groups which acquire their food from a fixed yearly phytoplankton production of 105 gC m^{-2}. The interactions are defined by size selection of food using the relation (5) mentioned earlier. For each plankton or benthic group and each fish species the mean and spread of the distribution is defined separately.

The main aim of the work is to simulate the changes in the North Sea fish stocks between 1960–70. Again the central problem is to define the year-to-year recruitment of juveniles into each of these stocks. Actual recruitment values are used for the most important North Sea species, when such data are available. Also, the main source of mortality after recruitment, fishing effort, is taken from observed data.

Examples of the results of the simulation, compared with observed yields of fish, show relatively good agreement (Table I). It is important to realize that because the parameters controlling recruitment and mortality are predetermined, the model is not generating the results for each species independently of the field data. The main test is whether the available energy from primary production can fuel a system as it changes from one state to another. Thus the overall yields (Table I) are a more detailed exposition of the general hypothesis of Steele (1965) and Jones (1976)—that energy is a limiting factor in the system and if the system is changed, the overall result will display the consequences of this limitation.

Within this context, the greatly increased yield from 1960–70 could be due to changes in recruitment or to these changes plus the changed

TABLE I Yield of 11 fish species in the North Sea as stated in the Bull. Stat. (left-hand columns) and as estimated by multi-species analysis (right-hand columns) Unit: 1000 tons

	Plaice		Dab		Long Rough Dab		Saithe		Cod		Haddock		Whiting		Norway Pout		Mackerel		Herring		Sand Eel		Total (11 species)	
1960	86	100	5	10	0	1	29	27	105	101	67	67	55	37	41	73	73	73	796	905	113	90	1370	1483
1961	86	87	4	11	0	2	31	33	106	97	67	63	83	45	34	91	86	84	690	819	84	100	1271	1432
1962	87	100	4	14	0	2	22	24	90	85	52	52	69	44	157	137	66	64	679	821	110	100	1356	1442
1963	107	127	5	17	0	2	28	28	106	104	59	70	99	46	167	122	55	56	805	572	162	101	1593	1245
1964	100	122	4	19	0	2	55	57	122	129	199	280	92	41	83	27	79	76	932	1059	129	76	1805	1888
1965	97	117	5	19	0	2	69	71	179	180	222	309	107	47	59	9	152	142	1230	1653	131	54	2251	2603
1966	100	122	5	16	0	2	87	86	220	263	269	374	155	94	53	12	505	513	1039	1186	189	41	2594	2706
1967	101	163	4	12	0	1	73	76	250	272	167	169	91	43	180	62	910	934	819	1009	194	47	2784	2788
1968	109	148	4	9	0	1	97	113	285	310	139	152	145	88	469	214	809	816	850	994	113	97	3101	2942
1969	122	122	4	8	0	1	106	132	199	249	639	445	199	143	135	425	714	678	725	599	191	206	2956	3017
1970	130	132	5	7	0	1	170	238	225	229	672	360	182	177	274	444	290	271	749	704	382	321	2888	2929
1971	144	176	7		0		206		320		639		112		359		228		644		358		2630	
1972	123		8		0		199		346		672		109		493		182		605				2636	
Total 1960–1970	1135	1394	49	142	0	17	767	885	1887	2019	2552	2341	1277	805	1652	1616	3739	3707	9314	10321	1577	1233	23969	24475

fishing effort. The conclusion from simulations with a constant recruitment for each stock (averaged over the 1960–70 period) and with either
the 1960 or the 1970 level of fishing is that the change in fishing effort
was the significant factor in the increased yields. The authors go on
from this point to consider how yields might be further increased by
more manipulation of the fishing effort and show that, within the context
of their simulation, total annual yields of 4·5 Mt can be obtained.

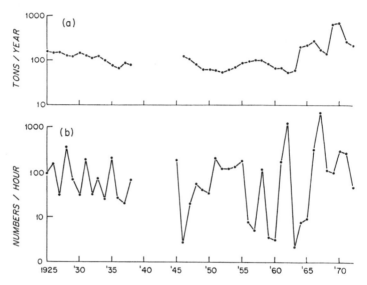

FIG. 6. (a) Yield of the North Sea haddock fishery; (b) number of recruits determined
from catches of 1-year-old fish by Scottish research vessels (from Jones, in press).

Essentially, this is achieved by simplifying the food web; for example, by
decreasing the cod stocks which are predators on other commercial
fish species.

There are many criticisms which can be made of this model. The
high yields of pelagic species in 1967–70 were the result of very heavy
fishing effort which caused a rapid decrease in the size of the stocks
leading to a virtual ban on fishing for herring in 1976–77. Thus the
ecosystem in 1970 could not be considered as providing a sustainable
yield.

The main problem, however, as with the other models, concerns the
assumption of constant recruitment levels, or levels derived from observation. We know that for the North Sea, the English Channel and the
eastern Pacific, the major observable factor is the large changes in
recruitment. Some of these changes may be attributable to stock-

recruitment relations although the evidence is seldom very good. Other changes, however, such as the very large haddock year-classes in the North Sea (Fig. 6b) are not explicable in this way.

Further, in all these cases, there were changes occurring in the lower planktonic levels of the food web and also changes in the physical environment. Such changes are a normal feature of the environment and will be due, in part, to long-term climatic trends. Can they also arise from changes imposed at higher trophic levels, so that the upper parts of the web, concerned with fishing activities, cannot be considered in isolation? Cushing (1976) has shown how the changes from herring to pilchard in the English Channel may have influenced not merely the plankton but, in turn, the concentrations of nutrients in this area.

D. PLANKTON COMMUNITIES

A model of plankton dynamics has been developed (Steele and Frost, 1977) where a range of phytoplankton has growth rates dependent on their size and on the nutrient concentration. These are fed upon by two herbivores, approximating to *Calanus* and *Pseudocalanus*, where the grazing relation is size-dependent according to the formula used by Andersen and Ursin (see equation 5). Within each size category of phytoplankton or herbivorous zooplankton there are, in reality, several species with different seasonal or geographical pattern and these variations are outside the scope of this model. Similarly, there are limitations imposed by considering only copepods as grazers. Other herbivores, such as pteropods, obtain their food by collecting particles on a mucous sheet and so may take a wider range of particle sizes than copepods. Various options are dealt with in detail by Steele and Frost, but here I wish to emphasize again the closure aspect. In this case, the problem is to specify the predation on the herbivores. This was determined by functional relations rather than by attempting to introduce "real" predators. Predation must be considered as a function of numbers of prey in different weight categories. For predation in terms of the numbers of animals in each size category the simplest relation, direct proportionality, was used. For predation as a function of the weight of prey, two functional forms were used: firstly, predation rate equal for all weights, and secondly, predation decreasing as $W^{-1/3}$. These were intended to simulate a generally balanced predator system and one where the removal of the larger predators (such as herring and mackerel) had led to a concentration on the smaller organisms.

The results of these two options were not only to alter the balance of the herbivores but also to affect significantly the size distribution of the phytoplankton as the productive season progressed (Figs 7–10). Thus changes at higher trophic levels can work their way downwards and alter the main features of the lower part of the ecosystem. Especially,

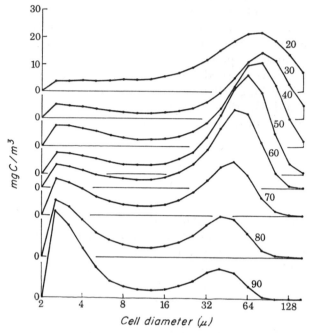

FIG. 7. Phytoplankton size structure at times after the start of the spring outburst (Steele and Frost, 1977), with a size-independent predation on the herbivores.

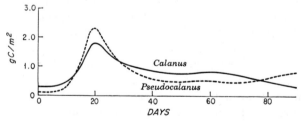

FIG. 8. Zooplankton populations in a simulation with size-independent predation.

they produced a switch from larger to smaller phytoplankton cells. These changes, in turn, affect the herbivores since, within the structure of the model, the size of phytoplankton cells affects the relative survival of the large and small copepods especially in terms of a suitably sized food for reproduction. The main interactions occur after the spring outburst when food is a limiting factor and affect not so much the general growth of the herbivores, as particular events in their life cycle. The model also demonstrates the general feature of multi-species

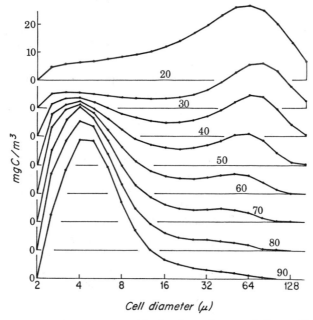

FIG. 9. Phytoplankton size structure with size-dependent predation on the herbivores.

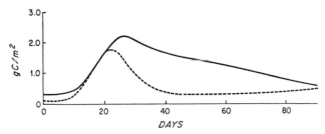

FIG. 10. Herbivore populations with size-dependent predation.

models, compared with the simpler food chain studies (Steele, 1974)— that within the same rates of energy flow there can be very marked changes in pathways and these changes can be due to events at higher as well as lower trophic levels.

There are again artificialities imposed by the closure of the model at a point within the total ecosystem. It can be seen that when predation is mainly on the smaller animals, there is, as one might deduce, a trend to preponderance on the larger herbivore species. If the system included interaction with the predators, then one might expect the balance to be redressed to some extent by changes back to larger predators. This does not happen within the model and is an obvious limitation in its usefulness.

Within the plankton ecosystem there have been models of one type of predator, fish larvae, which feed predominantly on planktonic herbivores in the spring. In particular, Jones (1973) has considered the effects of variable concentrations of copepods on the survival of fish larvae. He has shown that the numbers of larvae surviving the period after the end of the yolk-sac stage can be very sensitive to the quantity and, particularly, the size of copepods available. The larvae, at first feeding, require the smallest, naupliar, stages of the copepods. If food is not available at a sufficient concentration to provide a predetermined growth rate, then the larvae are assumed to die from starvation. This assumption closes the model for this period of development by eliminating the need for a relation with other components such as predators. There is experimental evidence for this effect of starvation on mortality (e.g. Rosenthal and Hempel, 1970). Results from this model showed that comparatively small variations in naupliar concentration, by a factor of two, could generate very large variations in numbers of larvae surviving the twenty days after start of feeding. If mortality is assumed constant for the remainder of the first year of life, then the calculated recruitment pattern was similar to the observed variability in haddock stocks (Jones and Hall, 1973). Observations over ten years in the North Sea showed very large variations in copepod populations in the spring (Steele and Henderson, 1977): certainly larger than a factor of 2, but the spatial variability in these distributions combined with the area of larval distribution may decrease this effect. However, the planktonic stage of the larvae lasts for a further 20–40 days and the haddock do not leave the pelagic system and go to the bottom for a further 100 or more days. Thus Jones's model indicates how variability in recruits may be generated early in the life cycle but the events in later life need to be considered as a process bounding the extent of these variations.

One other feature of Jones's (1973) model is that, although the fish larvae are critically affected by copepod numbers, the effect of their predation on the copepods is minimal. Instead, larval mortality is caused by lack of food. After metamorphosis from larvae to juvenile fish, growth is more plastic and, by changing food supply experimentally, can be made to vary over wide limits with little change in mortality (Edwards *et al.*, 1970b). Growth of larvae and juvenile fish fit the concept (Steele, 1976a) that when food is limiting but not affected by grazing rate, then rapid growth is a good strategy, whereas when food is limiting *and* its concentration can be significantly altered by predation, then the ability to decrease growth rate is important for competitive survival. The former may be relevant to larvae developing during the spring outburst when the match or mis-match of food and spawning is significant (Cushing, 1975). From metamorphosis onwards the latter situation could apply bringing in both energy and mortality as factors and so producing greater interactions with other parts of the ecosystem.

This brief consideration of computer models illustrates the separation of our ideas and knowledge into two areas—the planktonic environment including larval fish, and the commercially exploited stocks. One can draw food webs for the complete ecosystem and construct simulations of this larger entity. Such large simulations are unwieldly and the working concepts tend to close the system at predators for the plankton model and at recruitment for the fishery simulation. For fish stocks the missing links concern the period from larval feeding through metamorphosis to the juvenile fish, when the feeding niche can change radically.

The adult demersal fish stocks are assumed to feed predominantly on the benthic fauna but the process of transfer after metamorphosis from pelagic to benthic feeding can be gradual. This separation into larval, pelagic and later feeding would be acceptable if the two phases were not linked by an intermediate stage that depended on food and predation in both components of the system. Thus we have tended to think of an output from the first box (Fig. 15) as input to the third box, partly because we have least knowledge of the second box.

V. POPULATION VARIABILITY

For a particular species of fish the variability of recruitment, independent of the parent stock, would appear to place that stock at risk. If intensive fishing reduces the number of adult year-classes and there is a run of years with poor recruitment, then recovery might not be possible. Cushing (1975) calls this "recruitment overfishing". If, however, one considers a group of species such as the demersal gadoid fish in the North Sea, then imposed variability in recruitment could be regarded as a means whereby the range of species is maintained. Since the gadoids spawn at different times each year, a regular production cycle in the North Sea would favour one or two species by producing suitable food at the right time whereas other species would have poor year-class recruitment leading to a marked change in balance of populations and possible extinction of some species.

On this basis, larval fish in temperate waters are opportunistic (or r-selected; MacArthur and Wilson, 1967) so that large egg production, fast growth and variable recruitment are understandable responses to an unpredictable environment, but only in terms of limitation by other factors at a later stage.

Changes in the amount of variability can also have an effect on yield. This variability can be either in the initial number of larvae N_0 or in the mortality rate α. Assuming the simplest expression for mortality in the pre-recruit stage

$$\log N^* = \log N_0 - \alpha t^*$$

where N^* is the number recruiting at time t^*. Variability in the physical environment is likely to be normally distributed and, if the effect was instantaneous, could be associated with a change in N at one time, producing a normal distribution in the recruits. On the other hand, if the effect is over a period of time causing a normally distributed variation in α, then one arrives at the more biologically usual, log-normal, distribution for the recruits. For the period of good haddock years, 1962–70, the data on a log-normal scale show a large increase in variance compared with the pre-war years (Fig. 6). There is little apparent change in the mean but if we accept that fishery yield depends on number of recruits, then an increase in log-normal variance results in an increase in the arithmetic mean and so may account for some of the observed increase in yield.

Using data which estimate the total recruits for the period 1960–71 (Jones and Hislop, in press), the effect of the variable recruitment would be to increase yield by a factor of 2·5. This is comparable to the observed increase during this period in relation to the pre-war years (Fig. 6). If an increase in variance is to lead to an increase in yield from the fishery, then there must be an increase in food supply to this component of the system. This, in turn, implies a diversion of the energy flow and so requires changes in other parts of the whole eco-system.

For pelagic fish change of feeding habits at metamorphosis will be less marked and should appear as an increase in the size of copepods taken. The major herring stocks in coastal waters such as the North Sea spawn in the autumn and generally do not metamorphose till the spring. After an initial period of feeding in the autumn they will over-winter with reduced food available and with low growth rates. Thus the older larvae may have an adaptation to slow growth rates not normally observed in the larvae of the demersal species. There is some evidence of competition for food in the winter between herring and another pelagic fish, the sprat (Jones, G. K., 1976). Further, the metamorphosis of the herring may be adjusted in timing to the availability of food in the spring, in a manner comparable in principle to the timing of reproduction in their copepod food supply. In this way, the size structure and availability of food in the spring may also be important for certain pelagic fish.

The North Sea herring have been separated into stocks (Cushing, 1975) but feeding in the summer occurs mainly in the northern part of the North Sea, in the same general area in which the main stock of

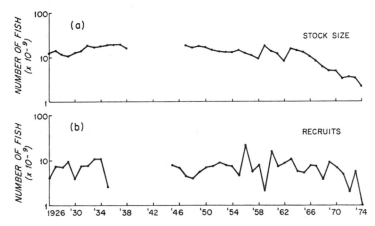

FIG. 11. (a) Size of North Sea herring stocks as numbers of fish 3-years or older; (b) year-class strength derived from estimates of recruits to the fishery (Burd, in press).

haddock occur. The variability of recruits (0- to 1-year-old) to the herring stocks (Fig. 11) is less than that of haddock (Fig. 6b) which might be related to the less marked change in feeding habits. The smoothing effects of age structure can be seen in stock numbers (2- to 3-years-old). There is evidence, however, of an increase in variability of numbers of recruits after 1955 and this variability becomes sufficiently large to be observed in subsequent stock size. The decrease in the stock after 1965 is the result of a very marked increase in fishing effort.

Some features of year-to-year variations in recruitment appear to have very large geographical extension giving simultaneous good years in regions as distinct as the North Sea, Iceland and Georges Bank. It is usually assumed that these must have some causal basis in climatic fluctuations since the stocks are, effectively, separate. On the other hand, certain fish stock fluctuations appear to be directly or inversely related so that in the North Sea good whiting years often occur during good haddock years and, conversely, in these years recruitment of cod and saithe are below average (R. Jones, pers. comm.). It is a common feature of the data that such direct or inverse relations can be seen for some of the largest or smallest year-classes but often show up only very weakly, if at all, under staistical test. This suggests that a wide variety of factors are significant.

The variable and unpredictable environment for a particular species at the larval stage consists not only of temperature, light and food, but also of predators. Thus, although part of the effect may be truly random in relation to input to the marine systems from outside, part of the unpredictability arises from the complexity of the interaction within the system.

The management problem is that the variability will have two sources. One part, fishing effort, is within, and another part, climate, is outside our control. Given the inherent importance of variability, a change in the total environment favouring one species would have its effect as a change in frequency of good, or bad years, or a change in amplitude of the good years. By implication, a change to the advantage of one or more species requires disadvantageous changes for others. There is a temptation to speculate that changes in frequency could result primarily from climatic factors whereas changes in amplitude will require a decrease in predation as well as an increased supply of food available for the larger brood.

A. STUDIES OF O-GROUP PLAICE (*Pleuronectes platessa* L.)

One detailed study of the population dynamics of newly metamorphosed fish can illustrate the probable ecological interrelations. O-group plaice settle on sandy beaches in the depth zone 0–5 m. It is this particular physical niche which makes them accessible to detailed study (Steele and Edwards, 1970; Steele *et al.*, 1970). For a semi-isolated beach in Loch Ewe the numbers and growth rates for four years (Figs 12 and 13) can be combined with experimental data on metabolism to determine population energy requirements (Fig. 14). These results show in microcosm the typical features observed for demersal stocks—that growth rates are much less variable than numbers. They also show that when numbers and growth are combined, there is a *relatively* constant rate of energy intake for any year. A detailed study of the benthos indicated that certain preferred food items were, generally, the limiting factor. The general hypothesis, for which there was circumstantial evidence, was that the recruits to the area in excess of the available benthic food were removed through predation by roundfish on plaice attempting to feed off the bottom. There was one apparent exception to the relation

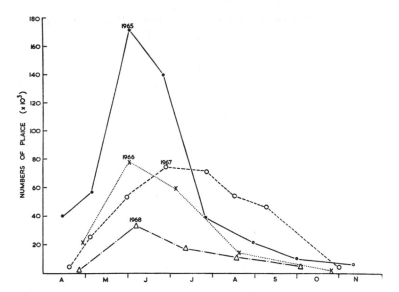

FIG. 12. Estimates of numbers of O-group plaice in Firemore Bay, Loch Ewe.

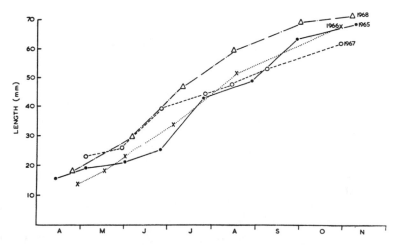

Fig. 13. Mean lengths of the plaice (see note on Fig.) populations in Firemore Bay, Loch Ewe.

between benthic food and numbers of fish in September to October. In 1967 mortality was low and the O-group plaice fed mostly on copepods, giving a larger final population than expected from the available benthic food.

Thus the populations recruiting, in the late autumn, to the main off-shore populations of older fish were determined by three factors:

　(i)　area of the physical niche;
　(ii)　supply of suitable in-faunal food;
　(iii)　intensity of predation on fish attempting to feed pelagically.

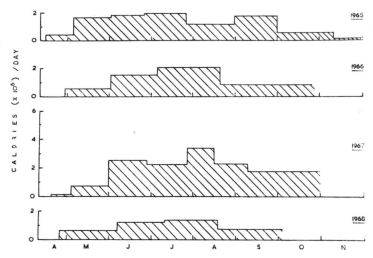

Fig. 14. Rate of energy intake by the plaice populations in Firemore Bay, Loch Ewe.

The initial numbers of newly metamorphosed fish did not seem to be a decisive component. The planktonic and epibenthic food supply did not appear to be limiting in this small-scale study.

It would be unacceptable to apply the results of this detailed study directly to larger systems such as the North Sea. They might be used, however, to provide working hypotheses, suggesting the nature of the links between plankton and benthos as food for the young fish, and the role of predation in determining not only numbers but growth rate.

The general implication is that for the demersal species at least, the simple division in Fig. 15 into separate boxes is unacceptable, particularly for the middle box, where the fish are going from the larval to the fully recruited stage. The detailed results for O-group plaice in Loch Ewe agree in principle with the proposal by Jones (1976) for the North Sea; that alterations in balance of stocks is dependent on the so-called demersal species taking a variable fraction of their food from the pelagic part of the ecosystem.

In this more general case there is not an unlimited supply of pelagic food but, from the energy calculations (Steele, 1965), the herbivorous pelagic production is about five to ten times as great as the available benthic production. Changes in feeding habits could obviously alter the yields of fish very considerably and it is this possibility which underlies the prediction of potential increase in yield made by Andersen and Ursin (1977). It is not possible to test the effects of these changes, in detail, for the O-group phase of the open sea species, such as haddock, cod, whiting, herring and mackerel, because we do not have the relevant metabolic and behaviour data to construct an adequate simulation.

Some possible consequences, however, may be derived in more general terms relating to qualitative changes in the structure of the food web. If we adopted the earlier view that the pelagic or demersal

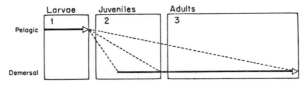

FIG. 15. Schematic division of demersal fish life cycle into 3 stages with varying transfer from pelagic to demersal mode of feeding.

systems were very loosely connected, then each could be considered as a separate entity not only for energy flow calculations but also for its resilience to perturbation, natural or man-made. The pelagic system has been fully discussed already. It is usually argued that behavioural responses of herbivores and pelagic fish to changes in their food density (Steele and Frost, 1977; Ware, 1975) have S-shaped (Holling, 1965) or threshold responses, which enable the system to absorb perturbations. For the demersal system the input of dead organic matter sinking from the upper layers provides a source of energy whose rate of input is independent on the dynamics of the benthic ecosystem. In turn, the the return of nutrients from the bottom sediments to the water depends directly on rates in the bottom rather than in the water. It has been pointed out (Steele, 1976b) that these "loose connections" between different components of an ecosystem tend to have a stabilizing effect in terms of the ability of the system to damp out fluctuations. If, however, the benthic predators start to take a significant part of their food supply from the pelagic sphere, this closer interrelation of the two components, although possibly more efficient energetically, could have detrimental effect on the resilience of the total system.

Thus there is some general, but very simplified, basis for suggesting that a system altered in the way proposed in Fig. 2 might at the same time become less able to accept environmental fluctuations.

A very simple illustration of this can be provided by a small simulation model. This model (given in Steele, 1974) was developed to show how slight changes in interaction could alter the whole response of relatively simple systems. Two initially separate prey–predator systems, S_1–S_2 and

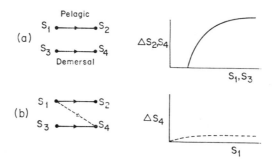

FIG. 16. (a) Two separate food chains with threshold feeding responses. (b) The demersal predator linked to the pelagic prey through feeding without any threshold.

S_3–S_4 (Fig. 16a), are able to absorb perturbations by the use of a threshold in their interactive responses. This permits quite large variations in parameters to be used with the response coming rapidly to a steady state. We can now link S_4 (the "demersal" predator) to the food supply S_1 (the "pelagic" food), using a functional response without a threshold (Fig. 16b). The upper limit to food intake of S_1 by S_4 is set at 10% of the main links. For equal harvesting rates on S_2 and S_4, the system still responds to an initial perturbation by rapid damping (Fig. 17a).

If, however, the harvesting rates are changed from 50% on each of S_2 and S_4 to 80% on S_2 and 20% on S_4, then not merely is there a change in the relative biomasses of S_2 and S_4 but a very marked alteration in the response to perturbation (Fig. 17b). S_4 is still relatively constant at a higher level but S_2 (the pelagic component) has violent oscillation and eventually becomes extinct. Thus the major impact of the linking of S_1–S_4 is on the survival of S_2. Within this very simple model, an alternative method of altering the system is to assume that the pelagic food becomes more accessible to the predator. If the upper limit on availability of S_1 to S_4 is put at 20% of the other links, then the system is still able to absorb an initial perturbation (Fig. 17c). If, however, the S_1–S_4 link is increased by a further 2%, then the system oscillates violently (Fig. 17d).

Such idealized simulations cannot pretend to relate directly to real problems. There is no overall limitation on rate of energy input to the system. Nor is there any age structure in the populations. The simulations demonstrate, however, the potential instabilities which result

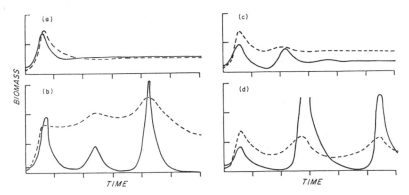

FIG. 17. Response of the system in Fig. 16(b) when (a) maximum intake of S_1 by S_4 is 10% of maximum intake of S_3, and harvesting of S_2 and S_4 are the same. (b) harvesting of S_2 is four times that on S_4. (c) harvesting equal but maximum intake of S_1 by S_4 is 20% of maximum intake of S_2. (d) harvesting equal but maximum intake of S_1 by S_4 is 22% of maximum intake of S_2.

from changes in structure or variation of parameters within an interacting prey–predator–competitor system.

Also, at this simple level the two types of change, harvesting and availability, might be considered to arise from very different causes (i.e. fishing and natural trends) yet show generally similar responses. Thus this theory and other, more complicated ones, might not distinguish between different management problems. Lastly, this simple example illustrates how constant rates of growth and mortality could lead to large fluctuations in population.

VI. The Use of Theory

The types of theoretical structure considered here may be put in three categories:

(1) The simplest energy flow diagrams concern transfer in one (vertical) direction along a food chain (Fig. 18a) which may divide

into separate legs at some stage. In a simple chain, changes in yield
depend largely on the original input at the beginning of the chain; or
on changes in the efficiency of transfer; or in the trophic level at which
the yield is taken. All these factors arise when, for example, comparisons
are made between upwelling, coastal, or open ocean systems in terms
of potential fishing yield (Ryther, 1969). Complications arise when
there are horizontal exchanges, but in general the flow of cause to
effect is still assumed to be from lower to higher trophic levels.

(2) The second simple picture (Fig. 18b) is of competition along
some gradient of a resource, or in terms of the gradient imposed by a

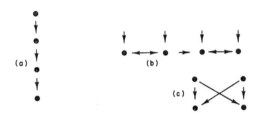

Fig. 18. Schematic representation of (a) a simple food chain, (b) simple competition
and (c) simple combined system.

predator behaviour. It is assumed, for simplicity, that the resource or
predator pressure remains constant, so that interactive variations occur
within a trophic level. In this sense, the models are one-dimensional
although, by using other niche characteristics, more than one dimension can be introduced (Pianka, 1976). In the case of plankton or
pelagic fish, the dimension is assumed to be size of organisms. The
expected trend is towards a relatively stable hierarchical structure
(Pianka, 1976).

(3) When these two aspects are combined (Fig. 18c), in even the
simplest four-unit structure, the results (Fig. 17) show that the major
problem arising is not necessarily differences in energy flow through
different sections, but changes in the variability of the components. In
the more detailed simulation of a plankton ecosystem (Figs 7–10) where
an overall energy limitation is imposed by rates of nutrient addition
through mixing, the same general features emerge—of switching
between major sectors of each trophic level in response to environmental
changes. Thus the combination of two basic scales—organism weight
and numbers in each weight category—displays the two main features
of parts of the marine ecosystem. There are considerable population
variations within the framework of overall energy limitation. Further,

these variations can arise from changes within the system, or from levels above or below.

There has been considerable study of the factors producing such variability in theoretical systems. As May (1976) has pointed out, one can count variables as the aborigines do—one, two, many. Linear or quadratic systems display relatively well-understood features, but beyond this there is a richness in dynamic behaviour which gives an effectively infinite set of responses to change. This leads to the general conclusion (Holling, 1973) that one must expect any relatively complex system to respond in quite unexpected ways. Further, such responses can include dramatic alterations from small changes in parameters. The examples given here can be considered as illustrations of these general conclusions.

In any application, however, the practical questions concern the "mechanisms" which may be important in generating a large variability in response of a particular species. Broadly, these might be divided into internal and external factors but this division is a function of the scope of the theory or model. Thus in the simple two-predator two-prey model, the critical factor was an "internal" link. But if only the pelagic component (S_1–S_2) were being studied, then the cause would be external.

In considering possible factors there are two apparently conflicting types of observation. Experimental studies of populations have revealed the wide variety of what can loosely be called "stabilizing" mechanisms. Holling's (1965) S-shaped curve has been shown to operate for a large range of organisms (Hassell et al., 1977). The evolution of such mechanisms within and between populations seems eminently sensible and would be expected to lead to relatively regular patterns of population through an ability to absorb the range of environmental variability. If this range of environmental variation changes suddenly or gradually, then the balance would also change again gradually or suddenly. We tend to concentrate attention on such changes—from herring to pilchard, from anchovy to sardine.

In many areas, however, field observations indicate that environmental variations are exaggerated rather than damped. Recruitment of fish stocks is a good example (Fig. 6). The general evidence suggests that recruitment may be influenced by external factors which can be derived from the physical environment, or from variation in predators. If either factor were constant, or if the species response removed the effects of the variation, then there would be a gradual elimination of certain species. In Lett and Kohler's model the elimination of one race of herring with constant mackerel predation is an example. In the plankton model, there can be a similar elimination of copepod species.

On this basis, the stochastic element in the real or theoretical environment may play a vital role in long-term community survival. If, however, this were the only mechanism, then there would still be the probability of a random walk to extinction of certain populations.

There is one obvious limitation on the utilization of variability by a species: the characteristic time-scale must not be too short and it must also not be too long. The survival of *Calanus* appears to depend on the occurrence of relatively large cells as food for the reproducing adults (Steele and Frost, 1977). This may depend on periods of rapid mixing to bring nutrients into the upper layer. In turn, this will result from high winds and so the whole cycle could, very speculatively, depend on the variability of weather. In theory, there is also a response of the copepods where feeding rate declines rapidly at low food concentration and this ensures a stock of cells available for the occurrence of suitable conditions. For a particular fish species, the year-to-year variation in recruitment may be balanced in part by the existence of several generations of reproducing adults. Changes in recruitment levels or in the age structure of the adult population could affect this balance. The assumption in stochastic models such as that of Jones and Hall (1973) is that successive year-to-year variations in larval food supply are not correlated; a result one might expect if the only factors derived from climatic variability.

VIII. Discussion

Resource management may be faced with two apparently different kinds of question. The first concerns future alterations in the system by additions such as potential pollutants or by removals such as fish. How, if at all, will the system be changed, and will the new structure be acceptable? The second question concerns past events. If the system has changed, do the causes of this change arise from natural trends or are they due to man's intervention? There is then a supplementary question —can we return the system to its earlier state?

These two questions are not really separate since most systems, if studied for long enough, show some kind of trend, and this must be incorporated into any prediction of future events. There is a further similarity in most applied questions: they usually require detailed information on the response of particular species, rather than general comments on the performance of the whole ecosystem. The argument here is that such detailed answers cannot be separated from the more general questions.

Detailed predictions of spatial patterns or of temporal sequences, would not appear to be an achievable aim for many areas where the environmental variability is large. The likelihood of overall energy limitations provides a possible framework for management in terms of total yields that may be taken from certain areas, if it is assumed that alternative harvesting strategies do not have side effects in terms of increased fluctuations. This, however, does not give the detail required for long-term management of individual stocks. For many fishery systems the inherent variability in recruitment precludes any effective prediction of yield from one species, in terms of year-to-year abundance for more than one or two years ahead.

Present methods for attempting to obtain a maximum sustainable yield from a fishery are often based on quotas which are adjusted on a year-to-year basis. A quota fixed independently of the population will generally tend to make the system less stable (Steele, 1976b). For a Schaefer (1954) type of fisheries model, Beddington and May (1977) have shown that a fixed quota combined with random fluctuations in the population growth rate can drive the population to extinction. Even with a fixed harvesting effort giving a yield proportional to the population, Beddington and May show that for heavily fished stocks with random fluctuations, there can be a slow recovery time from such perturbations. In conjunction with the age-specific character of fisheries, this could have severe effects on recruitment which are not included explicitly in the Schaefer logistic model (Doubleday, 1976).

Quota systems of management have an inertia in their response to fluctuations in the stock being harvested. For economic reasons, quotas will tend to be based on the average of several previous years, thus having both a lag and a smoothing effect in relation to year-to-year variation. Thus externally induced changes in recruitment, particularly on a year-to-year basis, will tend to be amplified by any failure to adjust the quotas. This can be balanced by the age structure of the harvested stock. If the age structure of the population covers a sufficient number of years, then year-to-year fluctuations may be smoothed out unless they are very large (Figs 5 and 6). If the population is dominated by a few year-classes, then much of the variability in recruitment is passed on the whole population (Fig. 3).

Evidence on the possible response of systems to perturbations can be derived from four sources: field data such as those from the North Sea during 1960–70; large enclosure experiments on planktonic ecosystems; computer simulations of the plankton or fish components of the whole ecosystem; and general ecological theory of responses in non-linear systems. Taken together these indicate that stresses imposed on the system are likely to produce major shifts in the species composition at several trophic levels without necessarily altering the overall energy flow through these main trophic levels. It is likely, however, that there can be major shifts in the pattern of energy flow within components of the food web. Such changes due to stress may often be accompanied by increased variability in population size and this factor could have a greater effect on management than changes in the longer-term mean. Much of this change may arise at lower trophic levels due to the response of the planktonic system to fluctuations in the physical environment with resultant effects on the larval fish populations. But the simulations and the large-scale experiments indicate that the effects of changes at higher trophic levels can be propagated donwards, affecting herbivore and phytoplankton communities. Thus field observations on their own cannot provide clear-cut evidence for the causal relations.

It has been pointed out by Jones (1976) that changes in management strategies for single fish species lead to marked changes in total food requirements by that species and these requirements are not normally included in management models based on variable number of fish but with fixed growth rates. Where changes in numbers of several species are involved, the problems are compounded. Thus the changes in population numbers and the balance of food requirements must be considered together.

The evidence indicates that initial high variance in numbers of commercial fish species can be induced early in the life cycle and this variability, seen in terms of the mix of species, may be essential for community survival rather than being viewed as "noise" on some hypothetical mean stock-recruitment curve. The later stages of life are dominated by mortality due to fishing with the so-called "natural" mortality being relatively minor. It is the intervening stage when major changes occur in the physiology, behaviour and habitat of most species. At this stage there can still be relatively large natural mortalities and also limitations arising from the interactions of the fish and their available food. The operation of these factors can be observed for particular species such as plaice.

It is proposed that similar mechanisms may apply to other demersal species whose feeding at an intermediate stage in life may be dependent on the availability of food in both pelagic and benthic areas, and on relative predation upon them in these areas. In this way the demersal fish may have an impact on the smaller pelagic fish or on the juveniles of the larger pelagic species.

The changes in the North Sea environment and in the fish stocks have led to discussion of possible interrelation between these stocks. The main decline in herring (and also mackerel) occurred after 1965 and was due to large increases in fishing. The increase in demersal stocks such as haddock and whiting was due to the occurrence of much better than average year-classes particularly in 1962 and 1967. Some of these changes might also depend on environmental factors (Hill and Dickson, in press) or be related to changes in availability of food (Jones, 1976). The timing of the changes would appear to preclude a simple explanation in terms of a decline in herring "causing" an increase in haddock. On the other hand, an explanation in terms of environmental factors alone ignores the problem of major changes in food requirements.

The one common factor is an increase in the variability of recruitment which was observed in most stocks and especially in haddock (Fig. 6) and herring (Fig. 11). This began before 1970 and is contemporary with, if not related to, general climatic changes that occurred after 1955 (Hill and Dickson, in press). Also, from a comparison of Figs 6 and 11, it can be seen that for the period 1955–74 there is an inverse relation between haddock recruits and herring stocks. This is statistically significant at the 5% level (R. Jones, pers. comm.). It suggests some interaction during this period rather than indicating any causal relation, and would support the concept that the stocks cannot be treated separately.

The inability to determine whether the increased variations are externally induced or derived from interaction within the ecosystem does not invalidate the fact that changes in variability can occur and these may be indications of major changes within the system. Further, such changes can have significant consequences for management through changes in the ability of the system to absorb added stresses from fishing or other activities of man.

It is proposed as a hypothesis that these alterations may be due to changes in the extent to which the system damps out fluctuations imposed initially at the fish larval stage. In turn, this would focus attention on events around the time of metamorphosis. This hypothesis is based on extrapolation from theoretical considerations (combined with a small amount of evidence) to the major fish stocks where no such data are available. The necessary data include not only information on the fish stocks but also on the dynamics of their various possible food supplies.

References

Andersen, K. P. and Ursin, E. (1977). A multispecies extension to the Beverton and Holt theory of fishing, with accounts of phosphorus circulation and primary production. *Meddr Danm Fisk-og Havunders.* N.S. **7**.

Beddington, J. R. and May, R. M. (1977). Harvesting natural populations in a randomly fluctuating environment. *Science* **197**, 463–465.

Beverton, R. J. H. (1963). Maturation, growth and mortality of Clupeid and Engraulid stocks in relation to fishing. *Rapp. P.-v. Reun. Cons. Perm. Int. Explor. Mer.* **154**, 44–67.

Beverton, R. J. H. and Holt, S. J. (1957). On the dynamics of exploited fish populations. *Fish. Invest.*, Lond., Ser. 2, 19.

Burd, A. C. (1978). Long term changes in the North Sea herring stocks. *Rapp. P.-v. Reun. Cons. Perm. Int. Explor. Mer.* (in press).

Caughley, G. (1976). Wildlife management and the dynamics of ungulate populations. *In* "Applied Biology" (Coaker, T. H., Ed.), Vol. I, 183–246. Academic Press, London and New York.

Colebrook, J. M. (1977). Changes in the zooplankton of the North Sea, 1948 to 1973. *Rapp. P.v. Reun. Cons. Perm. Int. Explor. Mer.* **172** (in press).

Cushing, D. H. (1975). "Marine Ecology and Fisheries." Cambridge University Press, Cambridge.

Cushing, D. H. (1976). Biology of fishes in the pelagic community. *In* "The Ecology of Seas", (Cushing, D. H. and Walsh, J. J., Eds), pp. 317–340. Blackwell Scientific Publications, Oxford.

Doubleday, W. G. (1976). Environmental fluctuations and fisheries management. *Int. Comm. Northwest Atl. Fish.* Sel. Pap. No. **1**, 141–150.

Edwards, R. R. C., Blaxter, J. H. S., Copalan, U. K. and Mathew, C. V. (1970a). A comparison of standard oxygen consumption of temperate and tropical bottom-living fish. *Comp. Biochem. Physiol.*, **34**, 491–495.

Edwards, R. R. C., Trevallion, A. G. and Steele, J. H. (1970b). The ecology of O-group plaice and common dabs in Loch Ewe. III. Prey-predator experiments with plaice. *J. Exp. Mar. Biol. Ecol.*, **4**, 156–173.

Gamble, J. C., Davies, J. M. and Steele, J. H. (1977). Loch Ewe bag experiment. *Bull. Mar. Sci.*, **27**, 146–175.

Hassell, M. P., Lawton, J. H. and Beddington, J. R. (1976). Sigmoid functional responses by invertebrate predators and perasitoids. *J. Animal Ecol.*, **45**, 135–164.

Hempel, G. ed. (1978). The changes in North Sea fish stocks and their causes. *Rapp. P.-v. Reun. Cons. Perm. Int. Explor. Mer.* **172** (in press).

Hill, H. W. and Dickson, R. R. (1977). Long term changes in North Sea hydrography. *Rapp. P.-v. Reun. Cons. Perm. Int. Explor. Mer.* **172** (in press).

Holling, C. S. (1965). The functional response of predators to prey density and its role in mimicry and population regulation. *Mem. Ent. Soc. Can.*, **45**, 5–60.

Holling, C. S. (1973). Resilience and stability of ecological systems. *Ann. Rev. Ecol. System* **4**, 1–23.

Jones, G. K. (1976). "A study of the distributional and feeding relationships between juvenile herring, *Clupea harengus* L and sprats, *Sprattus sprattus* (L) in the Moray Firth." A thesis submitted to the University of Aberdeen in partial fulfillment of the requirements for the Degree of Doctor of Philosophy.

Jones, R. (1973). Density dependent regulation of the numbers of cod and haddock. *P.-v. Reun. Cons. perm. Int. Explor. Mer.*, **164**, 156–173.

Jones, R. (1976). An energy budget for North Sea fish species and its application for fisheries management. ICES CM 1976, Demersal Fish (Northern) Cttee, F:36 (Mimeo.).

Jones, R. and Hall, W. B. (1973). A simulation model for studying the population dynamics of some fish species. *In* "The Mathematical Theory of the Dynamics of

Biological Populations" (Bartlett, M. S. and Hiorns, R. W., Eds.). Academic Press, London and New York.

Jones, R. and Hislop, J. R. G. (1977). Changes in North Sea haddock and whiting. *Rapp. P.-v. Reun. Cons. Perm. Int. Explor. Mer.* (in press).

Jones, R. and Richards, J. (1976). Some observations on the relationships between major fish species in the North Sea. ICES CM 1976, Demersal Fish (Northern) Cttee, F:35 (Mimeo.).

Lett, P. F. and Kohler, A. C. (1976). Recruitment: a problem of multispecies interaction and environmental perturbation, with special reference to Gulf of St. Lawrence Atlantic herring (Clupea harengus harengus). *J. Fish. Res. Bd. Can.*, **33**, 1353–1371.

MacArthur, R. H. and Wilson, E. O. (1967). "The Theory of Island Biogeography." Princeton University Press, Princeton, N.J.

May, R. M. (1976). Models for single populations. *In* "Theoretical Ecology, Principles and Applications", (May, Robert M., Ed.). Pp. 4–25. Blackwell Scientific Publications, Oxford.

Menzel, D. W. (1977). Summary of experimental results: controlled ecosystem pollution experiment. *Bull. Mar. Sci.*, **27**, 142–145.

Murphy, G. I. (1966). Population biology of the Pacific sardine. *Proc. Calif. Acad. Sci.*, **34**, 1–84.

Pianka, E. R. (1976). *In* "Theoretical Ecology. Principles and Applications", (May, Robert M., ed.). Pp. 114–141. Blackwell Scientific Publications, Oxford.

Platt, T. and Deman, K. L. (1975). Spectral analysis in ecology. *Annu. Rev. Ecol. System.* **6**, 189–210.

Reid, P. C. (1977). Continuous plankton records: large scale changes in the abundance of phytoplankton in the North Sea. *Rapp. P.-v. Reun. Cons. Perm. Int. Explor. Mer.* **172** (in press).

Ricker, W. E. (1954). Stock and recruitment. *J. Fish. Res. Bd. Can.* **11**, 559–623.

Riffenburgh, R. H. (1969). A stochastic model of interpopulation dynamics in marine ecology. *J. Fish. Res. Bd. Can.* **26**, 2843–2880.

Rosenthal, H. and Hempel, G. (1970). Experimental studies in feeding and food requirements of herring larvae. *In* "Marine Food Chains", (Steele, J. H., Ed.). Pp. 344–364. Oliver and Boyd, Edinburgh.

Ryther, J. H. (1969). Photosynthesis and fish production in the sea. *Science* **166**, 72–76.

Schaefer, M. B. (1954). Some aspects of the dynamics of populations important to the management of commercial marine fisheries. *Bull. Inter.-Am. Trop. Tuna Commn.* **1** 26–56.

Schaefer, M. B. and Beverton, R. J. H. (1963). Fishery dynamics—their analysis and interpretation. *In* "The Sea" (Hill, M. N., Ed.). Pp. 464–483. Interscience Publishers, J. Wiley and Sons, New York and London.

Smith, J. Maynard (1974). "Models in Ecology." 146 pp. Cambridge University Press, Cambridge.

Steele, J. H. (1965). Some problems in the study of marine resources. *Sec. Publ. Int. Commn. Nthw. Atlant. Fish.* (**6**), 463–476.

Steele, J. H. (1974). "The Structure of Marine Ecosystems." 128 pp. Harvard University Press, Cambridge, Mass.

Steele, J. H. (1976a). Comparative study of beaches. *Phil. Trans. R. Soc. Lond. B.* **274**, 401–415.

Steele, J. H. (1967b). Theoretical models in ecology. *J. Theor. Biol.* **63**, 443–451.

Steele, J. H. and Edwards, R. R. C. (1970). The ecology of O-group plaice and common dabs in Loch Ewe. IV. Dynamics of the plaice and dab populations. *J. Exp. Mar. Biol. Ecol.* **4,** 174–187.

Steele, J. H. and Frost, B. W. (1977). The structure of plankton communities. *Phil. Trans. R. Soc. Lond.*, **280,** 485–533.

Steele, J. H. and Henderson, E. W. (1977). Plankton patches in the northern North Sea. *In* "Fisheries Mathematics", (Steele, J. H., Ed.). Pp. 1–19. Academic Press, New York and London.

Steele, J. H., McIntyre, A. D., Edwards, R. R. C. and Trevallion, Ann (1970). Interrelations of a young plaice population with its invertebrate food supply. *In* "Animal Populations in Relation to Food Resources", (Watson, Adam, Ed.). pp. 375–388. Blackwell Scientific Publications, Oxford.

Ware, D. M. (1975). Growth metabolism and optimal swimming speed of a pelagic fish. *J. Fish. Res. Bd. Can.*, **32,** 33–41.

Ecological Principles for the Restoration of Disturbed and Degraded Land

M. S. JOHNSON AND A. D. BRADSHAW

Department of Botany, P.O. Box 147,
University of Liverpool, Liverpool

As a result of increased public pressure and legislation the restoration of disturbed and degraded land has become an important activity in many countries, supported by both public and private finance. There is not only the need to make good the disturbances taking place at the present time but also to reduce the areas of dereliction produced by industrial activity in the past. In Britain approximately 1500 ha of land are disturbed or degraded every year, adding to the 55 000 ha already accumulated; in the United States of America there are about $1·7 \times 10^6$ ha of land disturbed or made derelict by mining. Since many of these disturbances occur in areas of high population density, their effects on these countries are greater than the proportions of the land surface that they occupy, i.e. 0·44% and 0·2%, respectively.

In some situations it has been possible to use the land for other purposes such as housing or building, but in most cases the need has been to re-establish a vegetation cover to be used for amenity or agricultural purposes. The common feature of disturbed or degraded land is the disturbance, total destruction or absence of its original soil. As a result the critical problem to be overcome is the restoration of a functioning soil system with a structure, including content of available nutrients and water holding capacity, which will satisfy plant requirements. However, immediate replacement of a fully developed soil in the pedological sense, with recognizable horizons, is not necessarily required.

I. Natural Soil Development

It is self-evident that soil/plant ecosystems develop in natural conditions without human aid, on very different base materials: indeed there

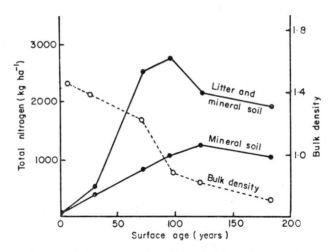

Fig. 1. Accumulation of nitrogen, and bulk density, in soils of different ages in the Glacier Bay chronosequence (from Crocker and Major, 1955).

are few areas where a vegetation cover and soil have not developed. But this process takes a considerable time, because most materials from which soils are derived are deficient in plant nutrients in forms available to plants. In particular they are totally deficient in nitrogen since this must be accumulated by the fixation of atmospheric nitrogen. Nitrogen is the mineral nutrient required in the largest amount by plants, and most evidence suggests that its rate of accumulation is critical in determining the rate of development of a vegetation cover. The soil chrono-sequence produced by retreating ice at Glacier Bay (Crocker and Major, 1955) provides good evidence for this, since the rapid development of vegetation does not begin until about 40 years after ice retreat when *Alnus crispa* begins to colonize, a species able to fix 40 kg N ha^{-1} year^{-1} (Fig. 1). However *Dryas drummondii*, a species which precedes it, is now known to fix nitrogen but at a much lower rate.

In areas where degraded land has been left undisturbed similar soil development can occur: one of the best analysed examples is that of ironstone overburden in the Mesabi Range (Leisman, 1957). In 50

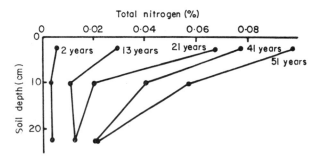

FIG. 2. Accumulation of nitrogen in iron ore spoil banks in the Mesabi region of Minnesota (from Leisman, 1957).

years the nitrogen and carbon content of the surface layers of the soil approach those of normal soils (Fig. 2). The total nitogen in the top 25 cm is about 1400 kg ha^{-1}, an annual rate of accumulation of about 30 kg ha^{-1}. This is paralleled by soil development on ironstone spoil banks in West Virginia (Smith *et al.*, 1971): 2500 kg N ha^{-1} have accumulated in the top 15 cm in 100 years, a level of nitrogen equivalent to that in neighbouring undisturbed soils.

The bulk density, one of the few standard measurements which gives an indication of soil structure, drops in the Glacier Bay chronosequence to below 1 at about 100 years. This does not occur in West Viginia, the 100-year-old spoils having an average bulk density of 1·47 while normal soils in the neighbourhood average 1·03. Nevertheless the developing soils support a substantial and vigorous vegetation both in West Virginia and the Mesabi areas, and trees at Mesabi growing on the older banks grow faster than trees of the same age on younger banks.

On china clay wastes in Cornwall, mainly coarse quartz sands, the importance of legumes in the colonization and soil development process has recently been shown (Dancer *et al.*, 1977a). These materials are extremely deficient in mineral nutrients, especially calcium and phosphorus, which precludes the invasion of a wide range of species. Nevertheless the legumes *Ulex europaeus, Cytrisus scopatrius,* and *Lupinus arboreus* are all capable of growing on calcium and phosphorus-deficient soils and are vigorous colonists. Once they invade, the soil/plant ecosystem, which has been a very poor community dominated by *Calluna vulgaris* and *Festuca ovina,* develops rapidly into woodland dominated by *Salix*

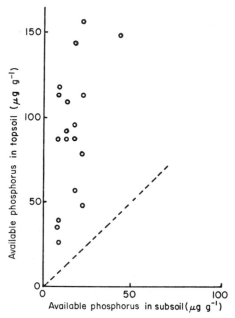

FIG. 3. Comparison of available phosphorus in the top soil and subsoil of afforested colliery spoil heaps of different ages (from Knabe, 1973).

caprea and finally *Quercus robur.* The critical level of nitrogen accumulation at which there is sufficient mineralization for rapid growth appears to be about 750 kg N ha^{-1}. This can be accumulated by the legumes in 10–20 years since they can fix 50–100 kg N ha^{-1} year^{-1}.

At the same time other nutrients are accumulating in an available form. Part of this is the result of the uptake of nutrients by plant roots from lower soil layers and their concentration in organic matter at the soil surface. But there is also a significant nutrient input in rain, particularly in polluted, urban areas. As a result the available nutrients in surface material are much higher than in the underlying original material: this can be seen in a range of afforested colliery spoils in Germany (Fig. 3) (Knabe, 1973).

During the process of soil development soil animals invade and multiply to form active populations. These will include the whole range of soil animals such as Diplopoda, Isopoda and Collembola (Neumann 1973). These digest and comminute organic matter thereby increasing its rate of decay (Thiele, 1964).

Nevertheless natural rates of development of fully functioning soil/plant ecosystems on derelict land materials are too slow for natural processes of soil and vegetation development to be feasible restoration methods. A closed plant community may take 50 years to develop on chalk (Tansley and Adamson, 1925). There are also many types of material with problems of toxicity or physical structure which may preclude any vegetation at all for 20 or even 50 years. On metalliferous wastes a closed vegetation cover may never develop. Steps have therefore to be taken to overcome these problems and hasten the more normal aspects of development of a viable ecosystem.

II. LAND USE OBJECTIVES

It is essential in any land restoration programme to have a clear idea of the ultimate land use objective, otherwise the appropriate steps may not be taken from the outset. This is particularly true in land restoration after recent mining activities, as opposed to reclamation of already derelict land, since the required soil handling etc. can be built into the mining operation from the beginning as an integral feature, using machinery already present on site. The alternative, which is to introduce machinery for the purpose afterwards, is usually considerably more expensive.

A. AGRICULTURE

Since in most cases land which has been disturbed or degraded was originally in agricultural use, restoration to agriculture is perhaps the most common land use objective. Although it is often considered that restoration cannot provide a soil as productive as the original, there is plenty of circumstantial evidence that this is not necessarily true if the work is carried out properly; for instance, in restoration of open cast coal workings in Britain (Whincup, 1974), and in the Bowen Basin Coalfield in Queensland where agricultural productivity is greater after mining when the brigalow scrub (*Acacia harpophylla*) has been replaced by rhodes grass pasture (*Chloris gayana*) (Coaldrake, 1973).

Nevertheless restoration of good agricultural productivity will require that substantial levelling is carried out; the amount being related to the type of agriculture proposed—arable crops or pasture (Fig. 4) (Kohnke, 1950). Great care will have to be taken in handling soils and overburden during the mining operation; in restoring lost nutrients and soil structure; and subsequently in maintaining fertility. The ways these can be achieved are discussed in the next section. It is self-evident that in some situations, such as metal wastes or hard rock quarries, return to agriculture will be possible only at considerable expense because of included

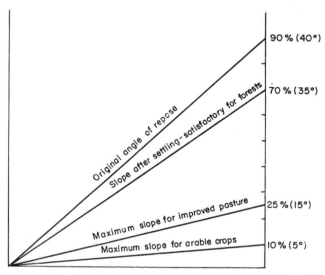

FIG. 4. The suitability of slopes for different land uses (from Kohnke, 1950).

toxic metals or topographical constraints. Alternative land uses should then be considered.

B. FORESTRY

Trees can be established on steep slopes at a natural angle of rest (Fig. 4), or even on rock faces, and they have fairly low soil fertility requirements. As a result, in earlier reclamation schemes when earth-moving equipment was not readily available and costs had to be kept low, forestry was a common land use objective in many countries, e.g. on ironstone overburden in Britain (Backhouse and Nimmo, 1956) and strip mining overburden in the USA (Limstrom, 1960). It is still an important land use, and particularly valuable on colliery spoil heaps where it is preferable not to spread the spoil over adjacent agricultural land e.g. in the Ruhr (Petsch, 1974), so that slopes are steep.

With the appropriate species and good management, commercial forestry is perfectly possible (Geyer, 1973; Jacoby, 1973; Medvick, 1973). But forested areas can also have important amenity values, a land use not always appreciated until the trees reach a reasonable size, but one which is important in areas of high population density where the original derelict land may represent a potentially important area for public access (Jacoby, 1973). In inhospitable situations such as sand dunes (Cornwell and Kiff, 1973) and slate waste (Sheldon and Bradshaw, 1976) trees may be the only practical reclamation solution.

C. COVER

Perhaps the simplest requirement is a stabilizing cover. The value of plants for this purpose is well recognized, but it is made particularly clear where the vegetation on a normal soil has been destroyed by overgrazing or pollution. An outstanding example is provided by the land in the vicinity of the nickel smelters at Sudbury, Ontario, where destruction of the vegetation by sulphur dioxide fumigation has caused erosion leading to the complete loss of all soil and exposure of bedrock.

It is always possible to use physical methods for erosion control, such as coverings of crushed rock, limestone chippings or granular slag (Dean et al., 1971). But these are visually unattractive and unless applied in large quantities, settle and expose unprotected material. Latex emulsions and similar materials, as well as mulches, are valuable as short-term coverings but have no permanence.

Restoration techniques which intend only to establish a simple vegetation cover can be straightforward and need only provide the basic pre-requisites for plant growth. This will usually mean that material can be upgraded as it lies, without earthmoving or elaborate soil improvements. Nevertheless some attention will have to be paid to means of maintaining soil fertility in the long term otherwise degradation of the plant cover will occur. Degradation is seldom recorded but is observable on many sites which have been reclaimed and subsequently given no maintenance.

D. AMENITY OR NATURE CONSERVATION

In industrial countries, areas of natural vegetation are disappearing at an alarming rate, because of advances in agricultural and industrial technology. As a result not only natural habitats but also individual species are threatened (Moore, 1962). Derelict areas represent land not being used for some productive purpose, where wild species are colonizing and multiplying unhindered by man's activities. Since the original mature soils and vegetation have usually been removed, they are also habitats belonging to early stages of ecological succession.

As a result many derelict areas are now refuges for rare or local species intolerant of competition (Ratcliffe, 1974; Davis, 1976) (Table I), and have been made into nature reserves. The outstanding example

TABLE I   Examples of rare or local species which occur in disused quarries and other disturbed areas (from Ratcliffe, 1974; Davis, 1976)

Aceras anthropophorum	*Herminium monorchis*
Anemone pulsatilla	*Herniaria glabra*
Astragalus danicus	*Hypochaeris maculata*
Crepis mollis	*Nardurus maritimus*
Epilobium lanceolatum	*Ophrys apifera*
Epipactis helleborine	*Ophrys muscifera*
Epipactis leptochila	*Orchis militaris*
Epipactis phyllanthes	*Salix nigricans*
Gentianella amarella	*Thesium humifusum*
Gentianella germanica	*Thlaspi perfoliata*

of this is the Norfolk Broads, now a concentration of local and national nature reserves but formerly mediaeval peat cuttings (Lambert *et al.*, 1960). But many other examples exist: limestone quarries, e.g. Millersdale, Derbyshire; chalk pits, e.g. Grays Quarry, Essex; mining subsidence flashes e.g. Alvacote Pools, Staffordshire.

Other areas have become colonized by trees, shrubs and other vegetation in such a way that, although they do not contain rare plants, they are valuable areas of public amenity. One very attractive area in a public park, the highest point of Hampstead Heath in London, was once a gravel pit satisfying the building requirements of Georgian London.

In these areas the only development necessary may be to provide public access or protection. But in some sites it may be necessary to encourage wild life by manipulation of land surfaces to create particular habitats, or by the introduction of appropriate species to overcome the slowness of immigration. Such creative conservation is a significant use for derelict land (Bradshaw, 1977). An excellent example, where plants have been introduced not only for their own sake, but also for the birds they encourage, is the Sevenoaks Gravel Pit Nature Reserve (Harrison, 1974).

III. Restoration Philosophies

The word "restoration" suggests the complete reinstatement of the original environment as it was before disturbance. We prefer to use the word, in the context of degraded land, to apply to restoration of a properly functioning soil/plant ecosystem. From a biological point of view the critical requirement is that an ecosystem consisting of soil, plants and animals is produced in which the original functions of plant growth, nutrient cycling, organic matter breakdown etc. are restored so that the system once again is properly active and self-sustaining.

The most obvious way this can be achieved is by reinstatement of all the original components, particularly the original soil. It is clear that where this is possible it should be carried out. In many situations topsoil can be removed in front of the operation, whether it be open cast mining or remodelling of old deep mine colliery spoil heaps, and replaced afterwards. In such circumstances haulage distances, if properly planned, can be small and costs consequently low. This point of view has been well argued by Doubleday (1973).

However, care has to be taken in such operations. For reinstatement of high quality agricultural land in England after sand and gravel extraction, the following instructions are given (DoE et al., 1977):

(i)   soil layers should be kept separate.

(ii)   storage piles should be managed to avoid repeated running over soil.

(iii)   soil should be kept in store for as short a time as possible.

(iv)   on reinstatement, vehicles must not traverse reinstated materials.

(v)   each reinstated layer must be scarified before the next layer is added.

(vi)   when the top soil is reinstated it should be lifted into place without being traversed by machinery.

(viii)   all work must stop if there is more than a specified amount of rain and not restarted until the material has had opportunity to dry.

This degree of care is unusual, but it serves to indicate that the removal and reinstatement of materials, so that the original structure is maintained, are not easy.

The retention and replacement of the original soil layers are the critical elements in a reinstatement strategy even if the methods of carrying this out vary. Topsoil reinstatement is required by legislation in many new mining and other disturbing operations, and elaborate methods are developed to enable it to be carried out at minimum cost. In all open cast coal mining in Britain careful reinstatement of soil is carried out (National Coal Board, 1974). The same is recommended for sand and gravel where the water table does not lead to flooding of worked-out pits (MAFF, 1971). A highly organized quarrying operation, which is associated with the production of cement, involving conveyor belt transport of topsoil across the workings, is being carried out at Dunbar in Scotland (APCM, 1970). The same sorts of methods are being developed in many areas of the world where land must be returned to its former use.

Nevertheless the extra handling of materials is costly and in many situations the replacement of topsoil is neither required nor practical. In the past, in the absence of appropriate machinery, topsoil has rarely been stripped initially. Thus in most of the degraded and disturbed land referred to earlier, topsoil has been lost. Sometimes it is possible to obtain topsoil from other sites in the vicinity which are undergoing developments for which it is not required. But haulage costs can make such material prohibitively expensive.

As a result for most derelict land the need is to develop techniques whereby the substrates can be improved directly, by cultivation, fertilization, liming etc. so as to allow a new vegetation cover to be established. If the treatments are carried out properly the individual limitations to plant growth can be overcome effectively and economically. However this requires that these limitations to plant growth are identified at the outset and appropriately treated. This point has been made very strongly in relation to restoration after surface mining of coal in the USA (EPA, 1974).

The major limitations to growth found in different derelict land materials are given in Table II. The subsequent sections appraise these limitations in turn and discuss how they can be overcome. Detailed analyses of the problems of individual materials are described elsewhere (Bradshaw and Chadwick, 1979). An extensive bibliography is also available (Goodman and Bray, 1975).

IV. Texture and Structure

Few derelict land materials have a texture or structure which compares with that of normal soils. In many cases they consist of particles of uniform size because they have been screened or ground to a standard specification (Table III). Moreover, they are usually deficient in the organic matter, clay minerals and microbial populations which are the

TABLE II The characteristics of wastes and degraded land of different origins likely to cause revegetation problems (from Bradshaw and Chadwick, 1978)

	Texture and structure	Stability	Water supply	Surface temperature	Macro nutrients	Micro nutrients	pH	Toxic materials	Salinity
Colliery spoil	○○○	○○○/·	○/·	○○○/·	○○○	·	○○○	·	●●●/·
Coal (strip mining)	○○○/·	○○○/·	○○/·	○○○/·	○○○/·	·	○○○/·	·	●●●/·
Fly ash	·	·	·	○	○○○/·	·	●●●/○	●	·/·
Oil shale	○○/·	○○/·	○○/·		○○○		○○/·		·/·
Iron ore mining	·	·	·		○○○	·	·	·	·
Bauxite mining	·	·	·		○○○		○○○/○	·	·
Heavy metal mining	○○○	○○○/·	○○/·		○○○	·	●●●/○	●/○	●●●/○
Gold mining	○○○	○○○	○○○		○○○		○○○/○	●/●	·
China clay wastes	○○○	○○	○○○		○○○		○○○	·	·
Acid rocks	○○○	·	○○○		○○○		○○○	·	·
Calcareous rocks	○○○	·	○○○		○○○		●/·	·	·
Sand and gravel	○/·	○○○/·	○/·		○○○	·	·/·	·	·
Coastal sands	○○/·	○○○/·	○/·		○○○	·	·	·	●/·

Deficiency
severe ○○○ moderate ○○ slight ○ adequate ·

Excess
slight ● moderate ●● severe ●●●

(relative to the establishment of a soil/plant ecosystem appropriate to the material: variations in severity are due to differences in materials and the climates of the areas concerned.)

principal agents controlling aggregation and therefore soil structure. The outcome of this is variable, for there are many natural materials, such as silty loams derived from marine deposits, and arid-zone soils, which are agriculturally productive despite their anomalous physical characteristics. However, in extreme situations severe constraints may exist.

Heavy clays such as those produced by brick–clay working and by ironstone mining in Northamptonshire are particularly intransigent

TABLE III   The particle size composition of some derelict land materials (%w/w)

	Sand >0·02 mm	Silt >0·002 mm	Clay <0·002 mm
Colliery spoil Yorkshire	64	27	9
Open-cast coal overburden			
Indiana	55	27	18
West Virginia	20	59	21
Pulverized fuel ash			
Yorkshire	38	59	3
Iron ore overburden			
Northants	39	6	55
Heavy metal tailings			
Derbyshire (old: 1961)	32	35	33
(new: 1975)	53	31	16
Gold sandwaste			
Johannesburg, South Africa	90	9	1
China clay			
Cornwall	97	2	1
Good loam soil	60	40	20

substrates which show marked seasonal variation in consistency and physical stability. Extreme consolidation and breakdown of soil structure are inevitable if such material is handled incorrectly. These problems can be reduced at the outset if all earth moving and levelling are carried out by crawler tractors preferably fitted with straked tracks. These vehicles exert significantly lower surface pressures ($0·5$ kg cm^{-2}) than rubber-tyred machines (5 kg cm^{-2}) which cause excessive surface compaction. Even normally more permeable dere-lict land materials, such as colliery spoil, are consolidated by the passage of wheeled traffic. If equivalent pressures are applied experimentally the bulk density of the matrix may double (Table IV). This introduces a physical barrier to root penetration and growth and inhibits infiltration of surface water, particularly in the absence of vegetation.

Where consolidation has occurred, the physical characteristics can be improved, at least temporarily, by ripping the surface to a maximum

TABLE IV   The bulk densities and infiltration rates of unvegetated colliery spoils in Yorkshire after subjection to different amounts of compression, compared with a normal soil (data from G. Bradley)

| | | | Infiltration rate (mm min^{-1}) | | |
| | | Bulk density (g cm^{-3}) | Uncompressed | Compressed | |
				0·5	5 kg cm^{-2}
Robin Hood	unvegetated	1·44	3·2	2·00	0·22
	vegetated	1·19	11·2	1·0	0·51
Grigglestone	unvegetated	1·69	1·0	0·15	0·07
	vegetated	1·46	4·0	1·3	0·52
Water Haigh	unvegetated	1·48	3·1	2·6	0·48
	vegetated	1·50	16·7	2·5	0·50
Walter Haigh	old pasture	0·89	111·0	58·8	2·94

depth of 50 cm using angled tines fitted to a crawler tractor, followed by shallower cultivation (Gemmell, 1973). However, the improvement will only be maintained if a plant cover is soon established, for the physical effects of root growth and associated organic matter additions are essential to the development of a good soil structure.

By way of contrast, many derelict land substrates do not retain percolating drainage water because of their very coarse texture. Primary wastes from the excavation of non-ferrous metal ores (Johnson and Bradshaw, 1977), spoils from slate extraction (Sheldon, 1975) and limestone quarrying (Humphries, 1977) are in this category. But in most cases the problem of drought is strictly a surface phenomenon. Even in apparently coarse wastes such as from slate quarrying, a high proportion of the material beneath the surface 30 cm is comprised of silt and clay-sized particles. These are derived from weathering of the surface but settle at depth due to movement through the spoil profile. The problem of surface drought and lack of a rooting medium may be overcome by blinding the tip with fine-grained material (<5 mm) or by incorporating organic matter or overburden to a depth of not less than 10 cm.

V. Stability

A large proportion of the waste material currently produced by the mining industry is intermediate in textural classification. For instance, tailings waste produced in the processing of metal ores usually have a particle size of less than 0·2 mm but include only a small proportion of material with clay dimensions (Table III). Treatment of these wastes is difficult for they are very unstable, readily windblown when dry and liable to erosion by surface drainage water. They are usually deposited as a slurry in tailings ponds or lagoons surrounded by high retaining walls. This effectively prevents water erosion but the problem of wind erosion arises as soon as the surface dries out. In the absence of an effective enclosing structure, or where the outer wall is itself constructed of finely divided metalliferous waste, erosion by water can be very severe. Several other spoil types, including the sand tips of the china clay extraction industry, and even colliery spoils with a fairly normal particle size range, are unstable and mobile.

Part of the problem can be ascribed to tip topography, because a lot of materials are dumped by conveyor belt or dragline to produce steep-sided heaps with a natural angle of rest of over 30°. Inevitably, these are liable to erosion. But deficiencies in soil structure due to lack of organic matter and micro-organism activity are equally significant, rendering soil liable to cap under the impact of rain and disperse under the influence of wind. On steep slopes there will be a double effect because the erosion will maintain the soils in a juvenile and nutrient-deficient condition (Kohnke, 1950).

Vegetation cover provides excellent stabilization even on steep slopes. However if a material is liable to erosion, from whatever cause, initial establishment may be difficult. Reduction of slope, terracing or stair-step grading (e.g. Hudson, 1971; Armiger et al., 1976) may have to be carried out to reduce liability to erosion. On flat ground surface treatment with crushed rock has been used, but is expensive and difficult to apply. Fibrous mulches of straw, shredded bark or wood wool are very effective stabilizers (e.g. Lal, 1977) (Fig. 5), particularly if tacked down with wood pulp or bituminous emulsion (Green et al., 1973), and provide good protection for germinating seedlings.

A wide range of chemical methods of stabilization has been developed, based on resinous adhesives, elastomeric polymers, alginates and bitumen (McKee *et al.*, 1964). These are widely used because of their convenience in sward establishment by hydroseeding. However they have unfortunate toxic effects on seedlings when used in this way (Sheldon and Bradshaw, 1977) (Fig. 6): only hydrophilic materials

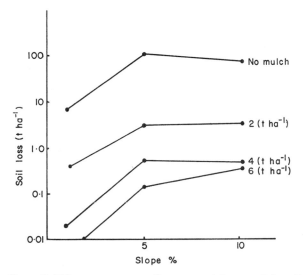

FIG. 5. The effect of different amounts of straw mulch on soil loss from different slopes in Nigeria (from Lal, 1977).

such as alginates, which are the most expensive, appear satisfactory. A list of the commonest mulches and stabilizers is given in Table V together with an assessment of their value in land restoration.

In situations where wind erosion is very severe, for instance in restoration after mineral sand-mining in coastal areas, brushwood coverings, plastic or brushwood fences may have to be employed (Brooks, 1976). Reed fences on a 4 m grid are used extensively in the establishment of a vegetation cover on the sand heaps left by gold mining in South Africa (James, 1966). However, costs are high. An alternative, more biological, method for loose sandy materials is to sow at low density a nurse crop of a stemmy cereal such as sorghum or rye. This does not have to grow particularly well: about 50 cm is sufficient. When the plants die the dead stems then persist for at least a year providing excellent protection until the main vegetation cover is properly established (Newey and Lewis, 1976).

Sward establishment is not always straightforward and the potential problems must be recognized. If the constraints are overcome, vegetation can be used to contend with unstable tips of 45° slope, or more, as the naturally colonized scree slopes of areas such as the English Lake District and North Wales imply. Progress has even been made in the revegetation of vertical quarry faces by artificial means (Humphries, 1977). The constraints of surface drought and instability are most

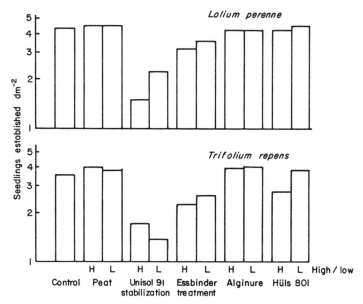

FIG. 6. The effect of peat mulch and different chemical stabilizers on the establishment of *Lolium perenne* and *Trifolium repens* on sand waste slopes (from Sheldon and Bradshaw, 1977).

important at seeding and during the initial phases of sward development. However, once a vegetation cover has been established, damage to it due to erosion is usually minimal.

VI. Water Supply

Any material with an extremely coarse texture has a low moisture holding capacity, and effective water retention only prevails when the substrate is dominated by particles of sand (2–0·02 mm), silt (0·02–0·002 mm), and clay (<0·002 mm). This textural control is progressive in that coarse sandy soils have poorer moisture-retaining properties than do heavy clays. However, plant-available water, defined as the difference in the volume of water held per unit of soil at field capacity

TABLE V Mulches and stabilizers suitable for derelict land reclamation

		Typical application rate (t ha^{-1})	Persistence	Stabilization	Effect on soil water retention	Plant nutrient input	Phytotoxicity
Mulches	Wood shavings	4	○○	○	○○○	·	·
	Wood chips	10	○○	○	○○○	·	·
	Shredded bark	4	○○○	○	○○○	·	·
	Peat moss	2	○	○	○	·	·
	Corncobs	10	○○○	○	○	○	·
	Hay	3	○	○	○	·	·
	Straw	3	○○	○○	○	·	·
	Glass fibre	1	○○○	○○○	○	·	·
Stabilizer/mulches	Wood cellulose fibre (as slurry)	1–2	○○	○○	○	·	·
	Sewage sludge (as slurry)	2–4	○	○○	○	○	·
Stabilizers	Asphalt (as 1:1 emulsion)	0·75	○	○○	○	·	○
	Latex (as appropriate emulsion)	0·2	○	○○	·	·	○○
	Alginate (as emulsion)	0·2	○○	○○	·	·	·

Excellent	Good	Fair	Insignificant
○○○	○○	○	

and at permanent wilting point, is somewhat less dependant on texture. Thus a light loam may hold more available water than a heavy clay, and a uniform fine-sand mine tailings more than the silty-clay over burden (Ludeke, 1973a) (Table VI).

TABLE VI　Average moisture percentages at different moisture tensions, and available water, in different materials produced in copper mining, compared with local desert soil (from Ludeke, 1973a)

| | Moisture tension (atmosphere) | | | | | Available water (%) |
Materials	1/3	1	5	10	15	
Tailing	10·2	7·1	3·6	2·6	2·2	8·0
Tailing-overburden	9·4	7·6	5·0	4·1	3·7	5·7
Overburden	11·0	8·8	7·3	6·1	5·9	5·1
Desert soil	4·8	4·2	3·9	3·0	2·9	1·9

The effectiveness of available water storage is also related to supply, in terms of total precipitation and its distribution throughout the year. In temperate climates true water shortage is rarely a problem, but in arid regions temporary irrigation may be essential to successful plant establishment. The need for irrigation on agricultural soils in the United Kingdom is calculable through the balance between potential transpiration and total rainfall, with its distribution in time and space (MAFF, 1967). But it must be remembered that mining and other derelict land materials are usually fairly deep, and the central mass of all but the coarsest substrates usually contains sufficient water for normal growth and development (Fig. 7). This is as true of arid zones as it is of temperate regions, and water moving upwards by capillarity is an integral part of the total available fraction and as important as that present in the rooting zone. Providing a plant has established deep roots it has a large store of water available to it.

It follows that water shortage is less of a problem than might be expected on degraded and disturbed materials providing that surface drought can be overcome. The different mulches and other treatments already discussed are important in this respect, but the climatic conditions occurring at the time of seeding are critical, particularly precipitation occurring in the fortnight before seeding (Sheldon and Bradshaw, 1977). For this reason sowing has to be limited to particular seasons of the year, and specific guidelines can be valuable, as for the establishment of swards on roadside materials in France (Henensal and Spake, 1974).

On coarse textured materials the arid surface layer may extend down to 50 cm in dry periods, and deep-rooting plants such as trees will be essential. But it will be necessary to provide them with a pocket of water-retaining material at the surface to provide adequate water supply until their roots are established. On rock waste this can be provided by a sphagnum–peat material, and the volume provided for each tree can be related to the likelihood of occurrence of dry periods (Hillestad, 1973; Sheldon and Bradshaw, 1976).

In very arid regions, for instance in Central Australia and Arizona, where the mean annual rainfall is less than 25 cm, irrigation may be

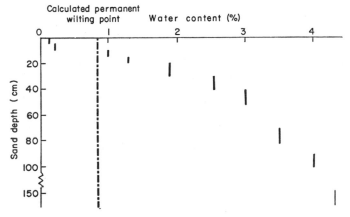

FIG. 7. The water content of the surface layers of a china clay sand waste heap in Cornwall after four weeks' drought (from Bradshaw *et al.*, 1975).

necessary, despite the water-retaining capacity of the material. However once the plants are properly established further irrigation may not be required. Fresh water is expensive but sewage effluent water has been found to be an admirable alternative at Broken Hill in Australia (Harris and Leigh, 1976).

It is equally common with derelict and disturbed lands to be confronted with the problems of impeded drainage. In most cases the infiltration rate or soil permeability is sub-optimal because of the unfavourable pore composition of the surface layers, or because of structural instability in the subsoil, or because there is no classical zonation in the profile of substrates derived from mineral grinding or screening operations. Consolidation can exacerbate this (Table IV). Less frequently, artificial drainage is necessary because of changes induced in the water table and in the position of the capillary fringe.

In either situation the restoration of a satisfactory drainage regime is a pre-requisite for the success of land reclamation schemes. Proper cultivation and soil management will rectify drainage defects, but only if aligned with an artificial system of surface ditches or a network of mole or tile under-drains. Complete replanning and construction of a drainage system may be necessary to take account of new topographical features.

VII. TEMPERATURE

A fundamental characteristic of continuous ground cover vegetation is that it reduces diurnal and seasonal fluctuations in soil temperature. Consequently, in the absence of a plant cover and its radiation absorptive properties, substrates behave very differently. On the dark bituminous strip-mine spoils of Pennsylvania, which have a low thermal conductivity even under conditions of intense solar radiation, high air temperatures and low soil moisture status, temperatures approaching 70°C have been recorded and sustained (Deely and Borden, 1973). Equivalent maxima for lighter mineral shales and sandstones were 50–55°C (Table VII), producing a mean temperature difference between the materials of 15°C. On black shale pit heaps in Durham, England, values as high as 57°C have been recorded (Richardson, 1958).

TABLE VII   Surface temperatures (maximum) recorded in July 1968 on various coal mining materials in USA grouped by predominant colour (from Deely and Borden, 1973)

Colour	Rock type	Max. temp. (°C)
Black	Bituminous coal	69·0
	Organic shale	69·5
	Organic shale	63·5
Dark red	Mineral shale	64·0
Dark grey	Sandy mineral shale	65·5
	Mineral shale	61·5
	Organic shale	61·0
Dark brown	Silty mineral shale	62·0
Yellowish brown	Sandstone	58·0
	Fine sandstone	50·0

High rates of seedling mortality in conifers and hardwoods occur when surface temperatures exceed 50°C even for short periods (Day, 1963; Horn, 1968). Herbaceous seedlings suffer from localized but lethal damage at the soil surface. Timing of seeding and planting programmes is therefore critical in certain situations. Alternatively, surface mulching with organic matter, or the use of rapidly establishing nurse crops, can be useful ameliorative measures.

The opposite temperature extreme can be equally damaging, although exfoliation of slate quarry and colliery spoils through frost shattering is an important initiator of soil formation and development in juvenile and raw substrates. Low temperature tissue-disruption in seedlings, and secondary damage through root tearing, are not infrequent causes of failure with late autumn seeding, so planning for optimum conditions at establishment is important, within the ungovernable constraints which always exist. Frost heaving can also be the initiator of instability, particularly on angular mine dumps and tips, because it disrupts the relatively stable surface crust thereby encouraging secondary wind and water erosion.

VIII. Nutrients

Deficiencies in essential plant nutrients are almost universal features of degraded and derelict land, and probably the single most important constraint on vegetation establishment. Totally inadequate reserves of nitrogen and phosphorus are the commonest limitations, though deficiencies of potassium, calcium and magnesium also occur (Table VIII). Supplies of micronutrients including iron, manganese, boron, copper, zinc and molybdenum are rarely limiting, though such nutritional disorders can be induced if established nutrient interaction and balance ratios are ignored. In derelict land materials, a more common feature of trace elements is their presence in excessive concentrations and the ensuing problems of phytotoxicity.

With normal soils correction of nutrient deficiencies or imbalance is quite straightforward and can be accomplished using modern single nutrient or compound fertilizers which are available in a range of formulations. On many derelict land substrates adjustment is more difficult because of their inability to retain nutrients against leaching processes and the tendency of certain elements to undergo fixation through reversion to insoluble compounds. Recognizing situations where this may occur, and the deployment of remedial measures, is critical to the long term stability of established swards.

Leaching of applied nitrogen is undoubtedly the commonest cause of

TABLE VIII Chemical characteristics of different wastes and degraded areas (from Bradshaw and Chadwick, 1978)

	N	P	K	Ca	Mg	pH	Ion exchange capacity	Salinity	Na	Heavy metals	Other toxins
Colliery spoil	○○	○○○	·	○○○/.	○/●	○○○/.	○○	./●	·	·	·
Coal (strip mining)	○○	○○○	○	○○○/.	○/●	○○○/.	○○	./●●	·	·	·
Fly ash	○○○	○○ ○	·○	○○	·	●/●●	○○	./●●●	·/●	./●●	boron
Oil shale						○/.		·/.		●	
Iron ore mining	○○	○○○	○	○/●	○/●	○/.	·		·	·	·
Bauxite (strip mining)	○○	○○	○								
Bauxite (red muds)	○○○	○○○	○	○○/.		●●●		●●●	●●●	·	aluminates
Heavy metal mining	○○○	○○○	○	○○○/●●	○/●●	●	○○○	./●●●		○/●●●	·
Gold mining	○○○	○○	○○	○○○/.	○/○	○○○	○○○	·	·	·	·
China clay wastes	○○○	○○○	··				○○○				
Acid rocks	○○	○○○	·	○○	○○	○○	○○○	·	·	·	·
Calcareous rocks	○○○	○○○	○	●	○	●	·		·	·	·
Sand and gravel	○○/.	○/.	○/.	○/.	○/.	○/.	○○		·	·	·
Coastal sands	○○	○	·/.	·	·	·	○○	./●	·	·	·

Deficiency — severe ○○○, moderate ○○, slight ○; adequate ·; Excess — slight ●, moderate ●●, severe ●●●

(relative to the establishment of a soil/plant ecosystem appropriate to the material.)

sward regression. Losses in percolating drainage water are encouraged on raw, man-made substrates by the absence of organic matter and clay minerals which together form the basis of the ion exchange complex of normal soils. Cation exchange capacities lower than 30 mEq kg^{-1} are not uncommon, and compare with values greater than 100 mEq kg^{-1} for many agriculturally productive soils. Where low nutrient retention properties are combined with high substrate permeability leaching is inevitable. The rate of profile movement can be quite dramatic (Fig.

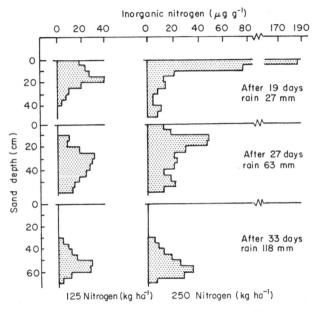

FIG. 8. The distribution of nitrate nitrogen, originally applied to the surface, in china clay sand waste after different periods of time (from Dancer, 1975).

8) irrespective of whether ammonium or nitrate fertilizer provides the nitrogen source (Dancer, 1975).

Leaching is a widely accepted problem which applies to derelict land substrates as diverse in physical and chemical properties as blast furnace slag (Gemmell, 1975), slate waste (Sheldon and Bradshaw, 1976), colliery spoil (Richardson and Dicker, 1972; Gemmell, 1973), urban clearance rubble (Bradshaw and Handley, 1972) and metalliferous tailings (Johnson and Bradshaw, 1977). In certain specialized circumstances, such as with alkaline pulverized fuel ash and calcareous chemical wastes (pH >8), volatilization losses of nitrogen may occur if ammonium-based nitrogen fertilizers are applied, due to formation of the unstable intermediate ammonium carbonate (Gardner, 1959; Hodgson and Townsend, 1973).

Leaching losses of potassium are usually less critical, for the initial nutrient status is normally higher than that of nitrogen. However where structural deterioration and clay mineral breakdown occurs, for example due to regeneration of acidity in colliery spoil, rapid release of potassium may result (Gemmell, 1977). Potassium fixation by electrostatic binding is an equally severe (though rare) problem of finely-ground

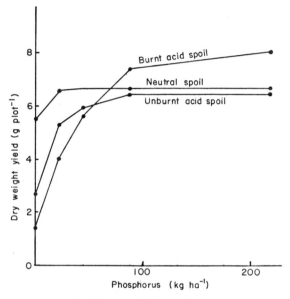

FIG. 9. Growth response to phosphate applied to colliery spoils differing in phosphorus fixation capacity (from Gemmell, 1977).

mineral wastes containing illitic, 2:1 layered aluminosilicates, which have undergone structural alteration and nutrient loss.

Nutrient fixation is however a common feature of highly acidic and alkaline materials. On very calcareous quarry and kilning wastes and on some chemical refining spoils, reversion of phosphate to insoluble higher calcium phosphates (e.g. $Ca_3(PO_4)_2$; $Ca_8H_2(PO_4)_6 . 5H_2O$) produces minimal residual nutrient values and low phosphorus availability (Gemmell, 1975). On basic metalliferous tailings this is less severe, but metal–phosphate interactions are equally efficient inducers of phosphate deficiency (Jeffrey et al., 1975). In acidic substrates, and particularly therefore pyritic colliery spoils, phosphorus fixation occurs through formation of insoluble ferric and aluminium phosphates and through adsorption on to amorphous ferric hydroxide (Doubleday, 1971). Gemmell (1977) has shown how the acidity and pyrite content of colliery spoil influence plant availability of phosphorus. Fixation increases following combustion due to the complexing properties of ferric compounds formed by pyrite oxidation (Fig. 9).

Recognizing the variety and heterogeneity of derelict land materials, there is often a need to predict the likelihood of nutritional disorders in advance of large scale revegetation work. Often this is accomplished by chemical analysis alone, but the predictive accuracy is invariably improved if the data is interpreted with the results of glasshouse bioassay experiments or small-scale field trials (Johnson, 1977). Nevertheless, forecasting nutritional problems by chemical methods has been refined considerably and the methodology has been described by several authors (e.g. Allen *et al.*, 1974). In principal, chemical analysis attempts to partition the total individual nutrient content of a matrix into several fractions which reflect the ability of a substrate to supply nutrients in plant-available forms. It may also be important to analyse the complexing power of the material: this is particularly true for phosphorus (Fitter, 1974). The data is then used predictively by comparisons with standard nutrient indices developed for normal soils (MAFF, 1973).

With many forms of derelict land it is not the existence of a nutrient disorder which presents a problem; it is knowing how to solve it on a permanent basis. Nitrogen is critical in this respect. A temporary solution to substrate nitrogen deficiency is readily available, and involves only the use of suitable chemical fertilizers such as ammonium nitrate, sodium nitrate or urea. However symptoms of nitrogen deficiency soon reappear in an establishing sward, and an inadequate supply of nitrogen is the single most common factor in sward deterioration on all forms of derelict land (e.g. Bradshaw *et al.*, 1975). This regression stems from the inability of coarse-grained, permeable substrates to retain readily soluble ions against leaching, and from the absence of an effective labile store of nutrients. The means by which this may be overcome have been studied recently.

Regular applications of nitrogen as a maintenance policy improve overall growth but these may have to be continued for several years, until an effective pool of organic material develops and nutrient cycling by microbial activity is fully established (Williams, 1975). This then introduces the generally unacceptable element of high maintenance costs. Use of slow-release chemical fertilizers has been advocated (e.g. sulphur-coated urea) and their value has been proven in several situations (Fig. 10). Such materials are, nevertheless, expensive and a single application at seeding, even at a high rate (100 kg ha^{-1}) is rarely satisfactory by itself (Gemmell, 1975). Considerably better slow-acting sources of nitrogen are organic amendments such as sewage sludge, mushroom compost and farmyard manure, though growth response to these amendments is also partly due to physical amelioration, particularly if they are incorporated (Goodman *et al.*, 1973; Humphries, 1977). On some substrates they may not mineralize rapidly enough for satisfactory plant growth.

Accepting that successful revegetation of land depends largely on maintaining a satisfactory nitrogen status, without regular maintenance

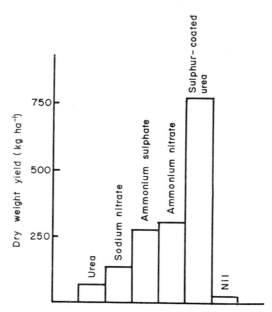

FIG. 10. Yield of a mixed grass sward on calcareous metalliferous tailings treated with 75 kg N ha^{-1} in different forms.

fertilizer treatments, the need for legumes becomes self-evident. Nitrogen fixation can be a more than adequate substitute for chemical and organic fertilizers. Table IX shows that clover cultivars on china clay sand waste can achieve nitrogen fixation rates, corrected for inherent fertility and rainfall inputs, of the order 100–150 kg N ha^{-1} year^{-1} (Dancer *et al.*, 1977b). This compares favourably with the 100–200 kg ha^{-1} year^{-1} reported by Stewart (1966), Date (1970) and others in agricultural situations. Accumulation of organic nitrogen can thus be quite rapid on some derelict land materials.

An important characteristic of legume fixed nitrogen is that it is readily mineralized because of low C:N ratios (below 20) so that transfer to the companion grasses and other components of the sward does occur. By contrast nitrogen accumulated in grass residues from

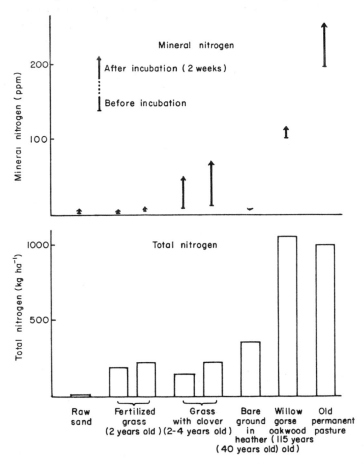

FIG. 11. The total nitrogen and its rate of release by mineralization in sand wastes reclaimed by different methods, compared with naturally colonized wastes and a local pasture (from Bradshaw *et al.*, 1975).

added fertilizer is much less readily available because of higher C:N ratios. This can be seen in incubation tests (Bradshaw *et al.*, 1975) (Fig. 11). Some materials may even have negative nitrogen release properties.

Successful root nodulation relies on the presence of appropriate nitrogen-fixing bacteria of the genus *Rhizobium*. In some cases artificial inoculation of seed by pelleting or the addition of peat cultures may be necessary due to the microbiological sterility of many raw mineral substrates (Hodgson and Townsend, 1973). Additional precautions must be taken to ensure successful legume establishment. Excessive nitrogen fertilizer treatment at seeding should be avoided; but applications in the range 30–70 kg N ha^{-1} are usually acceptable and indeed necessary for initial sward development.

TABLE IX   Nitrogen accumulation (kg ha^{-1}) for twelve legumes grown on china clay mica and sand wastes (from Dancer et al., 1977b)

Legume	Mica waste			Sand waste		
	1972	1973	Mean	1972	1973	Mean
Trifolium pratense (early)	100	463	281	65	236	151
Trifolium pratense (late, S-123)	205	333	269	76	205	141
Trifolium pratense (altaswede)	124	80	102	85	152	119
Trifolium repens (S-184)	74	200	137	89	181	135
Trifolium repens (S-100)	45	258	152	59	199	130
Trifolium hybridum (alsike)	80	273	177	79	143	111
Trifolium dubium (suckling)	44	136	113	31	99	65
Medicago lupulina (english trefoil)	88	234	161	48	216	132
Medicago sativa (lucerne)	65	214	140	61	168	115
Lotus corniculatus (birdsfoot trefoil)	100	319	210	67	166	117
Lupinus angustifolius (blue lupin)	108	—	108	32	—	32
Vicia sativa (vetch)	51	—	51	14	—	14

The potassium, calcium and in particular phosphorus status of the substrate should be determined and corrected as necessary. This is essential because a deficiency of one nutrient can be a severe constraint on performance in response to addition of another which is also in short supply, as shown on alkali waste (Fig. 12) and also on coal mine spoils (Berg, 1973).

In comparison with nitrogen, phosphorus is immobile in soils and less subject to leaching even in porous substrates. Thus in most situations phosphorus deficiency can be rectified simply by applying superphosphate, basic slag or, where necessary, slow-release forms (e.g. magnesium ammonium phosphate), usually at rates corresponding to 100–300 kg P_2O_5 ha^{-1}. In unfavourable materials treatment rates must

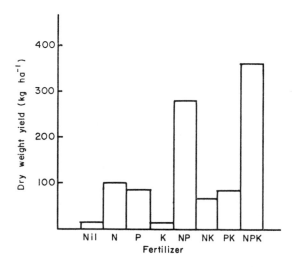

FIG. 12. Yield of a mixed grass sward on alkali manufacturing waste (pH 9·3) in relation to different fertilizer treatments.

compensate for fixation. For pyritic colliery spoils this may necessitate applications as high as 1000 kg P_2O_5 ha^{-1}, and also incorporation of the fertilizer after pH adjustment, so that root penetration and growth are encouraged.

Deficiencies of potassium are usually only marginal and, allowing for leaching losses, application rates greater than 75 kg ha^{-1} (as potassium sulphate) are rarely necessary. Moreover, except in the unique circumstances of pyritic colliery spoils and metalliferous wastes, calcium deficiency can usually be corrected by a single incorporated treatment of between 1000–5000 kg ha^{-1} of ground limestone (2 mm-dust). Dolomitic limestone (calcium-magnesium carbonate) can be used in most situations where deficiencies of both metals prevail.

IX. ACIDITY AND ALKALINITY

A major factor controlling plant growth on all soils and particularly on certain types of derelict land is pH. Extreme acidity or alkalinity imposes direct and indirect constraints on sward development, continuity and persistence. In many colliery spoils, for example, high acidity is of overriding importance because of inhibited root growth, reduced nutrient availability and adverse effects on soil structure. High acidity causes clay mineral breakdown and the release of toxic quantities of aluminium and manganese (Chadwick *et al.*, 1969). At the opposite extreme, in highly alkaline substrates produced by the chromate manufacturing and alkali industries, phosphate immobilization and induced micronutrient disorders are not uncommon (Gemmell, 1974).

The extent of acidity problems in colliery spoil differs considerably between the coalfields of the British Isles, with pH values showing regional and local variation between 1·5 and 8·0; the commonest pH range is 3–5. This variation derives partly from differences in the duration of exposure, the abundance of minerals with neutralizing properties and the factor of combustion (Gemmell, 1977). All these factors affect the principal determinants of pH conditions, namely the status and mineral form of iron pyrites in the material. Exposure and weathering of pyrite causes dramatic increases in acidity and a progressive decline in substrate pH. A series of oxidation and hydrolysis reactions, proceeding concurrently and assisted by ferrous ion oxidizing bacteria (e.g. *Thiobacillus ferro-oxidans*), cause pyrite dissolution and acid regeneration in certain colliery shales. The weathering process is complex but can be summarized by the following sequence:

$$4FeS_2 + 15O_2 + 14H_2O \rightarrow 4Fe(OH)_3 + 8H_2SO_4$$
(iron pyrites)

The severity of this constraint on vegetation establishment depends greatly on the mineral form of the pyrite, since grain-size distribution affects reactivity and the capacity for acid regeneration (Caruccio, 1973). Highly reactive spoils have a preponderance of framboidal pyrite inclusions measuring less than 10 μ in diameter; coarser-grained pyrite minerals are more resistant to normal decomposition processes.

However, the need to counter acid regeneration in colliery spoil revegetation work is not totally dependent on pyrite content and form, nor on the length of exposure. A critical feature of any model relating pyrite weathering to pH is the nature and composition of the associated minerals. Certain colliery shales have an inherent capacity to neutralize sulphuric acid produced by pyrite, because of their calcium and magnesium carbonate content. Thus the pyrite to carbonate ratio is a major determinant of substrate acidity and the consequent need for counter measures in revegetation schemes (Table X), and must always be

TABLE X   The relationship between pyrite content, carbonate content, pH and the response of ryegrass to liming on seven contrasting colliery spoils (data from P. J Costigan)

Colliery	Pyrite (%)	Carbonate (%)	pH	Response to liming[a]
Florence	1·72	4·39	6·6	1·04
Ham Heath	1·04	3·88	6·0	0·86
Bold	3·71	2·73	5·9	1·16
Sutton Manor	1·21	1·07	3·8	1·23
Littleton	0·58	0	2·3	2·30
Harrington	0·62	0	2·3	9·37
Silverdale	0·94	0·05	2·1	31·56

[a]Response to liming $= \dfrac{\text{shoot dry wt @ 20 t ha}^{-1} \text{ limestone}}{\text{shoot dry wt @ \ \ 5 t ha}^{-1} \text{ limestone}}$

determined. Combustion processes, of course, can destroy the potential acidity of unburnt pyritic shales by liberating the sulphur of the pyrite as gaseous sulphur dioxide.

The consequences of pyrite weathering are not unique to colliery spoils, for many metalliferous mine wastes exhibit similar and sometimes more pronounced problems in this respect. Ore dumps and spoil tips containing significant levels of pyrite ($>0·5\%$) are subject to secondary weathering reactions in which ferric sulphate, a powerful geochemical solvent, induces dissolution of toxic metals from associated non-ferrous metal sulphides. This secondary decomposition can be summarized by:

$$(M)S + 2Fe_2(SO_4)_3 + 2H_2O + 3O_2 \rightarrow$$
$$(M)SO_4 + 4FeSO_4 + H_2SO_4,$$

where (M) represents the non-ferrous metal. Because of acidity and enhanced metal release the substrate is extremely inhospitable to plant growth.

In all very acid materials it is not only the sulphuric acid which is soluble and mobile, but also many of the other products of weathering e.g. aluminium and other metal sulphates. These are liable to disperse in percolating drainage waters as acid mine drainage, and can cause severe pollution of receiving watercourses (Glover, 1975; Down and Stocks, 1976 and 1977). A well analysed example is the Brukunga mine, South Australia (Blesing *et al.*, 1975).

In the British Isles pyrite weathering in non-ferrous mine dumps is a local problem which is restricted mainly to abandoned lead–zinc mines in north Dyfed and Gwynedd in West Wales. In other countries metalliferous spoils with an acidic reaction (pH 3–6) are not uncommon

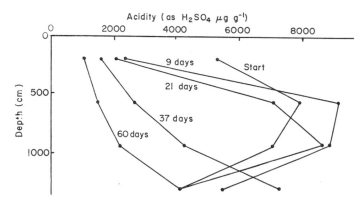

FIG. 13. Changes in the acidity of the surface layers of a gold slimes dam subject to artificial leaching (from James and Mrost, 1965).

but the low pH is itself a minor constraint on vegetative stabilization compared with metal toxicity.

Although pyrite oxidation is confined mainly to the surface strata of pit heaps (Doubleday, 1972), it remains one of the most difficult and critical factors to control in revegetation schemes. Natural leaching does ameliorate both low and high pH on colliery spoil (Knabe, 1973), but over long periods only. Artificial leaching by overhead irrigation has proved very successful on gold mine wastes in South Africa (James and Mrost, 1965): the acidity profile is rapidly and permanently modified (Fig. 13). But with high levels of pyrite continued production of sulphuric acid leading to sward deterioration is commonplace (Fig. 14) and alternative solutions must be adopted.

It is now accepted that artifical neutralization using ground limestone, slaked or burnt lime, or dolomitic limestone is the best treatment. The application rate and method must cater for both immediate and potential acidity. The countering of acid regeneration may demand limestone applications as high as 100 t ha⁻¹ on some colliery spoils, and rates of the order 50 t ha⁻¹ are not uncommon (Gemmell, 1973).

Surface treatment alone is unsatisfactory because most liming materials are immobile, particularly if structural deterioration of the substrate has occurred. Deep-ripping of the tip surface and incorporation of the liming materials are necessary before direct vegetation establishment becomes feasible. Where the total neutralizing requirement exceeds the equivalent of 20 t ha^{-1} of limestone, use of burnt or slaked lime should be avoided or extremely high pH conditions may result. Even if only limestone is applied, higher than normal rates of fertilizer

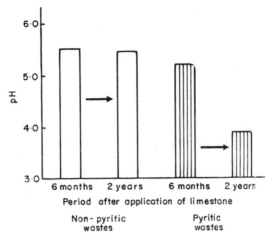

FIG. 14. The mean changes in pH of 6 pyritic and 6 non pyritic colliery spoils following addition of 10 000 kg ha^{-1} CaCO$_3$ (from Gemmell, 1977).

may be necessary to compensate for phosphate complexing and reversion, and for induced trace element deficiencies.

If serious redevelopment of acidity from the weathering of further unaccounted pyrite occurs, there may be total death of the vegetation. Since incorporation of large quantities of lime into the soil is difficult, it will be necessary to plough or deep-rip and then re-establish a new vegetation cover. However if the acidity has been adequately countered, subsequent soil development and the formation of a satisfactory soil structure with improved infiltration capacity, should lead to the disappearance of the acidity problem, although normal surface liming will still be necessary.

In many intractable cases, where the material has an extremely high pyrite content, it may be better if the material is buried at the outset under less acidic materials so that it is completely isolated (EPA, 1973).

Spoil materials displaying the opposite extreme of pH are relatively uncommon, and the principal waste in this category is pulverized fuel ash for which pH values of up to 12·0 have been reported (Townsend and Hodgson, 1973). Comparable values are known for substrates derived from the obsolete Leblanc process for manufacturing sodium carbonate (pH 11–12·6), blast furnace slags (9–10·5) and chromate smelter waste (11·8–12·7). Spoils displaying intense alkalinity are normally rich in hydroxides derived from the hydrolysis of oxides and silicates (Gemmell, 1974, 1975).

As with acidic colliery spoils, natural and artificial leaching are of limited value in amending high pH unless the matrix is very permeable. The latter is true of pulverized fuel ash where lagooning removes the active soluble hydroxides. In blast furnace slag a twelve month lapse between land modelling and seeding produces a marked decline in alkalinity and permits vegetation establishment without the use of top-soil or alternative amendments (Gemmell, 1975). However in materials where there is a high percentage of insoluble hydroxides, as in lime wastes, this is not possible because potential alkalinity reserves are higher. These cannot be removed by leaching and natural carbonation is restricted to the surfaces of lime aggregates. Even ten years after disturbance and exposure of unweathered Leblanc alkali waste, the decline in pH is marginal and restricted solely to the immediate surface layers (Table XI).

TABLE XI   pH Profiles of undisturbed and recently
exposed alkali waste

Depth (cm)	Undisturbed for 50 years	Exposed for 10 years
0	8·4	10·0
2	8·3	10·3
5	8·3	10·7
10	9·2	11·3
20	10·4	11·5
40	11·7	11·6
80	12·1	11·8

Deliberate acidification using aluminium sulphate, ferrous sulphate, gypsum or other chemicals used in the reclamation of alkaline and saline soils, is of limited, value, but can be used in exceptional circumstances (e.g. Gemmell, 1974). In many situations no alternative exists to revegetation systems based on amelioration with topsoil, subsoil or organic amendments. The potential of reciprocal reclamation between for example alkali waste and acidic colliery shale, remains an interesting but largely untried possibility.

X. Metal Toxicity

It is generally accepted that metalliferous mine and smelter wastes containing phytotoxic level of heavy metals are amongst the most difficult materials from a revegetation viewpoint. In Wales alone there are over 300 abandoned non-ferrous metal mines displaying spoil tips of a significant size ($>$ 1 ha), and similar sites are found throughout other metalliferous ore fields in Britain (Richardson, 1974). Furthermore one of the most extensive areas (325 ha) of derelict land in the British Isles is associated with former smelting operations in the lower Swansea Valley (Street and Goodman, 1967). Most mine and smelter waste tips exhibit a high level of metal enrichment because they were formed between 1750 and 1900 when ore separation and secondary refining were based on relatively crude gravity flotation and smelting techniques.

Lead, zinc and copper are the commonest toxic metals of polluted substrates in Britain (Table XII); they occur as sulphides and carbonates in mine spoils and as oxides and sulphidic complexes associated with ferrous silicates in smelter wastes. The physical and chemical properties of these derelict land materials have been studied repeatedly, both in respect of the principal metallic constituents and associated toxins such as cadmium, arsenic and nickel (Goodman et al., 1973; Davies and Roberts, 1975; Johnson and Bradshaw, 1977). The problems of erosion and release of metallic salts by weathering are widely recognized, and the need for preventive measures is clear from the effects of pollution episodes on adjacent land and water resources (Smith and Bradshaw, 1972; Jones and Howells, 1975).

Elsewhere in Europe, but particularly in Australia, North America and South Africa, mining has evolved relatively recently and is on a larger, more concentrated scale, and vast tracts of land have been polluted. Although stricter legislative controls are being developed and designed to at least maintain existing standards of environmental quality, metal pollution is extremely difficult to control. Even with modern mining techniques metal pollution of natural resources is not an infrequent event (e.g. Blesing et al., 1975; Down and Stocks, 1976).

Whilst many problems have yet to be solved, considerable advances have been made in the revegetation of disused tailings dams, low grade

Table XII Non-ferrous metals in spoil from abandoned mines in Britain

Mining region	Counties	Number of sites surveyed	Concentration range ($\mu g\ g^{-1}$)			
			Principal base metals			Associated metals[a]
			Cu	Pb	Zn	
SW England	Devon and Cornwall	16	65–6140	48–2070	26–1090	Ag:<5–350, As:68–7080 Cd:5–145, Sn:80–6200
W and NW England	Salop and Cheshire	12	15–7260	840–26000	980–21000	As:93–1970, Ba:<100–1400 Co:<5–95, Ni:17–720
N Pennines	N Yorkshire and Durham	8	—	605–13000	470–28000	Ba:400–62000, Sr:125–2530, Cd:<2–325
S Pennines	Derbyshire	17	—	10800–76500	12700–42000	Ba:<100–104000, Cd:<2–195, Cu:29–240, Sr:<50–8760
Lake District	Cumbria	7	77–3800	2070–6370	4690–7370	Ba:<100–3800
C Wales	Powys and Dyfed	10	—	1670–54000	475–8000	Ag:8–100, Cd:15–445, Cu:77–560
N Wales	Clwyd and Gwynedd	19	30–5750	6400–76000	11300–127000	Ag:18–95, Ba:<100–7500 Cd:70–510, Ni:30–695
S Scotland	Dumfries and Galloway	6	—	4730–28300	1600–31400	Cu:10–680, Ni:<5–665
Range in normal, uncontaminated soils			2–100	2–200	10–300	Ag:<1, As:1–50, Ba:100–3000, Cd:<1, Co:1–40, Ni:5–500 Sn:<10, Sr:50–1000

[a]Elements present in anomalous amounts at more than two sites.
Elevated levels of Bi, Ge, Li, Mo and Sb were also found occasionally.

ore tips and smelter wastes. Because of the unacceptable features of chemical and physical stabilization, greater attention has been paid to the constraints on revegetation and to the development of corrective measures. Vegetative stabilization relies on countering or avoiding the limitations of metal toxicity, nutrient deficiency, acidity, salinity and adverse physical conditions, all of which can occur singly or in combination.

The most severe problem is heavy metal toxicity. There has been considerable success of revegetation schemes implemented on various metalliferous tailings derived from modern processing mills. Technological improvements in metal recovery have developed to a stage where direct vegetative stabilization of tailings is, in many cases, a practical proposition, provided that extremes of pH, nutrient deficiency and physical constraints are overcome (Peters, 1970; Hill and Nothard, 1973; Jeffrey et al., 1975; Johnson et al., 1976). Of these, pH control is the most difficult, particularly in pyritic tailings and waste rock dumps (Nielson and Peterson, 1972). On such acidic substrates limestone treatments are doubly beneficial because they counter acidity and reduce metal availability through the antagonistic relationship between calcium and heavy-metal ions (Wilkins, 1957).

Stabilization of modern waste rock dumps (in contrast to modern tailings), older tailings, spoil tips, and smelter wastes is, however, much more difficult because of higher metal contents. Normal plant material fails to grow even with appropriate nutrients. In these cases the favoured technique is to alter radically the surface rooting-zone of the material by surface addition or incorporation of non-toxic ameliorants such as topsoil, subsoil, domestic refuse, sewage sludge and peat mixed with sand (Street and Goodman, 1967; Goodman et al., 1973; Johnson et al., 1977). Of the organic amendments, sewage sludge is the most widely used and is applied as a discrete surface layer (5–10 cm) or more commonly as an incorporated amendment. Its success on substrates as diverse as zinc and copper smelter wastes (Goodman et al., 1973) (Fig. 15) and pulverized fuel ash (Hodgson and Townsend, 1973) stems partly from physical amelioration, but mainly from an ability to render many toxic metals and some non-metals (e.g. boron) innocuous by chelation or by ion association processes. However, the persistence of vegetation established under these conditions is questionable because the gradual breakdown of organic matter is often accompanied by the reappearance of toxicity symptoms and by sward deterioration (Gemmell, 1977) (Fig. 16).

Dieback is caused mainly by metal inhibition of root growth, although this may be accompanied by a progressive decline in nutrient

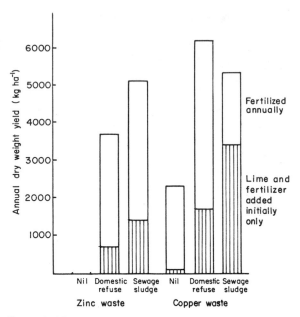

FIG. 15. The effects of different amendments on growth of grass on copper and zinc wastes in the Lower Swansea Valley (from Goodman *et al.*, 1973).

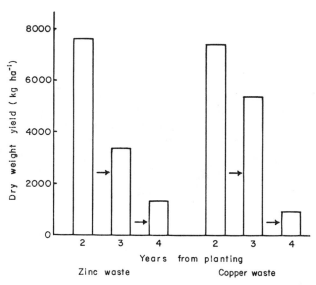

FIG. 16. Regression of grass swards due to the reappearance of metal toxicity on organically amended metalliferous wastes (from Gemmell, 1977).

status due to leaching of nitrogen and complexing of phosphorus. Annual maintenance treatments of 2–10 cm of organic matter are required to maintain sward stability (Goodman et al., 1973). A similar pattern of regression, although delayed in its initiation, occurs even if the amelioration treatment comprises 10–30 cm of topsoil or subsoil. Conversely on less toxic substrates including pulverized fuel ash, such a treatment may allow agricultural management in the form of crop production or high intensity grazing (Hodgson et al., 1963).

Recent developments of this technique have been concerned with physically isolating the surface from the toxic material beneath by using deep amendment layers. A surface layer of 75 cm of coarse-grained mineral waste will prevent the movement of metals into the surface vegetation. Materials such as non-pyritic colliery shale spread over toxic waste will support a satisfactory vegetation cover provided that nutrient deficiencies are corrected (Johnson et al., 1977). Potentially suitable amendments (e.g. slate and limestone quarry spoils and pulverized fuel ash) are themselves waste materials which are often available in sufficient quantities and at low cost, in close proximity to abandoned metalliferous mine and smelter sites. At Mount Isa waste rock-fines are a readily available and effective covering (Farrell, 1977). Essential features of the amendment are a high porosity and low cation exchange capacity, otherwise capillary movement of soluble metal ions causes dieback even in the absence of root penetration to the amendment/toxic waste interface.

Leaching of nitrogen must be countered by symbiotic fixation, so high initial applications of phosphorus ($100–200$ kg ha^{-1}) are essential to ensure successful establishment of legumes. The development of a soil ecosystem which is semi-independent of the underlying toxic matrix has other subsidiary benefits. These include eliminating both the need for regular fertilizer treatments beyond the normal maintenance period for reclaimed sites (1–2 years), and also the common problem of a gradual lowering of the nutrient status due to metal inhibition of microbial activity and organic matter breakdown.

A similar policy of separation using a porous subsoil (25 cm), together with ferrous sulphate and sewage sludge to overcome residual toxicity, has been used successfully to establish vegetation on chromate smelter waste (Gemmell, 1974). The prospects of the isolation approach are encouraging but insufficient time has yet elapsed to confirm its long term viability.

There is only one technique available for direct revegetation of waste materials containing phytotoxic levels of heavy metals. Certain species, although not innately tolerant, have the capacity to evolve heavy-

metal resistant ecotypes which occur naturally and persist on contaminated substrates (Gadgil, 1969; Antonovics *et al.*, 1971). These tolerant
populations also possess physiological and morphological characteristics which reflect environmental stresses apart from metal toxicity, and
are more tolerant of low nutrient status and drought conditions than
are normal populations (Humphreys and Bradshaw, 1977).

Copper and lead–zinc tolerant varieties of red fescue (*Festuca rubra*)
and common bent (*Agrostis tenuis*), suitable for establishment of a
vigorous vegetation cover, have been identified and are now available
on a commercial basis (Smith and Bradshaw, 1972) (Table XIII).

TABLE XIII   Metal-tolerant cultivars available on a commercial scale

Species	Cultivars	Application
Festuca rubra	Merlin	Calcareous lead-zinc wastes
Agrostis tenuis	Goginan	Acidic lead-zinc wastes
Agrostis tenuis	Parys	Acidic copper wastes

They are likely to prove invaluable where surface treatment is imprac-
ticable or where simple stabilization is all that is required. The largely
specific nature of tolerance, to the metal or metals present in the native
substrate, could be restrictive but only on spoil tips containing high
levels of several metals (Jeffrey *et al.*, 1975).

The superior performance of tolerant material compared with commercial varieties of the same species is quite dramatic, particularly if
fertilizers are applied (Fig. 17). Tolerance is of less significant value on
the less toxic tailings generated by some modern processing mills
(Fig. 18). On toxic spoils clear differences between tolerant and non-
tolerant populations are not always apparent in the early stages of
sward development (Smith and Bradshaw, 1972) but only the former
are capable of surviving in the long term.

Initially, major nutrient deficiencies may be overcome by applying
400–700 kg ha^{-1} of a granular, compound fertilizer (17 N:17 P$_2$O$_5$:
17 K$_2$O); but further maintenance treatments may be necessary to
maintain substrate fertility in the event of leaching of nitrogen and
complexing of phosphorus. Metal-tolerant populations of legumes are
not available, and commercial varieties are incapable of withstanding
high substrate toxicity.

Decisions as to the most suitable treatment policy for metal contaminated spoil tips must be based on several factors. Apart from

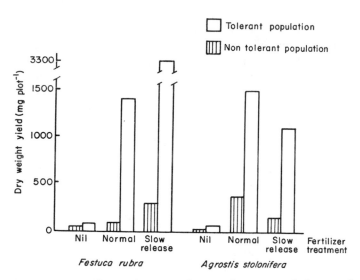

FIG. 17. Growth of lead/zinc tolerant and non tolerant populations on lead/zinc mining waste after seven months' growth (from Smith, 1973).

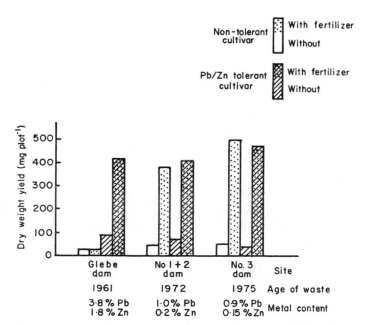

FIG. 18. Growth of lead/zinc tolerant and non tolerant populations of *Festuca rubra* on old and new metalliferous (Pb/Zn) fluorspar tailings (from Johnson *et al.*, 1976).

practical limitations of access, amendment availability, transport and application costs, the major consideration is the ultimate land use objective. In general, surface amendments provide for greater versatility because swards established directly on metalliferous waste cannot be used for grazing, even on a short-term basis, because of their high metal content. On the other hand surface treatment is considerably more expensive than direct seeding, irrespective of site location.

XI. SALINITY

Growth limitations attributable to high levels of soluble salts are characteristic of pulverized fuel ash, some oil shales, colliery spoils and metalliferous wastes, and certain relatively obscure chemical wastes (Doubleday, 1971; Dean et al., 1973; Hodgson and Townsend, 1973; Schmehl and McCaslin, 1973). Conductivities as high as 15 mmhos cm^{-1} have been reported in recently discarded metalliferous tailings (Wild and Wiltshire, 1971; Peterson and Nielson, 1973). Values of this magnitude often derive from injection treatments to adjust effluent pH, and from a progressive concentration of salts due to recycling of water in enclosed process systems, or from the presence of indigenous salts in the original material. But more commonly they arise from the interaction between pyrite weathering products and native carbonates, particularly of magnesium since its sulphate is soluble. Salt levels can therefore increase in a material as it is exposed to air.

High osmotic pressures in growth media caused by soluble salts can severely depress productivity, and an inverse relationship between yield and conductivity has been described for power station ash residues (Cope, 1961). Electrical conductivities in the range 7–13 mmhos cm^{-1} are not uncommon in certain types of waste, and compare with a critical level for most non-maritime plants of the order 4 mmhos cm^{-1}. Where salinity problems are caused by a single salt, ionic imbalance can also be a problem.

In situations where a high initial salinity is combined with a low regenerative capacity, natural leaching or irrigation can be valuable remedial measures, depending on seasonal fluctuations in water balance and movement, and on rainfall distribution throughout the year. Hill (1977a) has described a close inverse relationship between specific conductivity and total rainfall on non-pyritic gold, copper and nickel tailings (Table XIV).

In circumstances where reserves of acidity and alkalinity are high, of where evaporative losses cause surface accumulation of salts, leaching is less effective. This is particularly true in arid climates where ground water supplies may themselves be very saline. Where there is pyrite, neutralization by liming to counter active and potential acidity can be more effective than leaching processes. Use of dolomitic limestone should be avoided, otherwise substrate and leachate salinity will be maintained and even increased through the formation of magnesium sulphate.

Physical and chemical treatments are however expensive and may well have to be continued for long periods. A very promising new

TABLE XIV   Seasonal fluctuations in specific conductivity (mmhos cm^{-1}) of gold mine tailings at different depths (from Hill, 1977a).

Sampling date	Rainfall (mm)	Sampling depth (cm)				
		0–5	5–10	10–15	15–20	20–25
25.9.73		5·8	2·7	2·2	2·7	2·1
	28					
30.10.73		4·0	3·5	1·7	2·6	2·0
	126					
23.11.73		3·4	2·5	2·0	3·0	2·0
	307					
21.12.73		2·2	2·7	1·6	2·9	2·3
	672					
22.1.74		1·8	2·4	1·4	2·6	1·7
	910					
25.2.74		1·8	2·1	1·2	2·7	1·8

development, depending on the identification and use of salt-tolerant material, has recently been reported (Hill, 1977b). Salt-tolerant populations of various species, particularly *Sporobolus virginicus*, *Cynodon aethiopicus*, *Dactylotenium geminatum* and *Paspalum vaginatum*, have been identified and are being employed very successfully, by vegetative planting, to stabilize various saline metalliferous waste heaps in Rhodesia. It was originally thought that their superiority was due to metal tolerance but it now seems that the critical factor is their salt tolerance.

XII. Species Selection and Use: Ground Cover Vegetation

In addition to the growth limitations described, all of which may retard or prevent the natural development of vegetation on derelict land materials, one further factor must be considered. There are situations where the absence of plants is not due specifically to chemical or physical constraints of the substrate, but to the lack of opportunity for colonization. Species well adapted to extreme substrate conditions such as *Deschampsia flexuosa* and *Ulex europaeus* usually have limited powers of seed dispersal, while species with spectacular powers of dispersal such as *Taraxacum officinale* and *Sonchus asper* are usually natives of fertile soils. This is a reflection of "*k*" as opposed to "*r*" selected species (Harper, 1977). Problems of migration therefore often limit colonization of derelict sites.

The botanical composition of vegetation naturally colonizing disturbed sites depends on many factors, but species and population adaptation to edaphic constraints is of overriding importance. Thus a knowledge of species requirements and versatility is informative and can be an important guide to reclamation procedures. A mixed grass and legume sward is the standard objective of many revegetation schemes, but in Britain alone, which has a flora of restricted diversity, there are over 200 potentially suitable grass and legume species. Superficially any attempt to differentiate the most appropriate species appears difficult; but if the well defined growth characteristics and tolerances of commercial varieties are aligned with substrate features, climate, and the proposed after-use and maintenance policy for reclaimed sites, species selection is simplified. Usually grass species which are suitable for derelict land sites must combine rapid establishment and tolerance of low fertility: good examples are *Festuca rubra* in temperate regions, *Eragrostis curvula* in more arid regions and *Chloris gayana* in the tropics. But most agricultural species are available as several varieties, (including wild populations), which possess very different characteristics of hardiness, winter greeness, productivity and growth habit. The importance of varietal properties is evident from the contrasting performance of metal-tolerant and non-tolerant *Festuca rubra* on toxic mine waste. The need to compile seed mixtures at the varietal level may be equally crucial for other growth limitations such as salinity, drought and low nutrient status. For some species, particularly those with no agricultural value (e.g. *Deschampsia flexuosa* and *D. caespitosa*), seed supplies are restricted; but they should not be disregarded and can be collected as wild material for use in situations where they are particularly valuable (Farrell, 1977).

The selection of suitable legume species and cultivars for derelict land seed mixtures is less complex, for those used in agriculture provide the major requirement of high rates of nitrogen fixation. Legume species adapted to acid, low nutrient soils are common in warm climates, but unfortunately in temperate climates the best are shrubs such as *Ulex europaeus* and *Lupinus arboreus*. Table XV summarizes the most useful legume species for land restoration on a worldwide basis. Intra-specific variation is again significant so species and varietal selection must allow for climatic and substrate factors, particularly calcium and phosphate status. The development of cultivars tolerant of low base status soils

TABLE XV   Perennial legumes suitable for derelict land

	Species	Soil preference	Climate preference
Indigo bush	*Amorpha fruticosa*	NC	W
Centro	*Centrosema pubescens*	AN	W
Crown vetch	*Coronilla varia*	AN	W
Silverleaf desmodium	*Desmodium uncinatum*	AN	W
Mat peavine	*Lathyrus sylvestris*	NC	W
Lespedeza	*Lespedeza bicolor*	AN	W
Sericea lespedeza	*Lespedeza cuneata*	AN	W
Japan lespedeza	*Lespedeza japonica*	AN	W
Birdsfoot trefoil	*Lotus corniculatus*	NC	CW
Tree lupin	*Lupinus arboreus*	ANC	CW
Lucerne (alfalfa)	*Medicago sativa*	NC	CW
Sweet clover (white)	*Melilotus alba*	ANC	CW
Sweet clover (yellow)	*Melilotus officinalis*	ANC	W
Siratro	*Phaseolus atropurpureus*	ANC	W
Townsville stylo	*Stylosanthes humilis*	AN	W
Alsike clover	*Trifolium hybridum*	ANC	C
Red clover	*Trifolium pratense*	NC	C
White clover	*Trifolium repens*	NC	CW
Gorse	*Ulex europaeus*	ANC	C
		(acidic, neutral or calcareous)	(cool or warm)

from current breeding programmes, may be very important for derelict land revegetation in the future (Wright, 1976).

Sward establishment can usually be achieved using standard agricultural machinery and standard practices of cultivation, seed broadcasting and light consolidation. However, in situations where excessive consolidation has occurred, or where deep incorporation of ameliorants is necessary, specialized equipment may be required. This is equally true of large, inaccessible sites where the hydroseeding technique is useful if its limitations are recognized (Brooker, 1974; Sheldon and Bradshaw, 1977). Seeding rates must be adapted to suit species mixture composition and site conditions (50–100 kg ha^{-1}), but in general they will conform more to agricultural broadcasting rates (20–40 kg ha^{-1}) than to horticultural practices (250–500 kg ha^{-1}). Seeding rates higher than 100 kg ha^{-1} are rarely of value and do not compensate for inferior ground preparation, or other substrate limitations which remain uncorrected.

Temporary nurse crops which establish rapidly and aid sward development can be very useful, for example in the stabilization of continually shifting coastal sands (Brooks, 1976); but species selection must be planned according to the characteristics and requirements of individual sites and sowing density must be low to avoid competition with the main sward components. Sorghum, short rotation ryegrass (*Lolium italicum*) and cereal rye (*Secale cereale*) are commonly used. Vegetative propagation by planting tillers is a useful alternative method of stabilizing unstable materials, particularly for species with a low seed viability or restricted commercial interest. In the stabilization of coastal sands, marram grass (*Ammophila arenaria*) is established by hand planting, but in warmer climates sand spinifex (*Spinifex hirsutus*), which is a good seed producer, can be established very effectively from seed.

XIII. Species Selection and Use: Trees and Shrubs

Species selection must relate to land use objectives but as in the case of ground cover vegetation it must make allowances for specific site characteristics. The natural pioneers of abandoned sites can therefore be useful indicators. Commercially orientated planting schemes naturally rely on coniferous and broadleaved species of economic value in terms of timber production, wood fibre, pulpwood and associated products. Pines, firs and spruces are amongst the most important forest conifers and they tend to dominate softwood plantations on strip-mine spoils, though hardwoods including alder, birch and poplar are frequently interplanted or used in mixed shelter belt zones. Economically important hardwoods including sycamore, ash, beech and several oaks, are also widely used in commercial planting of derelict land materials but often with limited success in terms of productivity and timber quality.

Afforestation of derelict land in Britain has been on a very restricted scale because of different priorities and pressures on land redevelopment, and because of the diffuse distribution and small size of potentially suitable sites. By contrast, amenity planting has developed to a stage where it forms an integral part of many land reclamation schemes in both urban and rural environments. Unfortunately, establishment failures and inferior performance in the long term are not uncommon, and stem from a disregard of the need to relate species selection, planting material and techniques to the often severe constraints of derelict land substrates. The latter are so important that they demand priority (Schlatzer, 1973), particularly where species selected on substrate criteria conflict with landscape ideals and design. The significance of these considerations will become clear from a critical assessment of the success of tree planting, on derelict land in Britain, now being carried out.

On a worldwide scale the range of trees and shrubs suited to despoiled land is extensive and there are many recommendations (e.g. Hutnik and Davis, 1973). Species which are successful for degraded environments include *Betula pubescens* (birch), *Pinus nigra* (Austrian pine), *Pinus virginiana* (Virginia pine) and *Salix cinerea* (sallow) which are tolerant of low fertility. Nitrogen fixing trees such as *Robinia pseudo-acacia* (Black locust), and *Acacia saligna* (*A. cyanophylla*) in warm climates, are also important. Populations of trees and shrubs tolerant to zinc and other toxic metals are largely unknown. In such situations planting and amelioration treatments assume great importance.

Substrates which are prone to surface drought and leaching, or which exhibit extremes of nutrient deficiency or toxicity, may demand extensive treatment to ensure high rates of survival at establishment and satisfactory growth. Proven amelioration techniques involve planting into individual pockets or trenches filled with an innocuous amendment such as topsoil, subsoil or an organic matrix (e.g. sewage sludge), to which lime and fertilizer are added as appropriate (Humphries and Bradshaw, 1977; Johnson, 1977). If this approach is inappropriate, as for example with large scale planting programmes, treatment by surface amelioration or amendment incorporation is usually suitable. Where physical reshaping and surface treatment are impractical due to instability or topographical constraints, unconventional approaches can be equally acceptable. The value of pocket planting for slate and rock waste-tips in remote upland districts has already been discussed.

Many different planting methods have been used in derelict land situations. Transplanting of nursery stock comprising young seedlings or transplants, whips, or standard trees is the most common procedure, although direct seeding with surface mulching has been advocated for inaccessible quarry faces and is an accepted forestry practice for certain strip-mine spoils in North America. The optimum approach is not related exclusively to substrate and climatic considerations. Thus in amenity planting schemes the immediate visual gains from using advanced stock must be offset against the high probability of establishment failure, and increased expenditure from providing supporting stakes, ties and guards. For treatment of large areas, establishment from seed can be very effective because of the absence on disturbed soils of a competing vegetation cover. However, care has to be taken over choice of species, pre-treatment of seed to increase germination and time of sowing (Zarger *et al.*, 1973).

Fertilizer requirements show the same variation as in ground cover establishment and are dependent on all the factors controlling substrate fertility. Treatment rates should be kept to a minimum initially (100–300 g of NPK fertilizer (17:17:17) per 50 l of amendment) and can even be dispensed with if amendments of high inherent fertility are used (e.g. sewage sludge). Post-establishment maintenance applications of fertilizer (50–200 kg ha^{-1}, N:P$_2$O$_5$:K$_2$O) are usually critical: a good example is that of pine on spoil banks in Alabama where growth rates were doubled by addition of nitrogen and phosphorus. The effects of a decline in nitrogen status can be offset by including nitrogen-fixing tree species in the planting scheme. Considerable success has been achieved by the use of *Alnus glutinosa* and *Robinia pseudo-acacia* in particular. However, these will require nutrient addition, particularly phosphorus (Davis, 1973). Shrubs tolerant of very low nutrients such as *Ulex europaeus* and *Lupinus arboreus* may well prove extremely valuable (Gadgil 1971; Dancer *et al.*, 1977b). A continuous ground cover may be essential in the control of erosion during the early phases of tree and shrub development. Herbaceous legumes can be valuable because of their long term nitrogen supply, for instance in pulverized fuel ash (Hodgson and Buckley, 1975). However, stress caused by the herbaceous vegetation competing for nutrients, water and even light, must be minimized by careful selection of seed mixtures and, if necessary, by cutting or by controlled use of herbicides.

XIV. Species Selection and Use: Wild Material

Increasing attention is being given to the problems of restoring the original natural or semi-natural vegetation on land disturbed by mineral working. Whilst this approach is still in its infancy by comparison with other restoration techniques, changing social and legislative pressures in some countries suggest that it will assume even greater importance in the future. In many ways this is a more technically demanding landscape objective, for it assumes detailed knowledge not only of substrate characteristics and management needs, but also of community structure, species sensitivity, specificity and habitat requirements.

In some instances restoration of diverse semi-natural communities is impossible, either because land is released in a very difficult condition, or because the modified physical form is inconsistent with the original land use pattern. In other situations replacement will be possible provided that detailed knowledge is available concerning the biological composition of the undisturbed environment, and that seed or vegetative material of the native vegetation can be obtained and used effectively. There are also many circumstances where wild material has

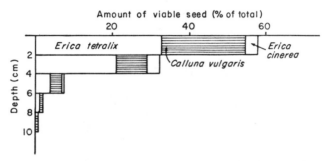

FIG. 19. The distribution of viable seeds of *Erica* and *Calluna* sp. in undisturbed moorland soil (Gillham, unpublished).

specific advantages over commercial stock, because the former will always be well adapted to its native habitat (Ludeke, 1973b; Farrell, 1977).

Recent research towards the objectives of true replacement has resulted in viable techniques for restoring heather moorland disturbed by pipeline installation (Gillham and Putwain, 1977), and the more complex heath vegetation of mineral-bearing coastal sands in Australia (Coaldrake, 1973).

In both situations the first consideration is to replace the surface soil layers in the correct sequence. The surface layer contains dormant seed and vegetative fragments which can provide propagules for much of the original vegetation, if removed and reinstated without delay. Since the buried seed is only in the top 5 cm (Fig. 19), this must be removed and replaced carefully, or it will be diluted with underlying material and many seeds will be buried too deeply to germinate and emerge after reinstatement. Some species will not be carried over in this way: these must be raised artificially and planted. This is now being carried out on a large scale, particularly for unusual but important species such as *Banksia serrata* and *B. integrifolia* (Newey and Lewis, 1976). Vegetational surveys are carried out before mining and after reinstatement to ensure that the original species balance is achieved. Nurse crops at low density are valuable, as well as some fertilizer treatments, particularly nitrogen, to replace that lost in the disturbance and to encourage growth of the wild species which otherwise may be slow in becoming established (Brooks, 1976).

There is no doubt that these techniques together with mechanical or manual collection of wild vegetative or seed material, at the appropriate time of the year, can provide enough material for complete restoration or at least for inoculation purposes; but further investigation is required. The reconstruction and colonization of semi-natural habitats is a field of growing interest and importance.

XV. AFTERCARE

The final step in restoration is to ensure that a self sustaining soil/plant ecosystem is established. If the initial problems have been overcome properly no further treatment should be required. It is self-evident that natural ecosystems are not given external assistance. But it is always possible that particular treatments will prove to be unsatisfactory or insufficient for the rapid development of a viable ecosystem.

Many of the problems that may arise have already been discussed. While individual sites will inevitably have specific constraints, the four crucial problems which are most likely to reoccur are nutrient deficiency, acidity, metal toxicity and salinity. The latter three are specific to particular sites and can be predicted on the basis of site characteristics.

Nutrient deficiency is more universal and because of this is not always understood or anticipated. A functioning ecosystem will have considerable quantities of nutrients within it, stored either in organic matter or soil mineral components from which they are eventually released by chemical or biological processes. Only a small fraction of this store is immediately available in soluble forms which can be absorbed by plants. Whether released by chemical or biological processes, the plant-available fraction will depend on the size of the store from which the nutrients are derived.

In derelict land materials the stores of readily available plant nutrients are very small indeed. The store of nitrogen may be non-existent and those of other nutrients very small. However nutrients such as phosphorus may be present locked up in minerals from which release is largely non-existent or very slow.

Restoration depends on increasing the size of these labile pools to a state where rates of release are adequate for vigorous plant growth.

For nitrogen this means a total value of the order 1000 kg ha^{-1} and for phosphorus 200 kg ha^{-1}. As we have seen these can be added in various ways, but there may be leaching losses of nitrogen, and fixation

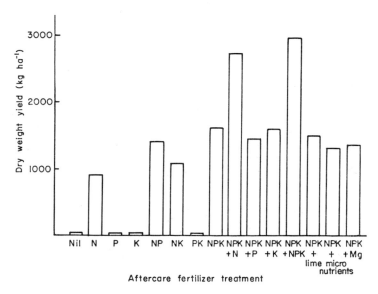

FIG. 20. The effect of different nutrients on the growth of a moribund grass sward established on china clay waste (Bradshaw *et al.*, 1975).

of phosphorus in unavailable forms. As a result, accumulation of appropriate stores of nutrients may not be achieved as rapidly or easily as expected.

From work on china clay wastes (Bradshaw *et al.*, 1975) and on a variety of colliery spoils and urban wastes (Bloomfield, unpublished), it is apparent that the nutrient most commonly in shortest supply, and leading to inferior growth, is nitrogen (Fig. 20). This deficiency can be overcome by fertilizer addition but the need for such treatment often goes unrecognized. Moreover, serious deterioration in ground cover vegetation is often attributed to causes other than nitrogen deficiency. Since nitrogen is the macronutrient required by plants in the largest amounts, and one which is lacking initially, nitrogen deficiency should be expected, and steps taken to remedy the problem.

Repeated fertilizer dressings are expensive and the use of legumes presents an obvious alternative which has already been discussed. However, many legumes are sensitive to deficiencies of calcium and phosphorus, and these must be added to maintain satisfactory growth (Fig. 21).

The recurrence of acidity, if not excessive, can be controlled by additions of lime, as in agricultural practice. The losses of calcium from normal soils and the assessment of lime requirement are well

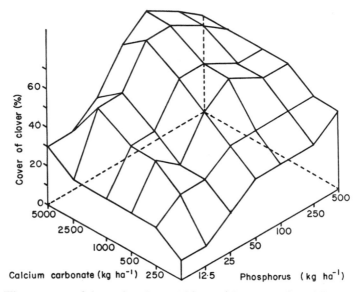

FIG. 21. The response of clover, in a 3-year-old grass/clover sward established on china clay sand waste, to aftercare additions of lime and phosphorus.

understood (Cooke, 1973). However, the regeneration of high levels of acidity, as on pyritic colliery spoils, cannot be treated with surface dressings of lime because of its immobility. It may then be necessary to rip the surface of the spoils and incorporate lime to an appropriate depth.

Since there is no readily available way of eliminating metals, recurrence of metal toxicity is difficult to deal with. However, as has already been indicated, phosphate and organic matter both complex heavy metals (Goodman *et al.*, 1973), so that vegetation already established on metalliferous waste is more likely to persist if high rates of phosphate fertilizer are applied. Not only the phosphate but also the increased organic matter produced by enhancement of plant growth will modify the toxicity.

Salinity, regenerated by interactions between the products of pyrite oxidation and native carbonates, will not be a problem in climates where precipitation is high. In arid climates it can be removed by irrigation, but if the soluble salts are not to return sufficient water will have to be provided to effect complete leaching from the soil profile, and the water table must be kept low (below 3 m) by adequate drainage (USDA, 1954).

Aftercare management of the vegetation cover is obviously necessary. In the absence of grazing or other management grass swards will degenerate and become invaded by shrubs: in many situations there will

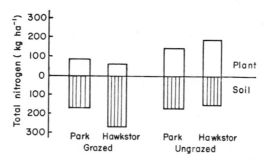

FIG. 22. The effect of grazing on the nitrogen accumulation in grass swards established on china clay sand waste.

be substantial lock-up of nutrients in undecayed organic matter. This will not occur if grazing takes place (Fig. 22). These sort of changes must be anticipated and planned for by appropriate aftercare treatments.

XVI. CONCLUSIONS

The reclamation of derelict and degraded land involves overcoming many problems: economic, social, technical and biological. The biological problem is to restore a functional and self-sustaining soil/plant ecosystem. Although the original soil should always be replaced when this is possible, there are many situations where this policy is not practicable.

The establishment of vegetation on a raw waste material, often originating from hard rocks far below the earth's surface, can seem a daunting prospect. But the natural processes of colonization of glacial and derelict land materials indicate that the restoration of a vegetation cover is quite feasible. However, natural colonization is nearly always slow, and the formation of fertile productive soils by natural processes is even more slow, because of physical and chemical limitations to plant growth.

If these limitations can be identified, they can be treated effectively and economically, as we have seen. The reclamation of derelict land has therefore three distinct elements which must be recognized if the end product is to be successful. The first step is identification of critical limiting factors, which can be by both analysis and experimentation. The latter can itself be an indicator of appropriate treatments. Only after this can the second step, the treatment, be undertaken. Inevitably, treatments often have to be applied without full and complete justification. In this case further experimentation should be undertaken by modification of the treatments themselves, at least over small areas. This then leads to the third step, aftercare. While the aim of many restoration schemes is to establish an ecosystem which requires no further maintenance, it is difficult to achieve this in practice with a single treatment. Attention to undesirable trends within the developing system is therefore essential.

The restoration of fully functioning soil/plant ecosystems on material as skeletal and deficient as those we have discussed is a considerable challenge, but the success of so many schemes in so many different areas of the world indicates that it is a challenge that can be met, providing sufficiently critical and well-planned exploratory investigations are undertaken.

References

Allen, S. E., Grimshaw, H. M., Parkinson, J. A. and Quarmby, C. (1974). "Chemical Analysis of Ecological Materials." Blackwell, Oxford.

Antonovics, J., Bradshaw, A. D. and Turner, R. G. (1971). Heavy metal tolerance in plants. *Adv. Ecol. Res.* **7**, 1–85.

Armiger, W. H., Jones, J. N. and Bennett, O. L. (1976). "Revegetation of Land Disturbed by Strip Mining of Coal in Appalachia." U.S. Dept. Agriculture, Agric. Research Service, Beltsville.

Associated Portland Cement Manufacturers (1970). "Dunbar Works—A Study in Conservation." Blue Circle Group, London.

Backhouse, G. and Nimmo, M. (1956). Afforestation of ironstone workings in Northamptonshire. *J. Forestry Comm.* **25**, 125–130.

Berg, W. A. (1973). Evaluation of phosphorus and potassium soil fertility tests on coal-mine spoils. *In* "Ecology and Reclamation of Devastated Land", (Hutnik, R. J. and Davis, G., Eds.), Vol. I, pp. 93–104. Gordon and Breach, New York.

Blesing, N. V., Lackey, J. A. and Spry, A. H. (1975). Rehabilitation of an abandoned mine site. *In* "Minerals and the Environment", (Jones, M. J., Ed.), pp. 1–21. Inst. Mining and Metallurgy, London.

Bradshaw, A. D. (1977). Conservation problems in the future. *Proc. Roy. Soc. Lond.* B **197**, 77–96.

Bradshaw, A. D. and Chadwick, M. J. (1979). "The Restoration of Land." Blackwell, Oxford. In press.

Bradshaw, A. D. and Handley, J. F. (1972). Low cost grassing of sites awaiting redevelopment. *Landsc. Des.* **99**, 17–19.

Bradshaw, A. D., Dancer, W. S., Handley, J. F. and Sheldon, J. C. (1975). The biology of land revegetation and the reclamation of the china clay wastes in Cornwall. *In* "The Ecology of Resource Degradation and Renewal", (Chadwick. M. J. and Goodman, G. T., Eds), Symp. Brit. Ecol. Soc. Vol. XV, pp. 363–384, Blackwell, Oxford.

Brooker, R. (1974). Hydraulic seeding techniques: an appraisal. *Landsc. Des.* **108**, 30–32.

Brooks, D. R. (1976). Rehabilitation following mineral sand mining on North Stradbrooke Island, Queensland. *In* "Landscaping and Land Use Planning as related to Mining Operations", (Australasian Inst. Min. Metall, Ed.), pp. 93–104. Australasian Inst. Min. Metall, Adelaide.

Caruccio, F. T. (1973). Characterization of strip-mine drainage by pyrite grain size and chemical quality of existing groundwater. *In* "Ecology and Reclamation of Devastated Land", (Hutnik, R. J. and Davis, G., Eds), Vol. I, pp. 193–226. Gordon and Breach, New York.

Chadwick, M. J., Cornwell, S. M. and Palmer, M. E. (1969). Exchangeable acidity in unburnt colliery spoil. *Nature*, Lond. **222**, 161.

Coaldrake, J. E. (1973). Conservation problems of coastal sand and opencast mining. *In* "Nature Conservation in the Pacific", (CSIRO, Ed.), pp. 229–314. Australian National University Canberra.

Cooke, G. W. (1973). "The Control of Soil Fertility." Crosby Lockwood, London.

Cope, F. (1961). "The agronomic value of power station waste ash." Ph.D. thesis, University of Leeds.

Cornwell, S. D. and Kiff, J. (1973). Trees and shrubs for difficult sites in Denmark. *Town Planning Rev.* **44**, 221–230.

Crocker, R. L. and Major, J. (1955). Soil development in relation to vegetation and surface age at Glacier Bay, Alaska. *J. Ecol.* **43**, 427–448.

Dancer, W. S. (1975). Leaching losses of ammonium and nitrate in the reclamation of sand spoils in Cornwall. *J. Env. Qual.* **4**, 499–504.

Dancer, W. S., Handley, J. F. and Bradshaw, A. D. (1977a). Nitrogen accumulation in kaolin mining wastes in Cornwall. I. Natural communities. *Plant and Soil.* **48**, 153–167.

Dancer, W. S., Handley, J. F. and Bradshaw, A. D. (1977b). Nitrogen accumulation in kaolin mining wastes in Cornwall. II. Forage legumes. *Plant and Soil.* **48**, 303–314.

Date, R. A. (1970). Microbiological problems in the inoculation and nodulation of legumes. *Plant and Soil.* **32**, 705–725.

Davies, B. E. and Roberts, L. J. (1975). Heavy metals in soils and radish in a mineralised limestone area of Wales, Great Britain. *Sci. Tot. Environ.* **4**, 249–261.

Davis, B. N. K. (1976). Wildlife, urbanisation and industry. *Biol. Conserv.* **10**, 249–291.

Davis, G. (1973). Comparison of fall and spring planting on strip mine spoils in the bituminous region of Pennsylvania. *In* "Ecology and Reclamation of Devastated Land", (Hutnik, R. J. and Davis, G., Eds), Vol. I, pp. 525–538. Gordon and Breach, New York.

Day, R. J. (1963). Spruce seedling mortality caused by adverse summer microclimate in the Rocky Mountains. Forestry Res. Branch. Publ. 1003, Can. Dep. Forestry.

Dean, K. C., Havens, R. and Valdez, E. G. (1971. USBM finds many routes to stabilizing mineral wastes. *Min. Engng* N.Y. **23**, 61–63.

Dean, K. C., Havens, R., Harper, K. T. and Rosenbaum, J. B. (1973). Vegetative stabilization of mill mineral wastes. *In* "Ecology and Reclamation of Devastated Land", (Hutnik, R. J. and Davis, G., Eds), Vol. II, pp. 119–136. Gordon and Breach, New York.

Deely, D. J. and Borden, F. Y. (1973). High surface temperatures on strip mine spoils. *In* "Ecology and reclamation of devastated Land", (Hutnik, R. J. and Davis, G., Eds.), Vol. I, pp. 69–77. Gordon and Breach, New York.

Department of the Environment. Ministry of Agriculture Fisheries and Food and Sand and Gravel Association (1977). "Joint Agricultural Land Restoration Experiments." Progress Report No. 1. (1974–77). Ministry of Agriculture, Fisheries and Food, London.

Doubleday, G. P. (1971). Soil forming materials—their nature and assessment. *In* "Landscape Reclamation", Vol. I, pp. 70–83. IPC Press, Guildford, Surrey.

Doubleday, G. P. (1972). Development and management of soils on pit heaps. *In* "Landscape Reclamation", Vol. II, pp. 25–35. IPC Press, Guildford, Surrey.

Doubleday, G. P. (1973). Top soil sometimes still the best answer in reclamation. *Surveyor* **142**, 31–32.

Down, C. G. and Stocks, J. (1976). "The Environmental Problems of Tailings Disposal at Metal Mines." DoE Research Report No. 17. Department of the Environment, London.

Down, C. G. and Stocks, J. (1977). "Environmental Impact of Mining." Applied Science Publishers, London.

Environmental Protection Agency (1973). "Processes, Procedures and Methods to Control Pollution from Mining Activities." U.S. Environmental Protection Agency, Washington.

Environmental Protection Agency (1974). "Environmental Protection in Surface Mining of Coal." U.S. Environmental Protection Agency, Cincinnati.

Farrell, T. P. (1977). Rehabilitation of Mine Wastes in a Monsoonal Semi-Arid Climate Environmental Workshop (1977). Australian Mining Industry Council, Canberra.

Fitter, A. H. (1974). A relationship between phosphorus requirement, the immobilisation of added phosphate and the phosphate buffering capacity of colliery shales. *J. Soil. Sci.* **25**, 41–50.

Gadgil, R. L. (1969). Tolerance of heavy metals and the reclamation of industrial waste. *J. Appl. Ecol.* **6**, 247–259.

Gadgil, R. L. (1971). The nutritional role of *Lupinus arboreus* in coastal sand dune forestry. 3. Nitrogen distribution in the ecosystem before tree planting. *Plant and Soil.* **35**, 113–126.

Gardner, H. W. (1959). Manuring barley on chalk. *Agriculture*, Lond. **66**, 396–7.

Gemmell, R. P. (1973). Colliery shale revegetation techniques. *Surveyor* **142**, 27–29.

Gemmell, R. P. (1974). Revegetation of derelict land polluted by a chromate smelter. Pt. II: Techniques of revegetation of chromate smelter waste. *Env. Pollut.* **6**, 31–7.

Gemmell, R. P. (1975). Establishment of grass on waste from iron smelting. *Env. Pollut.* **8**, 35–44.

Gemmell, R. P. (1977). "Colonization of Industrial Wasteland." Arnold, London.

Geyer, W. A. (1973). Tree species performance on Kansas coal spoils. *In* "Ecology and

Reclamation of Devastated Land", (Hutnik, R. J. and Davis, G., Eds.), Vol. II, pp. 81–90. Gordon and Breach, New York.

Gillham, D. A. and Putwain, P. D. (1977). Restoring moorland disturbed by pipeline installation. *Landsc. Des.* **119,** 34–36.

Glover, H. G. (1975). Acidic and ferruginous mine drainages. *In* "The Ecology of Resource Degradation and Renewal", (Chadwick, M. J. and Goodman, G. T., Eds.), Symp. Brit. Ecol. Soc. Vol. XV, pp. 173–196. Blackwell, Oxford.

Goodman, G. T. and Bray, S. A. (1975). "Ecological Aspects of the Reclamation of Derelict Land." Geo. Abstracts, Norwich.

Goodman, G. T., Pitcairn, C. E. R. and Gemmell, R. P. (1973). Ecological factors affecting growth on sites contaminated by heavy metals. *In* "Ecology and reclamation of devastated land", (Hutnik, R. J. and Davis, G., Eds), Vol. II, pp. 149–73. Gordon and Breach, New York.

Green, J. T., Blaser, R. E. and Perry, H. D. (1973). "Establishing persistent vegetation on cuts and fills along West Virginia highways—final report." Dept. Agronomy, Virginia Polytechnic Institute and State University, Blacksburg, Virginia.

Harper, J. L. (1977). "Population Biology of Plants." Academic Press, London and New York.

Harris, J. A. and Leigh, J. H. (1976). Stability of mine residues in Broken Hill, New South Wales. *In* "Landscaping and Land Use Planning as related to Mining Operations", (Australasian Inst. Min. Metall., Ed.), pp. 151–166. Australasian Institute of Mining and Metallurgy, Parkville, Victoria, Australia.

Harrison, J. (1974). "The Sevenoaks Gravel Pit Reserve." WAGBI, Chester.

Henesal, P. and Spake, A. (1974). "Engasonnement de l'emprise routiere". Ministere de l'Equipement, Laboratoire Central des Ponts et Chausées, Paris.

Hill, J. R. C. (1977a). Factors that limit plant growth on copper, gold and nickel mining wastes in Rhodesia. *Trans. Inst. Min. Metall.* **86A,** 98–109.

Hill, J. R. C. (1977b). Establishment of vegetation on copper, gold and nickel mining wastes in Rhodesia. *Trans. Inst. Min. Metall.* **86A,** 135–145.

Hill, J. R. C. and Nothard, W. F. (1973). The Rhodesian approach to the vegetating of slimes dams. *J. S. Afr. Inst. Min. Metall.* **74,** 197–208.

Hillestad, K. O. (1973). "Sprengstein Tipp og Landskap." Norges Vassdrags—og Elektristitetsvesen, Oslo.

Hodgson, D. R. and Buckley, G. P. (1975). A practical approach towards the establishment of trees and shrubs on pulverised fuel ash. *In* "The Ecology of Resource Degradation and Renewal", (Chadwick, M. J. and Goodman, G. T., Eds.), Symp. Brit. Ecol. Soc. Vol. XV, pp. 305–329. Blackwell, Oxford.

Hodgson, D. R. and Townsend, W. N. (1973). The amelioration and revegetation of pulverised fuel ash. *In* "The Ecology and Reclamation of Devastated Land", (Hutnik, R. J. and Davis, G., Eds.), Vol. II, pp. 247–271. Gordon and Breach, New York.

Hodgson, D. R., Holliday, R. and Cope, F. (1963). The reclamation of land covered with pulverised fuel ash: the influence of soil depth on crop performance. *J. Agric. Sci.* **61,** 299–308.

Horn, M. L. (1968). "The Revegetation of Highly Acid Spoil Banks in the Bituminous Coal Region of Central Pennsylvania." M.S. thesis, Pennsylvania State University.

Hudson, N. W. (1971). "Soil Conservation." Batsford, London.

Humphreys, M. O. and Bradshaw, A. D. (1977). Genetic potential for solving problems of soil mineral stress: heavy metal toxicity. *In* "Plant Adaptation to

Mineral Stress in Problem Soils", (Wright, M. J., Ed.), pp. 95–105. Cornell University, New York.

Humphries, R. N. (1977). The development of vegetation in limestone quarries. *Quarry Mgmt. and Prods.* **4,** 43–47.

Humphries, R. N. and Bradshaw, A. D. (1977). The establishment of woody plants on derelict land. *Scientific Hort.* **29,** 23–33.

Hutnik, R. J. and Davis, G. (Eds.) (1973). "Ecology and Reclamation of Devastated Land." Gordon and Breach, New York.

Jacoby, H. (1973). Growth and nutrition of beech trees on sites of different soil texture in the lignite area of the Rhineland. *In* "Ecology and Reclamation of Devastated Land", Vol. I, pp. 391–412. Gordon and Breach, New York.

James, A. L. (1966). Stabilizing mine dumps with vegetation. *Endeavour,* **25,** 154–157.

James, A. L. and Mrost, M. (1965). Control of acidity of tailings dams and dumps as a precursor to stabilization by vegetation. *J. S. Afr. Inst. Min. Metqll.* **65,** 489–495.

Jeffrey, D. W., Maybury, M. and Levinge, D. (1975). Ecological approach to mining waste revegetation. *In* "Minerals and the Environment", (Jones, M. J., Ed.), pp. 371–385. Institute of Mining and Metallurgy, London.

Johnson, M. S. (1977). "Establishment of vegetation on metalliferous fluorspar mine tailings." Ph.D. thesis, University of Liverpool.

Johnson, M. S. and Bradshaw, A. D. (1977). Prevention of heavy metal pollution from mine wastes by vegetative stabilization. *Trans. Inst. Min. Metall.* **86A,** 47–55.

Johnson, M. S., Bradshaw, A. D. and Handley, J. F. (1976). Revegetation of metalliferous fluorspar mine tailings. *Trans. Inst. Min. Metall.* **85A,** 32–37.

Johnson, M. S., McNeilly, T. and Putwain, P. D. (1977). Revegetation of metalliferous mine spoil contaminated by lead and zinc. *Environ. Pollut.* **12,** 261–77.

Jones, A. N. and Howells, W. R. (1975). The partial recovery of the metal polluted River Rheidol. *In* "The Ecology of Resource Degradation and Renewal", (Chadwick, M. J. and Goodman, G. T., Eds.), Symp. Brit. Ecol. Soc. Vol. XV. pp. 443–459. Blackwell, Oxford.

Knabe, W. (1973). Investigations of soils and tree growth on five deep mine refuse piles in the hard-coal region of the Ruhr. *In* "Ecology and Reclamation of Devastated Land", (Hutnik, R. J. and Davis, G., Eds.), Vol. I, pp. 307–324. Gordon and Breach, New York.

Kohnke, H. (1950). The reclamation of coal mine spoils. *Adv. agron.* **2,** 317–349.

Lal, R. (1977). Soil conserving versus soil degrading crops and soil management for erosion control. *In* "Soil Conservation and Management in the Humid Tropics", (Greenland, D. J. and Lal, R., Eds.), pp. 81–86. Wiley, New York.

Lambert, J. M., Jennings, I. N., Smith, C. T., Green, C. and Hutchinson, J. N. (1960) "The Making of the Broads." *R. Geog. Soc. Res. Series* 3. Royal Geographical Society, London.

Leisman, G. A. (1957). A vegetation and soil chronosequence on the Mesabi Iron Range spoil banks, Minnesota. *Ecol. Monogr.* **27,** 221–245.

Limstrom, G. A. (1960). "Forestation of strip-mined land in the Central States." Forest Serv. Agric. Handbk. 166, United States Dept. Agric. U.S. Dept. Agric. U.S. Govnmt. Printing Office, Washington DC.

Ludeke, K. L. (1973a). Soil properties of materials in copper mine tailings dikes. *Mining Congr. J.* **59**(8), 30–37.

Ludeke, K. L. (1973b). Vegetative stabilisation of copper mine tailing disposal terms of Pima Mining Company. *In* "Tailings Disposal Today", (Aplin, C. L. and Argall, G. O., Eds.), pp. 377–408. Miller Freeman, San Francisco.

McKee, W. H., Blaser, R. E. and Barkley, D. G. (1964). Mulches for steep cut slopes. *Highw. Res. Rec.* **93**, 38–43.

Medvick, C. (1973). Selecting plant species for revegetating surface coal mined lands in Indiana—a forty year record. *In* "Ecology and Reclamation of Devastated Land", (Hutnik, R. J. and Davis, G. Eds), Vol. II, pp. 65–80. Gordon and Breach, New York.

Ministry of Agriculture, Fisheries and Food (1967). "Potential Transpiration." *Tech. Bull. No.* 16. HMSO, London.

Ministry of Agriculture, Fisheries and Food (1971). "The restoration of sand and gravel pits." Ministry of Agriculture, Fisheries and Food, London.

Ministry of Agriculture, Fisheries and Food (1973). "Fertilizer Recommendations." *Bulletin No.* 209, HMSO, London.

Moore, N. W. (1962). The heaths of Dorset and their conservation. *J. Ecol.* **50**, 369–392.

National Coal Board (1974). "Opencast Operations—I." National Coal Board, Opencast Executive, Harrow. Eng.

Neumann, U. (1973). Succession of soil fauna in afforested spoil banks of the brown-coal district of Cologne. *In* "Ecology and Reclamation of Devastated Land", (Hutnik, R. J. and Davis, G., Eds), Vol. I, pp. 335–348. Gordon and Breach, New York.

Newey, C. O. and Lewis, J. W. (1976). Landforms and revegetation after mineral sand mining. *In* "Landscaping and Land Use Planning as Related to Mining Operations", (Australasian Inst. Min. Metall, Ed.), pp. 105–118. Australasian Inst. Min. Metall, Adelaide.

Nielson, R. F. and Peterson, H. B. (1972). Treatment of mine tailings to promote vegetative stabilization. *Bull. Univ. Utah. Agric. Expt. Sta.* No. **485.**

Peters, T. H. (1970). Using vegetation to stabilize mine tailings. *J. Soil. and Water Cons.* **25**, 65–66.

Peterson, H. B. and Nielson, R. F. (1973). Toxicities and deficiencies in mine tailings. *In* "Ecology and Reclamation of Devastated Land", (Hutnik, R. J. and Davis, G., Eds), Vol. I, pp. 15–26. Gordon and Breach, New York.

Petsch, G. (1974). Colliery spoil heaps in the Rhur, vegetational establishment and integration in the landscape as a means of improving the environment in densely populated conurbations. *In* "Green Colliery Spoil Banks in the Ruhr" (S.V.R., Ed.), pp. 201–223. Siedlungsverband Ruhrkohlknbezirk, Essen.

Ratcliffe, D. A. (1974). Ecological effects of mineral exploitation in the United Kingdom and their significance to nature conservation. *Proc. Roy. Soc. Lond.* **A.339**, 355–372.

Richardson, J. A. (1958). The effect of temperature on the growth of plants on pit heaps. *J. Ecol.* **46**, 537–546.

Richardson, J. A. and Dicker, R. J. (1972). Long term management of grass and tree plantations on colliery spoil heaps. *In* "Landscape Reclamation" Vol. II, pp. 53–63. IPC Press, Guildford, Surrey.

Richardson, J. B. (1974). "Metal Mining." Allen Lane, London.

Schlatzer, G. (1973). Some experiences with various species in Danish reclamation work. *In* "Ecology and Reclamation of Devastated Land", (Hutnik, R. J., and Davis, G., Eds), Vol. II, pp. 33–64. Gordon and Breach, New York.

Schmehl, W. R. and McCaslin, B. D. (1973). Some properties of spent oil shale significant to plant growth. *In* "Ecology and Reclamation of Devastated Land",

(Hutnik, R. J. and Davis, G., Eds), Vol. I, pp. 27–44. Gordon and Breach, New York.

Sheldon, J. C. (1975). The reclamation of slate waste. *Nature in Wales.* **14,** 160–168.

Sheldon, J. C. and Bradshaw, A. D. (1976). The reclamation of slate waste tips by tree planting. *J. Inst. Lands. Arch.* **113,** 31–33.

Sheldon, J. C. and Bradshaw, A. D. (1977). The development of a hydraulic seeding technique for unstable sand slopes. I. Effects of fertilisers, mulches and stabilisers. *J. Appl. Ecol.* **14,** 905–918.

Smith, R. A. H. (1973). "The reclamation of old metalliferous mine workings using tolerant plant populations." Ph.D. thesis, University of Liverpool.

Smith, R. A. H. and Bradshaw, A. D. (1972). Stabilization of toxic mine wastes by the use of tolerant plant populations. *Trans. Inst. Min. Metall.* **81A,** 230–237.

Smith, R. M. Tryon, E. H. and Tyner, E. H. (1971). "Soil Development on Mine Spoil." *Agric. Expt. Sta. Bull.* No. **604T.** West Virginia University.

Stewart, W. D. P. (1966). "Nitrogen fixation in plants." Athlone Press, University of London.

Street, H. E. and Goodman, G. T. (1967). Techniques of revegetation in the Lower Swansea Valley. *In* "The Lower Swansea Valley Project", (Hilton, K. J., Ed.), pp. 71–110. Longmans Green, London.

Tansley, A. G. and Adamson, R. S. (1925). Studies of the vegetation of the English Chalk. III. The chalk grasslands of the Hampshire-Sussex border. *J. Ecol.* **13,** 177–223.

Thiele, H. U. (1964). Bodentiere und Bodenfruchtbarkeit. *Naturwiss Rundschau.* **17,** 224–230.

Townsend, W. N. and Hodgson, D. R. (1973). Edaphological problems associated with deposits of pulverised fuel ash. *In* "Ecology and Reclamation of Devastated Land", (Hutnik, R. J. and Davis, G., Eds), Vol. I, pp. 45–56. Gordon and Breach, New York.

United States Department of Agriculture (1954). "Diagnosis and improvement of saline and alkali soils." U.S. Dept. Agr. Handb. No. 60. US Govnmt. Printing Office, Washington DC.

Whincup, G. T. (1974). Some aspects of opencast coal mining in South Wales. *Proc. South Wales Inst. Eng.* **86,** 15–34.

Wild, H. and Wiltshire, G. H. (1971). The problem of vegetating Rhodesian mine dumps examined. *Chamber of Mines. J.* **13,** 26–30.

Wilkins, D. A. (1957). A technique for the measurement of lead tolerance in plants. *Nature, London.* **180,** 37.

Williams, P. J. (1975). Investigations into the nitrogen cycle in colliery spoil. *In* "The Ecology of Resource Degradation and Renewal" (Chadwick, M. J. and Goodman, G. T., Eds.). Symp. Br. Ecol. Soc. Vol. XV pp. 259–274. Blackwell, Oxford.

Wright, M. J. (1976). "Plant Adaptation to Mineral Stress in Problem Soils", (Wright, M. J., Ed.). Cornell Univ. Agric. Exp. Sta. Ithaca, New York.

Zarger, T. G., Bengtson, G. W., Allen, J. C. and Mays, D. A. (1973). Use of fertilisers to speed pine establishment on reclaimed coal-mine spoil in northeastern Alabama. II. Field experiments. *In* "Ecology and Reclamation of Devastated Land", (Hutnik, R. J. and Davis, G., Eds), Vol. II, pp. 227–236. Gordon and Breach, New York.

The Quantification of Production Constraints Associated with Plant Diseases

W. CLIVE JAMES

Canadian International Development Agency,
Ottawa, Canada

P. S. TENG

Department of Agricultural Microbiology,
Lincoln College, Canterbury, New Zealand

I. INTRODUCTION

Ever since man changed from his nomadic ways to agriculture plant diseases, which represent a production constraint, have been a significant factor in his social development. Agriculture probably did not begin as a spontaneous activity but evolved as a natural extension and intensification of what man had been endeavouring to achieve over a long period of time (Harlan, 1976). Simultaneously agricultural systems evolved, based on crop monocultures (White, 1967), where the genetic homogeneity of crops increased as plant breeding methods improved. The vulnerability of these monocultures with respect to diseases and pests has been well discussed by Robinson (1976). As recently as 1970 the southern corn leaf-blight epidemics in the USA (Tatum, 1971) have reconfirmed that diseases can seriously disrupt world food supplies and trade patterns, despite the fact that plant protection measures are regularly practised. During the last 150 years there have been a few notable examples of devastating effects resulting from disease epidemics. In 1845 the potato crop in Ireland was completely destroyed by the late blight disease (*Phytophthora infestans*) and famine resulted. The coffee rust disease caused by *Hemileia vastatrix* led to a complete destruction of the coffee industry in Ceylon in 1870. Coffee production in Central America may now be threatened by the same disease, which was first observed in Nicaragua in 1976. Other examples are given by Carefoot and Sprott (1969) in their book "Famine on the Wind".

Although it is generally recognized that plant diseases constitute major constraints to food and fibre production, literature searches reveal that there are very few reliable data to identify and quantify these losses. This is a paradox because crop losses were the major reason for initiating studies on plant diseases and yet the quantification of production constraints has been grossly neglected. The lack of reliable data to define the importance of diseases in world agriculture may well have retarded the progress of plant protection as much as any other single factor. Identification and quantification of crop production constraints, associated with plant diseases and other elements in plant protection like weeds and pests, are a prerequisite to the development of any rational and economical plant protection programme. Irrespective of whether the control measures involved pesticides, resistant varieties, or integrated pest control, the magnitude and cost of the loss must be known so that it can be compared with the cost of control. Decision makers, especially those at a policy making level, must have reliable estimates of the crop production constraints in order to assign meaningful priorities and allocate resources in such a way as to optimize the returns for any given investment in research and development. Similarly the farmer must know the cost of the projected loss before he can decide how much to spend on a control programme. From a philosophical standpoint plant pathology can be regarded as a practical exercise in problem solving, aimed at the economic control of plant diseases. There are two elements involved in the resolution of a problem —the definition and the solution. Within the context of plant pathology the quantification of production constraints associated with plant diseases is the definition element. It is therefore a vital component in any plant protection programme because it is undesirable and illogical to attempt to solve a problem that has not yet been defined (James, 1979).

Within a global context there are probably more compelling reasons for the development of technology which will allow us to reliably identify our plant protection needs. Mankind is becoming increasingly conscious of its diminishing energy supplies and most of the current fungicides and other pesticides are derived from non-renewable petroleum products (Morrison and Boyd, 1973). There is probably even more concern about the increasing use of pesticides and the resulting long-term pollution problems. In 1973–74 the world pesticide market was estimated at US$7 billion but a more recent estimate would suggest that this has increased to approximately US$10 billion. The following table (Cramer, 1975) characterizes the use of pesticides on a global basis.

TABLE I   World pesticide usage (%)

By crop	%	By pesticide	%	By region	%
Cotton	21	Herbicides	39	USA/Canada	31
Maize	20	Insecticides	33	West Europe	22
Fruit/Citrus	16	Fungicides	10	Asia	16
Rice	8	Others (including hygiene and household)	18	East Europe	13
			100		
Potatoes	8			Latin America	12
Wheat	7			Africa	5
Soya beans	4			Australia and	
Others	16			New Zealand	1
	100				100

It is noteworthy that approximately 50% of total pesticides are used in developing countries with weak economies which are obliged to use limited foreign exchange to purchase pesticides from the industrialized countries. It is particularly important to note that 66% of the total pesticides applied to crops are used on food crops. In the long term the continuous input of high levels of pesticides into food production systems can create situations which are ecologically tenuous (Alexander, 1974).

However in the short- to medium-term fungicides and other pesticides must continue to remain one of the priority inputs for sustaining world food production, which currently is not keeping pace with demand. In 1975 the food deficit of the developing countries of the world was estimated to be 37 Mt, but this is expected to rise to between 120–145 Mt by 1990 (International Food Policy Research Institute, 1977). One way to attempt a partial resolution of this dilemma of high pesticide consumption, produced from non-renewable resources, and inadequate food supplies, is to rationalize fungicide usage. This rationalization would be based on an objective assessment of the plant protection needs and the corresponding benefits resulting from control measures. To achieve this objective it is essential to obtain a knowledge of the relationship between the amount of disease and the resulting yield/quality loss. Subsequently production constraints can be quantified and control strategies developed where both the benefits and corresponding hazards are objectively assessed. Although the major part of this review will deal with the details of assessing production constraints due to diseases, the subject will be introduced within a broader context thus allowing the reader to relate the specific details reported in the latter part of this review, to the overall philosophy of assessing production constraints.

The arguments for quantifying production constraints associated with plant diseases can be applied equally well to pests and weeds, and indeed any other constraint. It is important to note that production is the product of a multi-factorial equation in which all factors can be constrained and interact with each other. We may refer to plant protection constraints, agronomic constraints, economic constraints or infrastructure and political constraints. The latter constraints do not lend themselves as easily to quantification as the former but nevertheless assessments or judgements can be made. For the purpose of this review the self-explanatory organogramme (Fig. 1) shows how a programme can be developed to quantify the production constraints associated with pests, weeds and diseases within the context of the total production system. The objective is to establish a crop loss profile to indicate the relative importance of the different production constraints. For example the particular programme featured in Fig. 1 is capable of assessing the relative importance of pests, weeds and diseases and also the importance of the different pests, weeds and diseases within the respective groups. The organogramme is simply a model for demonstrating how these objectives can be achieved for plant protection elements; however in practice other factors, e.g., agronomy, economics, could be added to the programme to make it more comprehensive.

Figure 1 is made up of independent components thus allowing a flexible approach to cater for the diverse needs and objectives of a production constraint programme. In the vertical plane of Fig. 1 there are two major elements A and B. The crop loss profile is quantified in A by means of a two-part programme consisting of an experiment and a survey. In the experimental phase a network of field experiments is conducted in farmers' fields to obtain information for estimating crop losses. Such experiments would be easier to conduct at experimental stations but may not be representative of the constraints to increased production operative at the farm level, which the programme is specifically designed to identify. A typical experiment could include untreated plots and plots treated with fungicides, insecticides and herbicides separately or in combination. The pesticides are used only as tools to control to various extents the diseases, weeds and pests and also to establish the potential yield of the "healthy" crop in the absence of constraints. A comprehensive set of data is obtained for each experiment to characterize the pest, weed and disease status throughout the season. The data from these experiments can be accumulated over a period of years and used to generate crop loss models which characterize the relationship between the amount of disease/pest/weed and loss in yield. The limited number of experiments in the network will not allow valid conclusions to be drawn regarding the importance of pests, weeds and diseases on a national or regional basis. Therefore the experimental data can be supplemented by a survey of representative farmers' fields where the incidence or severity of pests, weeds and diseases will be assessed at appropriate times throughout the season. The same assessment methods should be utilized in the experiments and the surveys so that the data are compatible. With the aid of the yield determinations from the network of experiments, the survey data can then be interpreted to assess the importance of crop losses occurring in a representative sample of fields. Survey data from consecutive years can be used to identify variations from year to year, between regions, or differences due to cultural practices etc. Risk-prone areas can be identified and surveillance systems can then be concentrated in these areas to increase the sensitivity of the overall survey system. Collated information obtained from the experimental network and survey should allow the major constraints to be identified so that priorities can be assigned and effort directed to the solution of major problems.

The crop loss profile shown by A in Fig. 1 defines the problem but will to some extent reflect the usage of control practices used by farmers. It is equally important to determine the usage and specifications of control measures. This can best be done by conducting a survey of

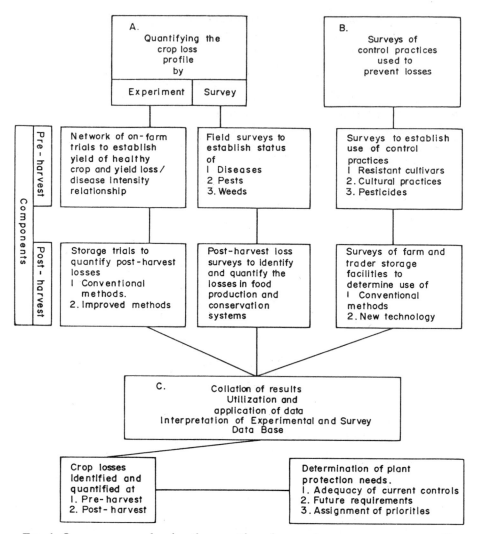

Fig. 1. Organogramme showing the operation of a crop-loss programme to quantify the production constraints associated with pests, weeds and diseases within the context of the total production system.

representative farms as shown in B in Fig. 1 to monitor the use of different control measures including cultural practices, resistant varieties, pesticides and any other practice leading to control. Such a survey will lead to a further understanding of how far, and in what way farmers have accepted control practices. It also may indicate what key factors motivate farmers to introduce plant protection programmes.

The programme proposed in Fig. 1 will give rise to information consisting of the crop loss profile (A) and the survey data on farmers' control practices (B). These data must be collated (C) before utilization and application. The collated data can then be used to judge the adequacy of current control programmes. Furthermore, and probably more important, the same data can be used to assess future plant protection needs and provide policy makers with information that will allow sound and efficient planning. At the same time the network of experiments can be used to demonstrate to the farmers the importance of pests, diseases and weeds as factors which limit production.

Recently much emphasis has been focused on the more easily recognizable post-harvest as opposed to pre-harvest losses, but little information is available about the relative importance of these types of loss in the total production system. The two components in the horizontal axis in Fig. 1 show how either or both types of harvest loss can be quantified in the same production system. This would involve assessments of the pre-harvest and post-harvest losses in the same crops and would allow the losses that occur at all stages from the time the crop is planted to the time the food is consumed, to be identified and quantified. With this information the relative importance of losses due to different factors at different stages of crop growth and food storage could be objectively assessed. The most important part of the activities outlined in Fig. 1 is the quantification of production constraints. It is considered that this should be a permanent feature of any national plant-protection programme to monitor changes in a dynamic system resulting from varieties becoming susceptible, the development of resistance to fungicides or a change in cultural practice leading to a decrease or increase in disease, pest or weed level. Such a system would allow the economic importance of pests, weeds and diseases in major crops to be monitored so that priorities can be regularly revised and new problems detected at an early stage (James, 1979).

The remainder of this review will deal only with techniques applicable to quantifying production constraints associated with plant diseases, although the same general principles will be applicable for pests and weeds. An attempt will also be made to demonstrate how the quantified data can be used in the development of control systems and procedures for reducing these losses. This review will complement other reviews on disease-loss appraisal by Chester (1950), Large (1966), James (1974) and the documentation published by the FAO Symposium on Crop Losses (FAO, 1967). Two major developments resulted from this symposium. Firstly, the publication of a Manual (FAO, 1971) consisting of chapters on general guiding principles in the conduct of field experiments and surveys, as well as detailed examples of specific methods for estimating losses due to particular diseases. This has been instrumental in standardizing methods of work throughout the world. Secondly, FAO has sponsored a series of workshops in different countries to provide practising plant pathologists with the necessary training to initiate programmes for assessing production constraints. Chiarappa *et al.* (1975) have noted that while the FAO programme has stimulated an increased activity in this area of research, there is still a need to accelerate research in the development, application, and standardization of techniques.

The strategy of disease-loss appraisal programmes and details of the corresponding techniques have been discussed in the reviews mentioned in the previous paragraph. The reader is referred to these because this review will only provide additional comment on material that has been published subsequent to the last detailed review (James, 1974). There are two main phases in a typical crop loss programme. The first phase involves a study of the relationship between disease and the corresponding yield loss, and is determined experimentally in field experiments from detailed studies of the host-pathogen system. This first phase comprises three stages.

1. Disease measurement, where a reliable means of quantitatively describing the disease must be devised.
2. Disease epidemiology, where disease development within the host population is studied over a period of time using the specified method of measurement. We do not propose to discuss the analysis of epidemics in this review and will only refer to epidemiology in relation to yield reduction.
3. Crop loss estimation, where information from 1. and 2. above are analysed in conjunction with crop-growth and yield data to characterize the relationship between disease and loss, i.e., the development of a crop loss model.

The second phase is a survey which makes use of the disease-loss model determined in phase one to estimate loss on a regional or national scale. However, surveys represent only one way of using the disease-loss relationship; this provides a post-damage evaluation of the economic importance of diseases, based on the amount of loss they cause. The disease-loss relationship model can also be incorporated into a disease management system which can be used to predict disease development and prevent production losses through the intervention of control measures. Methods for measuring disease will be discussed first, followed by an evaluation of techniques for deriving disease-loss models. The utilization of information on production constraints due to diseases will then be considered.

II. DISEASE MEASUREMENT

This is one of the most important aspects of any disease-loss appraisal programme because it is the process that produces all the factual information on disease development. While disease diagnosis methods are universally standardized, disease measurement methods are still at a stage of development when there is an urgent need for uniformity in methodology and agreement on criteria. Attempts have been made to standardize methodology by James (1971a,b, 1974), FAO (1971) and MAFF (1976). While James (1974) has pointed out the futility of semantic arguments over terms to describe the amount of disease, it is suggested that in the interest of clarity the term "disease measurement" (*sensu* Moore, 1943; Large, 1966) should be an all-encompassing term to include all methods of disease quantification, with "disease assessment" (*sensu* James, 1974) being considered one method of quantification. In this review, the term "disease intensity" is used to mean either disease incidence or disease severity in accordance with the FAO Crop Loss Manual. Disease incidence ($\%I$) is defined as the number of plant units infected, expressed as a proportion of the total number of units assessed, e.g., the percentage of infected plants. Disease severity ($\%S$) is defined as the area of plant tissue affected by disease expressed as a proportion of total area, e.g. the percentage of leaf area infected. The merits of using a percentage scale to describe incidence and severity will be discussed later.

A. DISEASE ASSESSMENT

Disease assessment includes any method where an estimate of disease is made in conjunction with a prepared standard. Disease assessment methods have a degree of subjectivity associated with their use, but this subjectivity can be reduced to a minimum if the method is simple to use and has been tested to give reproducible results between assessors. Disease assessment methods can be conveniently grouped into descriptive keys and standard area diagrams and a critical review of the respective advantages and disadvantages has been presented by James (1974). He considered that where possible assessments should be made on plant components e.g., specific leaves rather than whole plants. Also that arbitrary indices and rating systems be discouraged in favour of the percentage scale which has many advantages. The criteria for a successful assessment method are very demanding (James, 1971a) but two requirements are particularly important. Firstly the assessment method must be reproducible and not prone to errors resulting from human judgement. Secondly it should be rapid and easy to use. This latter requirement is extremely important when assessment methods are designed for survey or field use. Teng (1978a) has shown that the cost per unit efficiency (measured by the standard error of the estimate of %S) increases sharply if sample size has to be increased to compensate for a poorly designed assessment method.

1. Descriptive keys

Descriptive keys utilize arbitrary scales, indices, ratings, grades or percentages, to quantify disease. The best-known example of a descriptive key is that proposed first by Moore (1943) for potato late-blight measurement in the United Kingdom, and subsequently revised for general use (Anon., 1947). In its revised form the British Mycological Society (BMS) key (Anon., 1947) assigns categories of disease based on percentage. An appropriate description of disease severity is given for each category as shown below:

Late blight of potato disease assessment key (BMS)

Blight (%)	Description
0	not seen in field.
0·1	only a few plants affected; up to 1 or 2 spots in a 10·6 m radius.
1·0	up to 10 spots per plant or general light infections.
5·0	about 50 spots per plant or up to one leaflet in ten attacked.
25	nearly every leaflet infected, but plants retain normal form; field may smell of blight, but looks green although every plant affected.
50	every plant affected and about 50% leaf area destroyed; field looks green flecked with brown.
75	about 75% leaf area destroyed by blight; field looks neither predominantly green nor brown.
95	only a few leaves left green, but stems green.
100	all leaves dead, stems dying or dead.

The above key found wide acceptance because each blight category was a measure, within limits, of the actual percentage of leaf area destroyed (Anon., 1947). Because late-blight starts first in a potato crop as primary foci, James (1971a,b) published an addition to the BMS key for the early stages of the epidemic, where the area of the focus as well as the actual percentage of leaf area infected in each focus was estimated using %S diagrams. Fry (1977) further modified the above methods by introducing two extra categories, 0·01% disease (5 infected leaflets per

10 plants or 2 lightly infected leaves per 10 plants) and 0·1% disease (about 5 infected leaflets per plant or 2 lightly infected leaves per plant). Whereas the late-blight keys use the percentage scale, other descriptive keys do not use it to denote disease category. For example, the keys for *Septoria* spp. on wheat heads (Jones and Cooke, 1969), wheat foliage diseases (Hosford and Busch, 1974), *Cercospora* spp. on cowpea (Schneider *et al.*, 1976), banana leaf spot (Stover, 1971), South American leaf blight (Chee, 1976) and *Selenophoma donacis* on barley (Cooke and Brokenshire, 1975). The latter two authors categorized the severity of *S. donacis*, causing halo spot on barley, by means of a rating system of 1–6, each rating denoting respectively 1, 5, 10, 25, 50 and 75% infected leaf area. Chee (1976) graded *Microcyclus ulei* on rubber leaves as follows: 1 (less than 1% leaf area diseased), 2 (1%–5%), 3 (6%–15%), 4 (16%–30%) and 5 (more than 30%). Hosford and Busch (1974) assessed *Pyrenophora trichostoma* and *Leptosphaeria avenaria* on wheat leaves using ratings of 1–6, with each numeral representing 0, 1, 5, 25, 50 and 100% infected area respectively. The same authors allowed interpolation between the ratings, for example a rating of 3·5 representing 15% leaf area infected. It is of interest to note that in some cases, e.g. Chee (1976), the rating system would probably be better served by a standard area diagram which is less prone to error than the descriptive key.

Some descriptive keys are subject to a compound error because of the imprecision of the description (Chester, 1950, p. 240); for example the scale used for scoring all alfalfa diseases, except bacterial wilt, in the USA in the late 1940s (Newell and Tysdal, 1945), recognized nine classes of disease intensity from 1 ("very little") to 5 ("medium") to 9 ("very much"). With virus diseases the measurement of disease severity is complicated by the difficulty of diagnosing and quantifying symptoms on plant parts. Accordingly subjective assessments are often used, with arbitrary grades like healthy, moderate and severe (Hampton, 1975; Harper *et al.*, 1975). Some workers (e.g. Geh and Ting, 1973) have not attempted to assess severity and assumed total plant loss when measuring disease intensity of viruses.

Many assessment keys have been developed for use on selected plant parts that are important contributors to yield because there is a higher chance of establishing a relationship between amount of disease and loss in yield (James *et al.*, 1968). Other keys have been devised to measure disease of the whole plant; this is often done when preliminary knowledge is required on the relative importance of diseases under field conditions. Saari and Prescott (1975) have successfully tested a 0–9 scale for appraising the foliage diseases of wheat in different countries.

Their basic scale revolves around the value 5, which is defined as disease development up to the mid-point of the plant and the scale is accompanied by an adequate description. Aluko (1975), working on brown leaf spot of rice in Nigeria, has also used a descriptive key of 1–6 for the whole plant infection. Some descriptive keys have been used to assign a disease index from the ratings defined by the key for different plant parts. For example, Nelson *et al.* (1976) derived a *Septoria* Disease Index for *S. nodorum* by adding leaf and head ratings of 1–9. Kuhn and Smith (1977), working with maize dwarf mosaic virus (MDMV), calculated a MDMV Disease Index as follows: MDMV Index = $4W + 3X + 2Y + Z$, where W = total percentage of plants with symptoms 6 days after inoculation and X, Y, Z are the percentages at 11, 16 and 28 days respectively. These authors were able to relate percentage yield loss directly to the disease index.

2. *Standard area diagrams*

Assessment of plant diseases by comparison with a set of standard area diagrams appears to be the most reliable field method of disease measurement. Chester (1950) stated that "a high degree of uniformity in rating disease severity is possible when use is made of standards, representative of each of a series of grades of disease intensity". The literature on published standard area diagrams has been reviewed and documented by many authors (Chester, 1950; Large, 1966; James 1971a,b, 1974; MAFF, 1976). A self-explanatory example of a standard area diagram is given in Fig. 2.

Standard-area diagrams can be divided into two types, both based on percentage scales. The first has a graded series of severities where each grade represents the actual percentage infected area of a plant or plant part. The second series assigns a 100% value to the maximum severity observed in the field and all the other levels are pro-rated accordingly. The first, and certainly the most notable example of a standard area diagram showing actual percentage infected area was the Cobb Scale for assessing leaf rust of wheat. Cobb (1892) illustrated five grades, of disease severity—1, 5, 10, 20 and 50%. However, his method was modified by Melchers and Parker (1922) and Peterson *et al.* (1948) who assigned a 100% value to 37% actual infected area which they designated to be the maximum infection possible under field conditions. Similarly Eyal and Brown (1976), working on *Septoria tritici* found that the maximum actual leaf coverage by pycnidia was 22·8%. Accordingly, they designed a diagrammatic scale with grades designated 2·7, 5·7, 11·4, 17·2 and 19·9% (actual coverage) which was "rescaled to give coverage" of 12, 25, 50, 75 and 87% severity respectively. Other

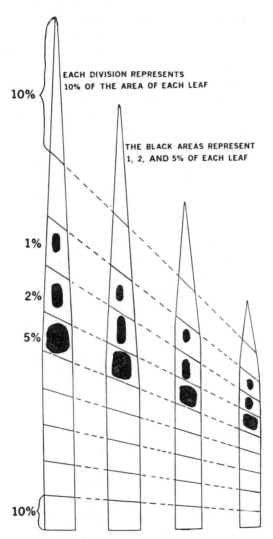

EACH DIVISION REPRESENTS
10% OF THE AREA OF EACH LEAF

10%

THE BLACK AREAS REPRESENT
1, 2, AND 5% OF EACH LEAF

1%

2%

5%

10%

FIG. 2. Assessment key for *Rhyncosporium* leaf blotch or scald of barley. Match the leaf to one of the diagrams and use the black areas (representing 1%, 2% and 5% of each leaf) as a guide in assessing the percentage leaf (lamina) area covered by small isolated lesions, and the 10% sections for the larger lesions that have coalesced. (After James *et al.*, 1968).

standard-area diagrams based on actual percentage infected area are those for powdery mildew on cereals (Grainger, 1947) and apple black-spot (Chester, 1950). Although most standard-area diagrams have been used to assess disease on designated individual plant parts,

Teng (1975) and Saari and Prescott (1975) have developed whole-plant diagrams for foliage diseases of rice and wheat.

Subsequent to the FAO sponsored crop-loss symposium in 1967 there have been efforts to prepare sets of standard area diagrams utilizing the same set of guiding principles and reflecting the actual percentage area infected by disease (James, 1971a,b; MAFF, 1976). James (1971a) proposed that the percentage scale be adopted as a standard for the following reasons: the upper and lower limits of a percentage scale are always uniquely defined; the percentage scale is flexible in that it can be conveniently divided and subdivided; it is universally known and can be used equally well for measuring proportion of plants infected (incidence) or the proportion of plant area damaged (severity); and it can easily be transformed for any subsequent epidemiological analysis, e.g. transformation to logits for calculation of the apparent rate of infection (Van der Plank, 1963). When designing a standard area diagram using the percentage scale, Large (1966) has cautioned against an irrational number of grades between 1–100% infection. Further-more, the number of grades on a percentage should take cognizance of the physical properties of the human eye for distinguishing between grades. Horsfall and Barratt (1945) have pointed out that according to the Weber–Fechner law, the human eye distinguishes differences according to the logarithm of the light intensity, and therefore disease grades should be based on equal ability to distinguish, not on equal amounts of disease. In practice this allows the human eye to detect grades which are approximately equal divisions on a logarithmic scale. The same authors further noted that on a percentage basis, the eye actually sees the amount of diseased tissue when infected area is less than 50%, but detects the amount of healthy tissue when disease is greater than 50%. A natural turning point for any percentage scale should therefore be 50%. Horsfall and Barratt's hypothesis regarding acuity of the human eye was subsequently confirmed in an extensive evaluation by Redman and Brown (1964). The relative merits of arithmetic or logarithmic divisions in an assessment diagram have been discussed by Chester (1950), Large (1966) and James (1974). Certainly from the standpoint of Van der Plank's (1963) analyses, a logarithmic scale is epidemiologically sound, and Large (1966) did note the coinci-dence with which disease-severity increments in standard area diagrams have largely conformed to increments on a logarithmic $(X/(100\text{-}X))$ scale, the logit transformation of Van der Plank (1963); the value X is the amount of disease measured at any time during the epidemic.

However, in the context of loss appraisal, diseases are not measured for epidemiological purposes but only as a means for relating disease intensity to yield reduction. It does not therefore follow that the same criteria should be used for defining disease grades for an epidemiological scale, as for a disease-loss scale. For example, from a disease-loss appraisal standpoint losses should ideally be estimated with equal and reasonable levels of precision at any level of disease; this is rarely achieved using equal divisions on a logarithmic scale, though it can be achieved with equal divisions on an arithmetic scale (James, 1974). James further noted that with the aid of standard area diagrams observers can often do better than the Weber–Fechner law suggests, by using their ability to judge relative differences and interpolating between values representing equal divisions on the logarithmic scale. Despite the fact that many workers (Horsfall and Barratt, 1945; Redman and Brown, 1964; Kranz, 1970) have studied the phenomena involved in the development of an acceptable scale, problems remain unresolved. This is an important area for future research because primary errors in disease assessment result in secondary and tertiary errors which cannot be corrected at a later stage (Kranz, 1975). Distribution of disease and sampling methods are two other areas that are not well documented, but which are very important to obtain reliable disease assessment data. Descriptive keys have in general been of more limited value than standard area diagrams in obtaining accurate disease assessments because of the more ambiguous nature of the description and the absence of a visual aid.

B. REMOTE SENSING

The term remote sensing is applied to the process of gathering information about an object from a distance and without physical contact with the object (Downs, 1974). In plant pathology remote sensing is dependent on the ability to measure differences in the radiant properties of healthy and diseased plants. These radiant properties are mainly in the visible (0.4–0.7 μm in wavelength) or the infra-red (greater than 0.7 μm in wavelength) portions of the electromagnetic spectrum, with the latter being of more practical importance. Remote sensing depends on the ability of sensors to detect spectral reflectance from the object or objects concerned. The form of detection can be as measurements of direct reflectance with reference to a standard, or as photographic transparencies (negatives or positives). In general, any infection of plant tissue which reduces vigour decreases the spectral reflectance of the tissue in the infra-red region, when compared to healthy tissue. Colwell (1956) explained that lowered infra-red (IR) reflectance in rust diseases, especially in the region of 0.8–1.1 μm. resulted from hyphal growth in the spongy mesophyll, which Jackson (1972) considered to be the main reflector of IR in the leaf. However, Gausman (1974) showed that near-IR reflectance, which is dependent on refractive index discontinuities of cell-wall/air-space interfaces in leaves, was also a function of plant maturity. As the plant matures, the leaf mesophyll becomes more spongy with increased air spaces and becomes a more efficient reflector of IR.

1. *Reflectance measurements*

As long ago as 1956, Colwell showed that rusted leaves of cereals had lower near-IR reflectances than healthy leaves. Ausmus and Hilty (1973) working with maize dwarf mosaic virus, also found significant differences between healthy and infected leaves in reflectance from wavelengths between 0·8–2·6 μm. The above two studies did not examine the effect of different disease severities on reflectance, but Teng and Close (1977) have since shown that barley leaf rust severities of 15, 30 and 70% can be distinguished from each other and from healthy leaves in the wavelength region 0·8–1·1 μm. Laboratory studies on single-leaf reflectances are mainly of academic interest but can provide guidelines for predicting whether plant canopy reflectances or photographic images are capable of detecting diseases. Commercial IR films are mainly sensitive to radiation from the 0·7–0·9 μm portion of the spectrum and Colwell (1956) listed four parameters which had to be known before the tone or colour of an object in an aerial photograph could be predicted. These were (a) reflectance of object, (b) sensitivity of film, (c) scattering by atmospheric haze, and (d) transmission of optical filters.

With the launching of the Earth Resources Technology Satellite (ERTS-1) in July 1972, considerable interest has been stimulated in the use of canopy reflectance properties for disease detection and measurement (Kanemasu *et al.*, 1974a,b; Kumar and Silva, 1974). The satellite has sensors with four band-passes corresponding to different portions of the electromagnetic spectrum. These sensors and their wavelength sensitivities are designated Multispectral Scanner 4—MSS 4 (0·5–0·6 μm), MSS 5 (0·6–0·7 μm), MSS 6 (0·7–0·8 μm) and MSS 7 (0·8–1·1 μm), with the last two being in the near-IR. Kanemasu (1974) studied the seasonal canopy reflectance patterns of wheat, sorghum and soya bean using a portable spectro-radiometer with sensors corresponding to the ERTS-1 MSS bands and it has since been shown that wheat-streak mosaic-virus severity and yield are significantly correlated with MSS4/MSS6 and MSS4/MSS7 values (Kanemasu *et al.*, 1974b). Casey (1978) has also reported promising results with spectro-radiometric measurements of soya bean rust. A great deal more research is needed in this area before ERTS imagery can be routinely used for disease–loss appraisal (Kanemasu *et al.*, 1974b).

2. *Infra-red photography*

The use of aerial photography, in particular false colour infra-red photography, for plant disease detection has received much attention after its potential was demonstrated on cereals (Colwell, 1956) and potato (Brenchley, 1966; Manzer and Cooper, 1967). Remote sensing by means of aerial IR photographic imagery can be used to measure both disease incidence and disease severity on a field scale.

On theoretical grounds, the estimation of crop loss using remote sensing would be easier in situations where loss is related to incidence, than where loss is related to severity. Powell *et al.* (1976) estimated losses in peanut fields due to *Cylindrocladium* black rot by assuming that all diseased areas had zero yield. In this example, the percentage yield reduction is equivalent to the percentage infected area as revealed by aerial false colour IR imagery. The technology concerned with converting false colour IR images into a form suitable for electronic scanning has been developed (Wallen and Jackson, 1971; Wallen and Philpotts, 1971). In a more recent study with bacterial blight of beans, Jackson and Wallen (1975), reported optical density differences in IR film images of healthy and diseased plots. The differences were particularly apparent at the later stages of the epidemic in diseased plots, when crop maturity was also a contributory factor to optical density differences between diseased and healthy plots. The same authors obtained data from ground studies on field plots and aerial IR imagery and developed the following model for estimating crop loss: Yield Loss = $AI \times ABP \times AvY \times YLF$, where AI = percentage area infected in a specific year (as determined by microdensitometer scans of IR photographs taken at a specified time). ABP = area in bean production in a specific year (ha); AvY = average yield in a specific year (kg ha^{-1}), and YLF = yield loss factor (%) derived from field plot experiments, to relate %AI to final yield loss.

The measurement of disease severity using remote sensing is difficult because IR reflectance can be affected by other stress factors as well as bare soil. However, Jackson *et al.* (1971) showed that the transmission density of false colour IR transparencies could be directly correlated to potato late-blight severities as determined by field studies. Scheider and Safir (1975) have shown that with sugar-beet, IR photography of plots could be rated 1–10 depending on amount of foliage remaining from blackroot disease caused by several fungi: 1 (cyan) denoting almost no foliage left and 10 (magenta) denoting healthy. Sugar beet root yields were significantly correlated with photograph ratings, and the study suggests a possibility of relating lowered reflectance, caused by multiple infections, to crop yield: a situation which is common in cereal diseases. Chiang and Wallen (1977) have reviewed the use of aerial photography for assessing crop losses and the reader is referred to their work for further details.

Remote sensing, used as a tool, offers several advantages compared with conventional methods for measuring disease. Foremost is the ability to monitor large areas in a short time and to obtain objective data which is not subject to errors of observation. However, the tool is still in its infancy and many practical problems remain, particularly those relating to interpretation, which can be confounded due to factors other than diseases expressing similar characteristics. We hope the current limitations will decrease as new techniques are developed but it will probably be some time before remote sensing replaces conventional methods as the principal method for obtaining data on disease measurement.

C. INDIRECT METHODS OF MEASURING DISEASE

Assessment of disease, particularly severity, can be a laborious and time-consuming exercise and some workers have, with limited success, explored indirect methods of measuring disease. These methods have principally involved the monitoring of other properties of disease which are well correlated with the amount of disease. Some workers have attempted to estimate the more easily monitored disease-incidence and then describe the relationship between disease incidence and severity. Others have endeavoured to relate the number of lesions or propagules to disease development and a few researchers have utilized chemical analyses for determining the mass of fungal tissue present in diseased plants.

1. *Relating disease incidence to severity*
The development of a disease epidemic depends on the spread of plant pathogens in space and time (Van der Plank, 1967). In the early phases of an epidemic infection foci are often present and the diseased host population resembles a binomial distribution, where disease per host unit is considered as being either absent or present. As the disease progresses, the distribution of disease severity amongst the host population usually tends towards normality. Even with an estimated mean percentage severity as low as 2·5%, the assumption of normality is still

statistically valid in *Puccinia hordei* in New Zealand (Teng, unpubl. data). In a study directed at determining the relationship between incidence and severity at low disease-levels of leaf rust and powdery mildew on winter wheat, James and Shih (1973a) demonstrated a linear relationship between the two properties for incidence values up to 65% and approximately 1% mean severity (see Fig. 3). The same

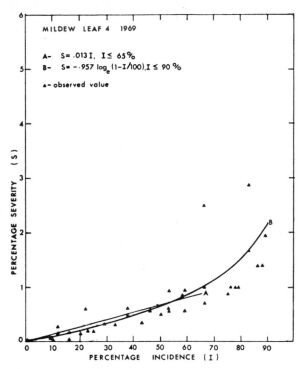

Fig. 3. Linear and semi-log equations for estimating severity for given levels of incidence of wheat powdery mildew. (After James and Shih, 1973a).

authors suggested that the ability to estimate severity from incidence using the linear equations $\%S = b \times \%I$ (where I is less than or equal to 65% and b is the regression coefficient for a specific leaf position and disease), could result in large savings when conducting a disease survey where many assessments have to be made. The incidence of coffee rust in the field is strongly localized and Rayner (1961) showed that rust severity could be estimated from the percentage rusted leaves incidence per bush. Furthermore since disease incidence is often related to foliage density, which in turn is related to crop yield, the estimate of percentage infected leaves may provide a good estimate of crop losses due to coffee rust. Gorter (1974) used disease incidence and severity for comparing the relative efficacy of different fungicides for powdery mildew of cucurbits caused by *Sphaerotheca fuliginea*. His results were similar to those of James and Shih (1973a) and he concluded that at low levels of disease (0–85% incidence or 0–2·1% mean severity) incidence was a good method for measuring disease. In general it can be stated that incidence can be used to predict severity during the early part of the epidemic when growth results from an increase in both incidence and severity. However when incidence reaches 100%, epidemic growth can only result from increased severity and thereafter incidence counts cannot be used to assess severity.

2. *Counts of lesions or propagules*

Severity is often calculated indirectly from lesion counts which are only feasible at low levels of disease. For example, Buchenau (1975) working on wheat rusts, counted all pustules if there were less than 25 pustules per stem or leaf. The same author used a modified Cobb scale (Melchers and Parker, 1922) for greater amounts of disease but converted the pustule counts at lower disease levels to conform with the modified Cobb scale. Burleigh *et al.* (1972a) showed that wheat leaf-rust epidemics can be characterized by uredinia counts, if time and labour are not constraints in a study. More recently, Eyal and Brown (1976) have counted the number of *Septoria tritici* pycnidia on wheat leaves using a television beam to scan 35 mm photographic transparencies of infected leaves. However, the method was used only during the development of an assessment key to establish the relationship between numbers of pycnidia and the percentage coverage by the disease.

Other indirect methods estimate disease severity from a measure of the signs of disease, for example, fungal propagules. Zadoks (1972) suggested that counting the number of propagules could serve either as an alternative for, or a complement to disease assessment. The validity of these methods can be upheld on the technical grounds that propagule counting may be fast, accurate and non-destructive, and does not disturb the crop and its microclimate. With the cereal rusts, cumulative urediniospore counts have proved reliable indicators of disease severity (Romig and Dirks, 1966; Burleigh *et al.*, 1972a; Eversmeyer and Burleigh, 1970), and Johnson and Taylor (1976) have demonstrated that spore counting is a means to show differences in host resistance and pathogen growth. Shearer and Wilcoxson (1976) used a destructive sampling method for obtaining conidia of three *Septoria* spp. on wheat and showed that the epidemics caused by each of the three fungi could be characterized by the area-under-the-sporulation curve. With current technology the use of spore counts (disease signs) as a means of field measurement of disease is unlikely to replace the principal and conventional method of measuring disease severity (disease symptoms), unless its accuracy can be shown to override the ease and low cost of symptom assessment. The evidence to date (Burleigh et al., 1972a; Eversmeyer et al., 1973) suggests that predictive equations for cereal rusts using severity as the disease variable have proven more accurate than those with numbers of spores as the variables. Although spore counts are not often used directly in crop-loss assessment, they can play an important role within the context of disease management. For example, for identifying risk periods when inoculum potential is high and when meterological conditions are suitable for infection (Polley and King, 1973). Spore counts are more suitable for monitoring those diseases which produce abundant quantities of airborne spores; particularly when the generation time is short. Although estimates of spores at any particular time will reflect differences due to sporulation conditions and other factors, cumulative spore counts can be said to be analogous to disease severity (Zadoks, 1972). On the contrary, diseases with low spore-production or where spores are dispersed by water cannot be monitored by spore counts because suitable trapping methodology has not been developed.

3. Chemical analyses

These determine the chitin content of fungal cell walls and therefore can be used for all fungi with the exception of the Phycomycetes (Sturgeon, 1974). Chemical analyses are laboratory-based, and although capable of accurately determining the mass of fungal tissue in host plants, they are time consuming and do not have much practical value in field epidemiology. However they are useful from a crop loss assessment standpoint because they provide physiological or biochemical explanations of the effect of fungi on crop yields, when these are accurately monitored in a detailed field experiment.

The first method was developed by Ride and Drysdale (1971) to determine the amount of *Fusarium oxysporium* f. *lycopersici* in stems of infected tomato. Chitin, a polymer of N-acetyl-D-glucosamine, was enzymatically hydrolysed using chitinase, and the acetylglucosamine subsequently assayed by a colorimetric method. Ride and Drysdale (1972) later modified the above procedure and shortened it to five hours. Toppan et al. (1976) have stipulated four steps which they considered essential for determination of the mass of chitin-containing fungal tissue in plants using hydrochloric acid hydrolysis for glucosamine release. These steps were: (a) isolation of the chitin-containing fraction from an infected plant, (b) selection of a suitable hydrolysis method, (c) purification of the hydrolysates, and (d) glucosamine determination by a specific method. These authors confirmed Wu and Stahmann's findings (1975) that the extra purification step using ion-exchange chromatography, prior to glucosamine estimation, gives a more accurate and reproducible result irregardless of the plant part being investigated.

III. Generation of Data to Describe the Disease-loss Relationship

The major objective of the experimental phase referred to earlier, in any crop production constraints programme is to generate reliable data to characterize the relationship between disease incidence or severity and loss in yield or quality. This involves experimentation with healthy treatments and others with various levels of disease, to obtain a set of independent variables (disease assessments) that can hopefully be related to the dependent variables (yield or quality loss). It can be stated at the outset that it is always preferable to set up experiments specifically for crop losses, rather than attempt to extract the data from secondary sources derived from experiments designed for other purposes. Most institutions have large bodies of such data from fungicide variety trials etc., that have accumulated over a period of years. Kelber (1975) explored the possibility of utilizing such secondary data and despite the fact that a voluminous quantity of data was analysed, very few data were found to be satisfactory. The most frequent problems were lack of quantitative disease data and the absence of yield data for crops in the absence of the disease under study. Following the application of critical standards to a large body of data, Kelber was only able to suggest three models for *Septoria nodorum* on wheat, *Erysiphe graminis* on barley and *Cercospora beticola* on sugar beet. Kelber's work points to the need for careful pre-planning and co-operation in the conduct of plant pathology experiments, so that with a little extra effort involving the collection of specific disease and yield data, secondary data could be infinitely more useful.

Two approaches have been used to generate crop loss data. The traditional approach has utilized conventional field plots in standard experimental designs to study the effect of disease on the crop. More recently the use of single plants or tillers within the crop has been explored. A critical discussion of selected references utilizing the two approaches follows.

A. CONVENTIONAL FIELD EXPERIMENTS FOR STUDYING THE EFFECT OF DISEASE ON THE CROP

1. Location design and specifications

Similar experiments have usually been conducted over a period of three years or more in all areas where the crop is important, featuring the major varieties cultivated under the range of conditions found under normal farming practice. The paired plot design, i.e. untreated and treated with fungicides (Large and Doling, 1962) is not as efficient as multiple treatment experiments (Romig and Calpouzos, 1970) which allow the effects of more than two epidemics to be compared at one location. Required precision of results, particularly yield estimates, is an important consideration during the planning phase. The optimum size and shape of plots for various levels of precision have been determined, for certain host–pathogen combinations, by James and Shih (1973b). The standard experimental designs, randomized block, latin square and split plot have been successfully used. It may be useful to note that a large body of data is inevitably produced and therefore pre-planning with statisticians and computer programmers is necessary to select optimal designs and facilitate the orderly and efficient processing of data.

2. Modifying epidemics

It is important to note at the outset that irrespective of the technique used to modify the epidemics, the principal effect should be to promote or delay the epidemic. If it leads to secondary effects that may increase or decrease yield this can invalidate the technique, if the yield differences are significant. The methods selected for modifying epidemics are different for each disease and largely depend on the biology of the pathogen, in particular the infection rate and its mode of spread. Van der Plank (1963) has reported that for diseases with low infection and spread rates e.g. loose smut of barley *Ustilago nuda*, altering amounts of initial infection by varying the proportion of healthy to infected seed (Semeniuk and Ross, 1942), will achieve lasting differences in disease levels between contiguous plots. However pathogens with high rates of infection and spread e.g., airborne diseases like rusts and powdery mildews of cereals will not allow differences to be maintained in contiguous plots following inoculation with different levels of inoculum. The rapid movement of spores from plot to plot as a result of interplot interference (Van der Plank, 1963; James *et al.*, 1973) precludes the possibility of maintaining differences in disease level between neighbouring plots.

Although it is preferable to conduct experiments with natural epidemics, experience has shown that in the majority of cases the success rate is low because of the unpredictability of epidemic development. To increase the chances of success workers have resorted to manipulating the level of natural infection by artificial inoculation. Seeds of wheat have been inoculated with spore suspensions of *Fusarium nivale* (Millar and Colhoun, 1969) and wheat plants have been inoculated with *Septoria nodorum* or *tritici* at different growth stages (Jones and Rowling, 1976). However care should be taken that the epidemics resulting from direct inoculation of the host crop are representative of natural epidemics, otherwise the results are only of academic interest. In an attempt to circumvent the problem associated with direct inoculation different amounts of inoculum have been placed on the surface of the soil in plots (Jones and Davies, 1969). Alternatively perimeter areas around the plots are infected (Chamberlain *et al.*, 1972). In both these cases the pathogen spreads "naturally" on to the host plants because the source of inoculum is either infected debris, or infected plants, which are not a part of the population under study.

The use of diseased and healthy propagating material has been widely utilized to study the effect of viruses on potatoes (Wright, 1970; James, 1974) and for fungal pathogens in the same crop (Hide *et al.*, 1973). The level of disease can be easily controlled by mixing different proportions of healthy and infected stock. Also the availability of a clean stock allows viruses and pathogens to be reintroduced singly or in different combinations at different incidence levels, thus allowing a study of the interaction effects of different diseases (James, 1974). This method is likely to become increasingly important in the future.

Another effective way to vary disease is to locate experiments in different geographical areas expected to have different levels of disease (Calpouzos *et al.*, 1976; Emge and Shrum, 1976) over a period of years. Varieties with varying susceptibility to disease, but with approximately the same yield potential in the absence of disease, can also be used, with the proviso that disease susceptibility is not highly correlated with potential yield (James *et al.*, 1968). The use of isogenic lines (Schaller, 1963) provides further safeguards that yields are similar but even the introduction of the resistance genes may have pleiotropic effects which result in different yield potentials for the two lines. For example, Schwarzbach (1975) has shown that the introduction of the ml-o gene responsible for powdery mildew resistance in barley also reduces potential yield by decreasing ear and grain number as well as grain size. In general, soil-borne diseases present more problems than airborne diseases because they do not easily lend themselves to epidemic modification. Cultural methods and different rotations (Slope and Etheridge, 1971) have been used to build up different levels of inoculum in the soil.

In practice fungicides have been more widely used than any other technique to modify epidemics. When used in conjunction with different varieties, location and years, fungicides are a powerful tool and they allow maximum flexibility for varying disease level (James, 1974; Calpouzos et al., 1976). However, like other techniques there are disadvantages, particularly secondary effects resulting from phytotoxicity or beneficial effects which usually result in an increase or decrease in yield respectively (Thomas, 1974). The use of isogenic lines in conjunction with fungicide probably represents one of the most accurate means of determining disease-loss relationships. The fungicides can be used to vary the level of disease in the susceptible isogenic line whilst any errors due to phytotoxicity or beneficial effects can be measured by comparing the yield of the resistant isogenic line with and without fungicide, and appropriate yield corrections made if necessary. The advent of eradicant and systemic fungicides (Marsh et al., 1977) has considerably increased the flexibility of fungicides as a tool for modifying epidemics. With the simultaneous use of more than one target-specific fungicide, the effect of more than one disease can be studied at the same time in the same experiment. In practice there is often no alternative to using fungicides to modify epidemics, and if used with care they will probably continue to be the most important technique for modifying epidemics.

All of the above techniques are subject to some degree of error due to secondary effects and these have been discussed in detail by James (1974). However, in general the disadvantages are minor compared with the advantages. The use of these techniques in conjunction with conventional experimental designs will probably continue to be the principal method of obtaining information for describing the relationship between disease and yield.

3. *Identification of host growth-stages*
Whenever disease assessments are recorded the growth stage of the crop should be noted so that disease progress can be related to host development. This allows useful comparisons of epidemic development at different locations where the time and length of growing season may be different. Growth-stage keys have been published for most of the major crops and the FAO Manual (1971) with its continuing supplements provides a good reference. The Feekes Scale for cereals (Large, 1954) is probably the best known. Zadoks et al. (1974) have published an

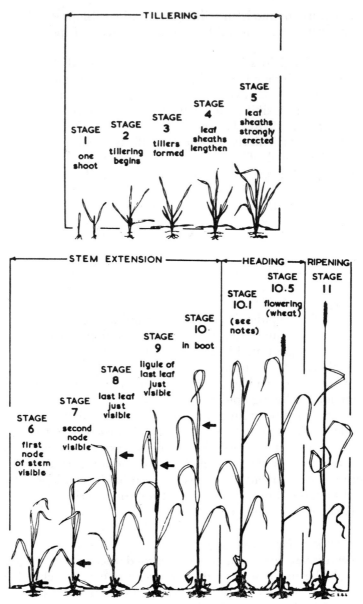

Fig. 4. Growth stages in wheat, oats, barley and rye. (After Large, 1954).

improved version of the Feekes Scale which clarifies some important growth stages and also utilizes a decimal code to facilitate recording; Feekes' scale is reproduced in Fig. 4 to serve as an example. Calpouzos *et al.* (1976) also modified the Feekes Scale to provide more detailed descriptions of post-flowering growth stages. In the second supplement, issued in 1977, of the FAO Manual (1971) many new growth-stage keys of diverse crops have been published.

B. THE USE OF SINGLE PLANTS OR TILLERS

The use of single plants to determine yield loss is not a new technique (Chester, 1950; Gaskill and Schneider, 1966). The method is particularly suited for late-developing diseases with a systemic-type infection where effective yield loss is total e.g. *Pyrenophora graminea* on barley (Richardson *et al.*, 1976). For such diseases the percentage loss in yield is the same as the percentage of infected tillers in the crop, because with late infection, little or no compensation occurs from neighbouring plants. However more recently the same technique has been used (Richardson *et al.*, 1975, 1976; King, 1976) to estimate losses associated with other cereal foliage diseases where the losses are only partial, and where the relationship between disease and yield is more complex as a result of epidemiological differences, earlier infections and corresponding yield compensations. It is not sufficient to record these diseases on a present or absent basis (i.e. incidence). Quantitative assessments (i.e. severity) are necessary in order to characterize the yield losses associated with different degrees of disease severity. Richardson *et al.* (1975) have claimed that the single tiller method has more advantages than the conventional experimental methods for quantifying losses resulting from these more complex diseases. It is pertinent therefore to examine the merits and problems of the single tiller method by referring to three single tiller studies in some detail and making the necessary comparisons with the conventional method. The three single tiller studies are on powdery mildew of barley (Richardson *et al.*, 1975), yellow rust of barley (Richardson *et al.*, 1976) and yellow rust of wheat (King, 1976).

Details differ for each reported experiment but the basic principle is the same. Between 50 and approximately 2000 individual tillers were tagged and the amount of disease recorded only at one growth stage. At maturity each ear was harvested and individually threshed and a regression analysis was used to describe the relationship between disease assessments (X) and corresponding yield-loss estimates (Y). Richardson *et al.* (1975) selected the tillers in pairs and the yields of adjacent infected and healthy tillers were compared in the hope that differences resulting from other yield constraint factors would be reduced to a minimum. However the pairing did not improve the precision and the paired data were not used subsequently. King (1976) selected only primary tillers within narrow transects running through foci of infection in a commercial crop of wheat, whilst Richardson selected tillers at random within one small area of 45 m².

"Greatly increased precision in the estimation of the slope of the regression" (approximately 10% error) of loss on disease was claimed to be an important advantage of the single tiller technique (Richardson et al., 1975). However later studies by the same workers (Richardson et al., 1976) showed that the error can be as high as 31% (standard error of b expressed as percentage, $b = -0.054$ = standard error 0.017) which in fact is higher than all the corresponding average errors associated with conventional experiments: 9%, Mundy, (1973); 24%, James et al. (1968); 25%, Doling and Doodson (1968); 30% Large and Doling (1962, 1963). The standard errors of b have been quoted above because this was the criterion chosen by Richardson et al. (1975) for evaluating the relative precision and the acceptability of the two techniques. However, given that the objective of the study is to develop a model that will allow estimates of loss to be predicted for any given level of disease (r^2), the percentage variability explained by the equation is a more relevant criterion for judging acceptability than the standard error of b. It is important to note that without exception the r^2 values for all single tiller studies have been extremely low: 10–13% Richardson et al. (1975); 2% Richardson et al. (1976); 9–28% King (1976). These figures compare very unfavourably with corresponding figures from conventional experiments: $r^2 = 98\%$ Romig and Calpouzos (1970); 64% Burleigh et al. (1972b); 87% Mundy (1973). Although Richardson et al. (1975) noted that the low r^2 values were not surprising due to the high level of variation associated with other factors, it does not follow that low r^2 values are acceptable. On the contrary low r^2 values do not complement the objective of the study, which is to develop a reliable model for estimating the losses due to disease.

Crop-loss assessment is a practical field exercise involving the development of suitable methodology for measuring the effect of a disease on crop yield. The use of the single tiller differs fundamentally from the conventional approach in that the effect of disease is studied on single tiller yield rather than the crop yield. If the effect on the single tiller yield differs from that on the crop yield, and this is possible for example as a result of compensation, then the single tiller technique can be said to be subject to a representational error because tiller yield does not accurately represent crop yield. Such a representational error could have occurred when Richardson et al. (1975) characterized the loss in yield due to powdery mildew of barley. Yield loss was reported to be caused by a decrease in number of grains per head and in single grain weight but the single tiller technique used could not detect a decrease in number of tillers per plant. Griffiths *et al.* (1975), working on the same disease, have produced evidence that mildew can significantly decrease the number of tillers per plant. If this occurred undetected in Richardson's studies it would lead to a misrepresentation of the yield-loss relationship and an underestimate of loss. The failure of the single tiller method to detect a yield reduction in cereals caused by a reduction in number of tillers per plant can be overcome by using single plants (Aluko, 1975) as opposed to single tillers. However with the use of plants, the economy of labour associated with single tillers is eroded and any compensation between plants may still be difficult to detect. Compensation between tillers and between plants as a result of disease is complex and is not well understood. Yield of cereal plants can be considered to consist of three components: number of tillers per plant, number of grains per ear and individual grain weight. The relative contribution of each of these components to final yield is affected at various stages in the plant's growth (Gaunt, 1978); for example, the total number of tillers that reaches maturity is determined before the early boot stage (stage 10 on the Feekes Scale) by genetic, environmental or stress factors including disease. The weight of grain per ear is similar for the primary and first secondary tiller but is significantly greater than the yield of other secondary tillers on the same plant. The amount of disease on tillers of the same plant can also vary (Teng, unpubl. data) which adds to the difficulty of interpreting yield-loss relationships based on single tiller data and is probably one of the factors responsible for the low r^2 values. However with the use of plots this type of variation is evened out by the greater size of the sample (Richardson *et al.*, 1975). Indeed, many workers have emphasized the need for adequately sized plots to allow yield loss due to disease to be measured with reasonable precision (Chester, 1950; Gaskill and Schneider, 1966; James and Shih, 1973b). Yield variability due to factors other than disease is probably one of the principal problems that limits the usefulness of the single tiller technique. Differences in soil fertility can have a major influence on yield variability in diseased populations (Gorter, 1974) but in the conventional method suitable blocking can be utilized to minimize this effect in a field plot experiment. In the single tiller technique such a correction can only be attempted by the use of adjacent and healthy tillers, but Richardson *et al.* (1975) found that pairing did not improve the precision of the data; a possible reason for this was inherent high variability in both the single and paired tiller data. The data of King (1976) confirms the high variability in yield per tiller due to factors other than disease. He reported that 69% of the variability in yield per ear was due to variability in number of grains per ear which was not dependent on the level of yellow rust. Single grain weight per ear was the only component of yield affected by yellow rust (King, 1976). The late development of the epidemic and its singular effect on seed weight probably accounts for the fact that the yield-loss equation of King, utilizing the single tiller method, is similar to that of Mundy (1973) who used the conventional plot method. A similar comparison of yield-loss equations for powdery mildew of barley, utilizing single tillers (Richardson *et al.*, 1975) and conventional methods (Large and Doling, 1962, 1963) is unfortunately not possible because different assessment methods were used. Richardson *et al.* (1975) have also noted that one of the advantages of the single tiller method is that a complete range of disease severities can be obtained during a single growing season. While this may be so, single tiller estimates still have to be based on several crop seasons and varieties to check the effects of different factors on the variety/disease responses. We may conclude that if further studies prove that the single tiller technique is satisfactory it is likely to be useful only for late epidemics, particularly those affecting the crop at a time when single grain weight per ear is the only component of yield that is not fixed and where there is little chance for compensation. King (1976) and James (1979) have both noted that further validation of the single tiller technique is necessary and that this can easily be achieved by conducting concurrent trials utilizing single tiller and conventional methods in adjacent experiments. If the results of such investigations confirm the usefulness of the single tiller technique there are advantages of economy and experimentation. For example, the observations could be repeated at a number of locations annually to provide current loss estimates for situations where varieties are changed frequently (King, 1976).

The foregoing is a critical discussion of the single tiller technique, for the purpose of developing a reliable crop-loss model to predict the loss in yield at any given level of disease. The same limitations may not apply if the single tiller technique is used as a descriptive, as opposed to a predictive, tool, within the framework of a general crop-loss programme. It is conceivable that the technique, with suitable modification, could be utilized as a first step in a crop-loss programme to provide an approximation of the relative magnitude of production constraints associated with disease and other factors. Techniques are being developed (Stynes, 1975) for evaluating the data that could be obtained from such an evaluation.

IV. CHARACTERIZING THE DISEASE-LOSS RELATIONSHIP

In order to obtain a useful relationship between disease and yield loss, data has to be generated from field experiments where epidemics with different characteristics have effected varying levels of yield loss. The data is obtained over a period of years and must represent the range of cultural, agronomic and environmental conditions. Finally an attempt is made to summarize the characteristics of the data in the form of a disease-loss model which is usually defined by a mathematical equation. The general approach to model fitting is discussed below and followed by a selective review of specific disease-loss models that have been evolved.

A. THE FITTING OF DISEASE-LOSS MODELS

The mathematical equations used to describe crop-loss models are the summary of the experimenters' observations, represented in symbols. The equation simplifies the calculation of loss and the crop-loss model facilitates some biological rationalization of the phenomena that are involved. However, it does not follow that an acceptable equation can be considered evidence of a cause and effect relationship. The majority of the equations that have been evolved for describing disease-loss models are of the regression type where percentage yield loss is the dependent variable and one or more disease intensity values are the independent variables. Butt and Royle (1974) noted that most of the regressions have been inherently linear. Simple and multiple regression techniques have been used and readers are referred to standard statistical texts (Draper and Smith, 1966; Koutsoyiannis, 1973) for detailed discussion of the statistical considerations and the mechanism of computation. Within the context of this review it will suffice to discuss some of the important criteria for judging the acceptability of regression equations for describing disease-loss models.

Prior to the fitting of any regression equation it should be ascertained that there is no lack of normality in the data. In a regression model the independent variable is also assumed to be measured without error, but this is impossible to achieve for most crop-loss models because most disease assessments are estimates and are therefore subject to error. Nevertheless the numerical technique of regression is useful for obtaining an equation which can later be accepted to rejected, based on evidence as to whether it was a reliable predictor of loss. Any regression model also assumes homoscedasticity and the absence of auto-correlation in the data and these should be tested for prior to regression analysis. Homoscedasticity can be illustrated by considering a simple linear regression of the form:

$$Y_i = b_0 + b_1X_1 + u_i$$

OR

| variation in Y_i | = | systematic variation (explained) | + | random variation (unexplained) |

Y may be the dependent variable of percentage yield loss, X may be the percentage on flag leaf at a certain growth state, and u_i is the error or stochastic term. The error term, u_i, can be considered the cause for the random dispersal of observations of yield loss on either side of the true regression line that estimates percentage yield loss from X in the example: u_i can also be described as the stochastic part of the response of Y which is not fixed by the parameters of b_0 and b_1. If the percentage yield loss associated with respective values of percentage is homoscedastic, then the variance of u_i about its mean is constant at all values of X, i.e., for all values of X, the u's will show the same dispersion around their mean. Homoscedasticity is easily checked in a one-independent variable situation by plotting a scatter diagram of percentage yield loss against percentage severity. If the dispersion of points is fairly uniform, then the data can be assumed to be homoscedastic. However, if there is increasing, decreasing or uneven dispersion of observation points along either axis, heteroscedasticity is present. An example would be when at say 20% severity, percentage yield loss points are dispersed in a range of 10%, but at 80% severity the percentage yield loss points are dispersed in a range of 60%. Heteroscedasticity can be statistically tested and corrected for (Koutsoyiannis, 1973). Butt and Royle (1974) noted that small deviations from homoscedasticity can probably be ignored.

Auto-correlation or serial correlation is said to be present when successive observations of a variable are not independent, i.e. when the value of an observation at time t is dependent on its value at time $t-1$. Auto-correlation can occur either with the dependent variable or variables, or the error term; it should not be confused with inter-correlation (Butt and Royle, 1974), which is the dgree of association between two dependent variables used in a regression. A distinction should also be made between "biological" auto-correlation and "statistical" auto-correlation because biologically, the amount of disease on a certain day is in part dependent on the amount of disease on a previous day. Biological auto-correlation, or "biological stickiness"

(Butt and Royle, 1974) is often unconsciously eliminated if samples are not taken every day, i.e. it is reduced if the sampling interval is increased. Statistical auto-correlation can be tested for and corrections can be made when the source of the problem has been identified (Koutsoyiannis, 1973).

Provided that the data satisfies the assumptions discussed above, equations can be produced using the regression technique. To judge the acceptability of the equations several statistics can be used. These include the r^2, r, F, t and s statistics or tests. The r^2 statistic, or coefficient of multiple determination, is computed from regression sum of squares per total sum of squares, and is considered the proportion of total variation of the dependent variable (percentage yield loss) that is explained by the independent variable or variables, (percentage severity). For example, if $r^2 = 0.90$, the regression explains 90% of the total variation of percentage yield loss values around their mean. The remaining 10% of the total variation in yield loss is unaccounted for by the model and may be due to random error or undefined variables. r^2 is probably the most important indicator of the reliability of a regression model and very often a critical point model (James, 1974) with low r^2 will show great improvement when more disease assessments are added as independent variables to make it a multiple point disease-loss model. Butt and Royle (1974) have suggested that the ratio of regression mean square per total mean square may be more useful for comparing equations since it is the proportion of total variance accounted for by multiple regression. The correlation coefficient, r, describes how well the original data is fitted to function and is the square root of the coefficient of multiple determination, r^2; r is an additional statistic to describe model reliability, but unlike r^2 it can be tested for significance at the 5% or 1% probability levels (Snedecor, 1957). The F statistic in the analysis of variance of a regression model provides a test of the overall significance of the model, as well as of the significance of the improvement in fit obtained by the introduction of additional variables in a multiple regression. However, as Draper and Smith (1966) noted, the F Statistic is derived from regression mean square per deviation (residual) mean square, and although a significant F-value shows that the model has satisfactorily accounted for data variation, it is not necessarily an indication that the model is useful for predictive purposes. The often used t statistic or test can be used to test the significance of a regression coefficient (when there is more than one independent disease variable). The t statistic is obtained by dividing the estimated (partial) regression coefficient with the standard error of the (partial) regression coefficient and it can be used to assess the relative contribution of a parameter to the overall significance of the regression model. The t test can be useful when many disease assessments have been made on different plant parts at many growth stages and no *a priori* postulation of the disease-loss relationship is possible. S is the standard error of the estimate of the dependent variable (percentage yield loss), and is computed as the square root of the deviation mean square in the analysis of variance table. The smaller the value of S, the more precise will be predictions from the model.

B. MODELS FOR ESTIMATING YIELD LOSSES

The disease-loss models that have already been developed are grouped to give a clear perspective of developments published in the literature. The three main types of disease-loss models are critical point, multiple point, and area-under-curve and they have been characterized by James (1974). Critical point models estimate yield loss for any level of disease at a particular growth stage of the crop (James *et al.*, 1968; Large and Doling, 1962; Romig and Calpouzos, 1970; Mundy, 1973; Ayers *et al.*, 1976) or at a given time when a specified level of disease is reached (Large, 1952; Olofsson, 1968). Multiple point models estimate yield loss based on sequential disease assessments during a crop's growth (Burleigh *et al.*, 1972b; James *et al.*, 1972). Area-under-curve models estimate the amount of yield loss from the area under a disease progress curve measured in arbitrary units (Van der Plank, 1963; Buchenau, 1975; Schneider *et al.*, 1976). The utility of the three types of models for estimating yield loss will be compared.

The discussion is best introduced by considering an example of a pathogen–host system for which many models have been proposed, e.g. the rust-wheat system. The fungi concerned are **P.** *graminis* f.sp. *tritici* and **P.** *recondita tritici*. Yield loss is the result of the interaction between epidemic development and yield production. As noted earlier the three components of cereal yield are number of tillers, number of grains per tiller (which can be further subdivided into number of spikelets per tiller and number of grains per spikelet) and individual grain weight (Thorne, 1973). The properties of an epidemic such as the duration, the onset date and the stability of its infection rate, will be major factors in determining the type of model that will be appropriate. In wheat, early infections during tillering and apical development may reduce the number of tillers produced and the number of spikelet primordia, although this may result in compensatory effects by the crop at a later growth stage; if the epidemic is short and early, these will be the only two effects expected. In a long duration epidemic, commencing at about growth stage (g.s.) 2 on the Feekes scale, there is evidence that barley mildew will impair root development (Brooks, 1972) which is a form of source-limitation. Long-duration epidemics which commence early, may also reduce the number of fertile florets per ear which in turn decreases the number of grains per ear. On the other hand, a late epidemic would be expected to exert its major influence by reducing seed weight, through imposing stress factors during the grain filling stage. These stress factors include source limitation (through reduction in photosynthetic area due to disease), increased evapo-transpiration through pustules (Wal and Cowan, 1974) resulting in water stress at a very sensitive period in a cereal's growth (Salter and Goode, 1967), or simply fungal metabolism (Wood, 1967). The critical point models which have been successfully applied to cereals have been for late epidemics occurring near the time of grain-filling, between Feekes g.s. 10·5 and 11·3. Examples of such epidemics and their critical points are leaf blotch on barley, g.s. 11·1 (James et al., 1968), powdery mildew on barley, g.s. 10·5 (Large and Doling, 1962), stem rust on wheat, g.s. 11·2 (Romig and Calpouzos, 1970), and leaf and stem rusts on wheat, g.s. 11·1 (Keed and White, 1971). In the light of the discussion on yield components, these late epidemics would be expected mainly to decrease kernel weight, and this has been substantiated by the work of James et al. (1968) on barley leaf blotch, Brook's (1972) work on mildew and the studies of King (1976) on yellow rust of wheat. The critical point model for estimating yield losses at the 75% kernel-growth stage due to stem rust of wheat (Romig and Calpouzos, 1970) is reproduced in Fig. 5. Critical point models imply that there is one critical point when the crop is particularly sensitive to disease. In fact the critical point is simply that particular growth stage which allows the most reliable estimate of loss. It does not follow that less accurate estimates of loss cannot be made at other growth stages.

The precision of the critical point model can almost always be bettered by increasing the number of assessments (i.e. transforming the critical point to a multiple point model) but this will be at the expense of extra resources. The work of Burleigh et al. (1972b) on wheat leaf-rust provides a good illustration. These workers examined the relationship between yield loss and percentage leaf rust on flag leaf or whole tiller at four growth stages—boot, heading, early berry and early dough. They found that percentage severity at early dough alone (a critical point model) explained only 64% of the variation in yield loss, whereas the best predictor was a multiple point model of the form:

$$\% YL = 5{\cdot}3788 + 5{\cdot}5260 X_2 - 0{\cdot}3308 X_5 + 0{\cdot}5019 X_7$$

where X_2 = percentage severity per tiller at boot, X_5 = percentage on flag at early berry and X_7 = percentage severity on flag at early dough. This equation explained 79% of the variation in yield loss and had a standard error of prediction of 9%. Two points should be noted in the equation. The negative sign of the partial regression coefficient

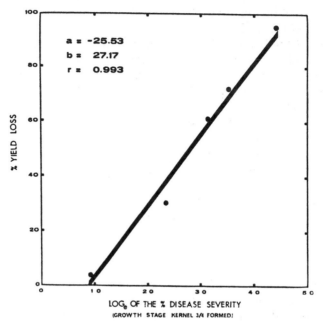

FIG. 5. Critical point model for estimating losses due to stem rust of wheat. Regression of percentage yield loss on the $\log_e$ of stem rust severity at a growth stage when the caryopsis had reached three-fourths' of final size. The untransformed disease data points from left to right are 2·6, 10, 23, 35 and 81%. (After Romig and Calpouzos, 1970).

at the early berry stage (X_5) is interesting as it implies that disease at that growth stage actually increased grain yield. Gaunt (1978) has noted that this is physiologically feasible by reducing the "correlative inhibition" of other plant organs and allowing more grain to mature. The second point is that in the absence of disease, percentage yield loss is equal to 5·3788, but this is within the 9% standard error.

Working on potato late-blight (*Phytophthora infestans*) James *et al.* (1972) developed a multiple point model for estimating loss in tuber yield. Multiple regression was used to derive an equation utilizing disease increments during nine weekly periods as the independent variables, and loss in yield as the dependent variable. The model is shown in Fig. 6 and the difference between estimated loss and actual loss is less than 5% in nine cases out of ten. The equation passed through the origin with a multiple correlation coefficient of 0·976. The estimate of loss is the sum of the products of the partial regression coefficient

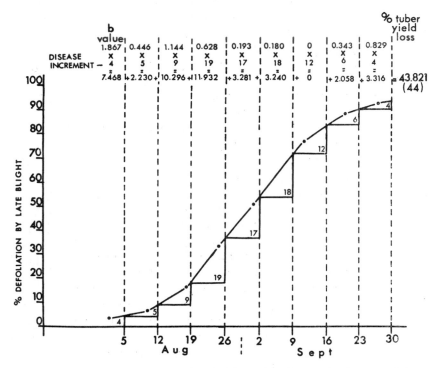

Fig. 6. Multiple point model for estimating losses in tuber production caused by late blight of potato (*Phytophthora infestans*). To estimate loss in tuber yield calculate weekly increments in disease and multiply by the relevant b values; the sum of the weekly products, 48.821, is the percentage loss in total tuber yield. (After James *et al.*, 1972).

and its corresponding disease increment for each week during the epidemic. The equation of James *et al.* (1972) was later modified by MacKenzie and Petruzzo (1975) to a more generalized expression involving simpler procedures so that its application could be broadened. Latin and MacKenzie (1976) have developed a further model for use in conjunction with the disease-loss model which allows disease to be projected throughout the season at different rates of infection which in turn allows tables of expected losses to be developed. It is noteworthy that James *et al.* (1972) did not select any equations with a negative partial regression coefficient similar to that of Burleigh *et al.* (1972b). This selection was justified on the basis that all experimental evidence showed that an increase in disease increased loss, whereas a negative coefficient would imply that an increase in disease actually increased yield. Prior to developing the multiple point model, James *et al.* (1971) tested the critical point models developed by Large (1952) and Olofsson (1952) for estimating losses from the same disease. The results showed that the critical point models lacked the desired accuracy. Large's method is based on the assumption that when 75% of the foliage is affected by blight there is no further tuber production. Accordingly, with the aid of a bulking curve giving the accumulation of yield throughout the season, it is possible to calculate the loss as that percentage which has not been accumulated at the time when 75% blight is reached. Van der Plank (1963, p. 156) noted that Large's method can be considered as equating yield losses with the area under the disease progress curve, except that there is a correction for the change in rate of tuber bulking with time. The Large method has the disadvantage that blight must reach 75% before an estimate can be made. Also the estimate of loss is the same for an early and late epidemic which reaches 75% at the same time, whereas the actual losses are greater from the former. Considering that potato yield is accumulated over approximately half the growing season and that late blight can effect a decrease in yield at any point during the accumulation process, it is not surprising that a multiple rather than a critical point model is necessary. In contrast to the long epidemics and lengthy yield accumulation period associated with late blight and potatoes, the short epidemics and short dry-matter accumulation periods in cereals can be characterized by critical point models.

The estimation of yield loss from area under the disease progress curve models was first proposed by Van der Plank (1963) after he analysed wheat stem-rust data published by Kirby and Archer (1927) and Kingsolver *et al.* (1959). Although he obtained linear relationships between percentage yield loss and area-under-curve in arbitrary unit Van der Plank (1963, p. 153) cautioned that the ratio between different areas-under-curve is independent of the infection rate; with cereals, this will not allow the relative importance of disease at different growth stages to be detected. James (1974) noted that a multiple point model has this capability to apply a different weighting to disease, relative to time, by varying the value of the partial regression coefficients. Romig and Calpouzos (1970) attempted to evaluate both a critical point and an area-under-curve model for estimating yield loss due to stem rust in spring wheat. While their data supported a critical point model and did not support an area-under-curve model, the small number of epidemics studied did not conclusively discount the use of area-under-curve models for yield-loss estimation in stem rust. More recently, Buchenau (1975) reported a significant relationship between percentage yield loss and area-under-curve of stem and leaf rust measured together. Buchenau considered that the common correlation coefficient obtained between percentage yield loss and area-under-curve of -0.93 (about 86% of total variation explained) was sufficient evidence to indicate a $1:1$ relationship between percentage yield loss and area-under-curve. No area-under-curve or multiple point models have been developed for early and prolonged cereal epidemics to enable a comparison to be made between them, for estimating yield reduction due to several yield components.

Schneider *et al.* (1976), working with Cercospora leaf spot of cowpea in Nigeria, evaluated a critical point and an area-under-curve model for yield-loss estimation. The disease commonly occurs after flowering and is of short duration. Schneider *et al.* reported that an area-under-curve model of the form percentage yield loss $= 0.43\ AUC + 14.95$, with 70% of total variation explained, was a better estimator of yield loss than a critical point model based on the time after flowering when the Disease Severity Index equalled 1. The authors concluded that the area-under-curve models are suited to the same conditions described by James (1974) for critical points models, i.e. epidemics must be short and late in crops where yield is accumulated in a short period of time.

Although a primary purpose for grouping models is to give a better perspective of the literature, it is not possible to put all models into the three chosen groups. A notable example is the model for estimating yield loss due to stem rust proposed by Calpouzos *et al.* (1976). The model is in essence a multiple point model but yield is plotted as a response surface which is a function of the slope of the epidemic and the growth stage at the time of epidemic onset, i.e. $Y(\%\text{loss}) = f(X_1 X_2)$ where $X_1 =$ slope of the epidemic infection rate, $X_2 =$ growth stage at epidemic onset. The three-dimensional model is shown in Fig. 7 and has an r^2 value of 0.69. The model can be used to predict losses provided that values of X_1 and X_2 are available which can be calculated as follows. By utilizing equal divisions for growth stages, linear relationships were described between rust severity and growth stage (time). The linear relationship is used in conjunction with two or more disease assessments to determine the slope of the line (X_1) and to extrapolate the growth stage at epidemic onset (X_2).

The models discussed above reflect the volume of research on fungal pathogens causing significant yield losses in cereals and potatoes. Much less work has been done on other crops and on viral and bacterial pathogens. Of the limited published literature on virus losses, authors have often related yield loss to incidence of infected plants. For example, A'Brook and Heard (1975) noted that for percentage infected plants of 0, 40 and 80%, yield of ryegrass swards eight weeks after infection with ryegrass mosaic virus were 2·12, 1·44, 1·52 t ha^{-1} respectively. Singh and Singh (1975) estimated that in eggplant, each 1·5% incidence

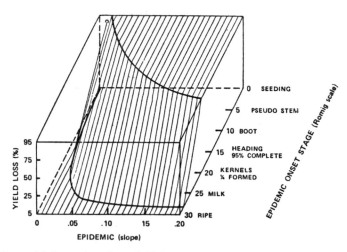

Fig. 7. A model for estimating yield loss due to stem rust of wheat. The three-dimensional illustration shows the response surface of yield loss to the two parameters of the epidemic; the epidemic onset stage and the epidemic slope. (After Calpouzos et al., 1976).

of eggplant mosaic virus caused 1% yield reduction. Scarborough and Smith (1977) reported that with tobacco and tomato ringspot viruses on geranium, virus incidence was directly expressed as reduction in the number of florets, which is the economic "yield".

Other workers have managed to relate percentage yield loss to mild or severe symptoms shown by infected plants, e.g. in potato leaf roll (Harper et al., 1975) and bean yellow virus (Hampton, 1975). Steadman et al. (1975), found that by rating roots of mature plants with a scale 0–5 they could estimate fairly accurately yield reduction in beans with each unit increase of root rot. Similarly Basu et al. (1976), working on Fusarium root rot of pea suggested that a conservative estimate of percentage losses in growers' fields may be equal to 0·57 × percentage of severely infected plants.

The characteristics of the epidemic and the required precision of loss estimates are the major factors which dictate the type of disease-loss model. The critical point model requires less input than the area-under-curve and multiple point models and is therefore less precise. The multiple point models, although more demanding in resources, provide the maximum flexibility and can cater for short or long epidemics where the onset, rate and level of infection may vary.

Very few disease-loss models take into account the quality losses which often accompany losses in yield. The work of Main *et al.* (1973) is an exception in that it represents a study on the effect of brown spot of tobacco on quality. The multiple regression technique was used to relate the effect of disease on many quality factors and an equation describes the relationship between disease severity and economic loss.

V. Disease-loss Surveys

Church (1971) commented that "when a problem is intractable and there is no obvious method of tackling it, a frequent suggestion is to do a survey". In the context of estimating disease losses, it may even be premature to assume that there is a problem before conducting a survey, because the principal objective of the survey is to establish whether there is a problem. Experience has shown that impressions of pathologists regarding the size of losses are often not confirmable when detailed surveys are conducted. One possible reason for such a discrepancy is the dominance of experimental data in plant pathology which is often not representative of the constraints associated with plant diseases at the farm level. Another reason is that farmers known to extension plant pathologists may not be representative of the total production system. *Ad hoc* surveys are just as likely to provide misinformation. Well-conducted surveys are the only way of determining the status of disease in crops, and the significance of the results and conclusions can have major impact. When compared with methods for deriving disease-loss models, survey methodology is relatively underdeveloped, probably because in the past most surveys have been conducted in an *ad hoc* fashion and consequently been regarded by plant pathologists as unproductive exercises. However, continuing survey programmes in England and Wales initiated by James (1969) and continued by King (1972, 1977a, 1977b) and in Scotland by Richardson (1975), have demonstrated their usefulness in keeping agricultural administrators, researchers and farmers aware of the status and importance of diseases on cereal crops. If conducted properly disease-loss surveys can provide much useful information not only about the magnitude of crop losses but also about the effectiveness and acceptability of control practices, provided that the latter information is collected simultaneously, as shown in Fig. 1. The practical application of knowledge developed in research and development in plant protection is probably a more difficult task than in most industries. Information on losses and control practices can lead to a further understanding of how far and in what way farmers have accepted control practices. It may also indicate what key factors motivate farmers to introduce plant protection programmes. Most disease surveys do not attempt to measure yield but involve collection of disease data to be used later for estimating losses in conjunction with a disease-loss model established by experiment. However, a few workers (Richardson, 1975; Stynes, 1975; Pinstrup-Andersen et al., 1976) have attempted to measure yield as well as disease, utilizing a survey approach. Church (1971) has reviewed sampling methods and techniques appropriate to crop-loss surveys and readers are referred to more detailed texts on survey methodology (Hansen et al., 1953; Yates, 1960; Zarkovich, 1966; Sukhatme and Sukhatme, 1970). Within the context of this review basic survey methodology will be presented and selected disease-loss surveys will be discussed.

Prior to initiating any disease-loss survey it is important that the objectives are defined. These include the area to be surveyed, the desired precision of the estimates, and the sub-classes for which estimates are required (e.g. districts, varieties, etc.). The methodology for disease assessment, usually developed during the experimental phase, must be well defined and used for training disease assessors, so that error between observers is minimal. All available information relating to the distribution and characteristics of the crop and the diseases under study must be collated so that the best sampling schemes and procedures can be developed. Church (1971) has noted that survey findings can lead to more efficient use of resources but that surveys must not use too much of what they aim to conserve. His statement underlines the importance of conducting a pilot survey to check all aspects of the operation, so that appropriate modifications can be made prior to the large scale survey.

The selection of representative samples from the whole population is an extremely important aspect of any survey because the sample represents the only data source for defining characteristics of the whole population. For example, for a plant disease-loss survey a sample of representative farms or fields must be selected to give a true estimate for the region and any sub-classification of the data into districts. Similarly within each field a truly representative sample of plants must be selected and assessed to establish the amount of disease within that field. The operational aspects of a survey may be conveniently discussed at two different levels of operation: procedures for selecting a sample of fields and procedures for assessing within fields.

A. PROCEDURES FOR SELECTING FIELDS

For the purpose of this review fields represent the sample points which can be defined as the basic entities for which disease estimates are to be recorded. In practice, farms could also be selected as sampling points. An important consideration is the sampling fraction which is the ratio of sampling points and the total population; this is often calculated on an acreage basis. As the sampling fraction increases so will the precision of the estimates. Although no fixed guidelines exist a sampling fraction of 0·01 is considered reasonable and is often used if little information is available about disease distribution and level. The sampling fraction will also vary according to the type of sampling used, e.g. simple random, stratified random sampling, stratified sample with variable sampling fraction and multistage; these are discussed below in more detail.

1. *Simple random sampling*
Simple random sampling is the most rudimentary method, in which every sample point (i.e. field) in the crop population under study has an equal chance of being included in the sample. For example, if it is known that there are 8000 wheat fields in the population (Table II) with a sampling fraction of 1/80, 100 fields can be selected at random with the use of a random number table (Barnett, 1974). Church (1971) has provided a guide-line formula for determining sample size: (n), the number of fields, for a given standard deviation (SD) and standard error (SE) as

$$n = \frac{SD^2}{SE^2}$$

In the absence of data on distribution of disease he suggested that a standard deviation of $\pm100\%$ is reasonable with a standard error of $\pm10\%$; this would give $n = 100^2/10^2 = 100$ (Table I). The precision of the final estimates of loss will not only reflect the precision of the assessment of disease as defined above, but also the precision of the crop-loss model for estimating loss for a given level of disease. Many of the crop-loss models have standard errors of approximately 20% and in these cases no gain would be effected by using *SE* estimates of less than 20% in the above equation. In practice simple random sampling is difficult to implement, because the fields are widely scattered throughout the region being surveyed.

2. *Stratified random sampling*

Simple random sampling is seldom adopted because disease-loss information is required on a district basis within a country. In stratified random sampling fields are selected at random from each strata, usually in proportion to the size of the district. Stratified random sampling is used when the proportion of population in the strata are known and where the standard deviation of disease estimates within strata are less than that for the whole population using a simple random sample. Strata can also apply to other variables e.g. variety or soil type. In Table I, assuming a standard deviation of $\pm 80\%$ within districts the number of fields is reduced to 64 $(80/10)^2$ and a sampling fraction of 1/133 compared with simple random sampling. A variation of stratified random sampling is the stratified sample with variable sampling fraction; this is used where estimates are needed for each district with a similar standard error. In Table II if a standard error of $\pm 15\%$ is

TABLE II Comparison between simple random and stratified random samples (after Church, 1971)

District	Total No. of fields	I Simple random sample		II Stratified sample		III Stratified sample with variable sampling fraction		Estd. average disease incidence
		Sampling fraction	Expected number[a]	Sampling fraction	Expected number	Sampling fraction	Expected number	
A	800		10	1/133	6	1/28	28	3
B	1600		20	1/133	13	1/57	28	6
C	1600		20	1/133	13	1/57	28	13
D	4000		50	1/133	32	1/142	28	16
	8000	1/80	100	1/133	64		112	

[a] Actual number will be different.

required for each district then the total number of fields is 112, $(80/15)^2$ = 28 per district. In practice a stratified random sampling procedure has been frequently used by plant pathologists (James, 1969; King, 1972; Richardson, 1975; Teng, 1975). Grainger (1967) illustrates the calculation of percentage severity means from strata of equal and unequal size, and in general it can be said that selecting a number of fields from each stratum proportional to the size of the stratum facilitates later calculations. Apart from the administrative and logistic reasons for using stratified random sampling to select fields, the method is also more efficient than simple random sampling. The stratified random mean reduces the variance of the population mean, especially when variation in disease severity between districts is large compared to within-district variation.

3. Multistage sampling

Where the cost of visiting random farms selected by the above methods is prohibitive, multistage sampling is often used. Multistage sampling for the selection of sample points can be considered a process of sub-sampling at different levels of the population. For example, in a three-stage procedure, the first stage may be two districts selected from four; the second stage, a number of villages selected from each of the two districts; and the third stage a number of farms selected from the villages. The computation of the mean and variance of each stage and of the population are outlined by Cochran (1963) and Sukhatme and Sukhatme (1970). The major gain from multistage sampling is the concentration of survey activities which leads to more economic sampling procedures compared with other schemes.

B. PROCEDURES FOR ASSESSING DISEASE WITHIN FIELDS

Disease assessment keys and diagrams have been found to be the most useful methods in disease survey work. The assessment method used in a survey also has to be comparable to that used in a disease-loss model if disease data from the survey is intended for loss estimation, and in this context, the growth stage at which assessments are made must also be comparable. For example, in the surveys by James (1969) on barley in England and Wales, fields were sampled at Feekes g.s. 11·1 because the loss model for leaf blotch called for assessments at this growth stage (James et al., 1968). In situations where there are more than one field of the crop under study, care has to be taken to select the field at random. James (1969) outlined a simple procedure where the fields were listed and numbered consecutively so that one field (the sample point) could be selected with random numbers.

1. *Sampling procedure*

In this context, sampling procedure is the selection of sampling units (e.g. tillers) from a field to obtain a representative estimate of the true disease situation in the field. The sampling procedure should be as free from human bias as possible, and should not be influenced by the accessibility of the sample or its presumed value. One common sampling procedure is to walk across the diagonal of the field and select at random the predetermined number of tillers or plants. The tillers may be removed for laboratory assessment or assessed *in situ*. For fields of unequal size, James (1971c) selected 3 wheat culms per acre up to a maximum of 25 culms per field, while Teng (1975) assessed 50 per 3 acre field in an area with fairly similar field sizes. Selection of the first tiller or plant may be achieved using a random procedure or by ensuring it is a minimum distance away from the edge of a field to reduce border effects. Although taking samples in a diagonal is convenient, variations like a "W" pattern across a field can be used (James, 1971c). An important guide-line is that the sampling procedure should cater for the distribution of disease in a field.

The individual unit of the crop population on which disease or loss measurements are made is termed the sampling unit. In temperate cereals, the sampling unit commonly sampled is a single tiller, with one or more leaves per tiller being assessed for disease. Specific leaves are often assessed at particular growth stages (James, 1969). In most rice surveys, the sampling unit is a hill of rice tillers, each hill comprising three to four seedlings grouped during transplanting. In some surveys, extra numbers of tillers are removed for laboratory testing of pathogen races, or for verification of crop growth stage (James, 1969; King, 1977b).

2. *Sample size*

Several factors are considered before determining the number of sampling units (tillers) to be removed from a sampling point. These include the sampling costs, the time available for sampling and the accuracy required (Teng, 1978a). The size of the sample may also have to account for fluctuations in field size (James, 1971c). The accuracy of a disease estimate is measured by the standard error of estimate of the sample mean. In general with an increase in sample size, the cost per unit precision rises. However, with very small sample sizes the increased cost for increased precision may be worthwhile; the diminishing return becomes more obvious as sample size increases. There is a lack of data on distribution of disease and this precludes the development of optimal sampling procedures. For example with more information on disease distribution, more use could be made of sequential sampling similar to that developed by Strandberg (1973) which saved much time and effort.

3. *Data recording and reporting*

All surveys produce a voluminous amount of data and computer processing facilitates efficient analysis of results. However this has meant that the coding of data from a sample has become more important as a pre-survey consideration. Many standard statistical packages are now available to users for analysing survey data (Nie *et al.*, 1975). Programmes have also been specially written for particular projects (James, 1969; Mogk, 1974; Arnold, 1977) but specifications generally conform to the 80 column standard computer card. The designing of a field coding sheet which will allow direct card punching will therefore expedite data transfer and analysis and result in minimal errors. Reporting of results to all personnel involved in the survey including co-operating farmers is an extremely important aspect for the continued success of repeated surveys. Computer processing allows such reports to be prepared sufficiently fast to ensure retention of interest amongst co-operators.

C. OPERATIONAL DISEASE-LOSS SURVEYS

A series of surveys on barley-foliage diseases initiated by James (1969) in England and Wales in 1967 and continued by King (1972, 1977b) probably provides the most convincing evidence of the usefulness of surveys. The first survey conducted in 1967 demonstrated the significance of powdery mildew and the probable need for chemical control measures previously considered unnecessary. Approximately 300 fields totalling 5250 acres of spring barley were sampled and approximately 7500 tillers were assessed for diseases on the flag and second leaf at g.s. 11·1. The average severities for the disease present on the top two leaves are given below with their associated standard errors.

Disease	*% lamina affected*
Mildew	11·0 ± 0·6
Brown Rust	4·3 ± 0·4
Leaf Blotch	1·7 ± 0·2
Yellow Rust	1·0 ± 0·2
Halo Spot	0·1 ± 0·05

The loss due to mildew was estimated at 13–18% and total losses due to foliage diseases estimated at 20–25%. A similar survey concentrated in the south west of England during the same season independently confirmed the importance of mildew (Melville and Lanham, 1972). The usefulness of the barley survey has ensured its repetition every year with the exception of 1971, and furthermore it has prompted the development of a similar annual survey on wheat by King (1977a) in 1970. Since 1967 barley mildew has consistently caused significant losses and with the exception of 1970 and 1975, it was the most severe foliage disease recorded despite the increasing use of mildew fungicides. During the period 1967–70 mildew was estimated to cause an average loss of 9% (King, 1972). Analysis of survey data led King (1977b) to conclude that in 1974 and 1975 at least 60% of the untreated crops could have been treated with fungicide to economic advantage.

In all the surveys on spring barley in England and Wales, a stratified random sampling procedure was used to select fields, with each stratum being based on administrative regions. The number of fields sampled in each region was proportionally allocated depending on barley area in each region. On farms with more than one barley field, the field for sampling was selected randomly (James, 1969). As noted earlier, this facilitates computations of national mean due to equal weightings in each region. Fifty tillers were removed at random along the diagonal of a field, and despatched to a central laboratory for assessment. A subsample of 25 each of flag and second leaves were assessed for diseases, and the remaining leaves used for virus testing or race identification. The disease data were punched directly on to computer tape and a specially written programme was used for analysis of the data. The detailed procedure is outlined by James (1969) and revisions reported by King's subsequent reports (1972, 1977b). In the later surveys, Wales was over-sampled to provide more accurate estimates, and an additional growth stage was included in some samples for better mildew-loss estimation. Recently King has also utilized the more critical decimal code of Zadoks *et al.* (1974) for recording growth stage. The results of the winter wheat surveys in England and Wales for the period 1970–75 have been reported by King (1977a). *Septoria nodorum* was found to be the most severe leaf disease in all years except 1970, when mildew was most severe, and in 1975 when brown rust (*Puccinia recondita*) was most severe. Due to the lack of disease-loss information, the estimation of yield losses has been hampered. King estimated that for the years 1970–75, on average mildew caused 3% annual loss while *Septoria* caused 2% loss. Both the barley and winter wheat surveys are now conducted annually, with continuous modifications to provide comprehensive information on foliage and other foot-rot diseases.

Richardson (1971) has used a different survey technique which directly determines yield in the survey fields. The technique attempts to partition loss in yield due to different diseases and other constraint factors at different growth stages during the season. For each crop, the seedling population is checked and the final yield as well as the three components of yield—ears per plant, seeds per ear and seed weight—are determined from a sample of ears. Richardson reported on the mechanism of the technique as follows; three yield-component potentials are estimated:

1. An estimate of the potential ear population from the particular seedling population;
2. An estimate of potential yield from the actual ear population;
3. An estimate of potential yield from the potential ear population.

Using these three estimates in conjunction with actual yield, the following losses are calculated:

(a) The differences between potential yield from the seedling population and that from the actual ear population is considered to be a loss due to ear deficiency;
(b) The difference between potential yield from the actual ear population and actual yield is a loss due to a deficiency in seed number per ear or seed size;
(c) The total loss is the difference between the potential yield from the seedling population and the actual yield, with the addition of losses due to the non-functional ears.

A self-explanatory example for a particular crop is shown below in Table III: (after Richardson, 1971).

Richardson's method aims to estimate losses within the total production system and the approach is claimed to be successful despite the problems of estimating potential yield. Richardson has not utilized the sophisticated statistical techniques employed by Stynes (1975), who successfully analysed similar data to assess the relative significance of different constraint factors within the total production system. Examining and partitioning losses from surveys cannot however be a substitute for the experimental phase which is necessary to prove a cause and effect relationship. Surveys at different growth stages during the growth of a crop can indicate that certain factors may be important, but experimentation is still required to confirm the finding and characterize the relationship between disease and yield.

To date, aerial surveys have not been used as a matter of routine for monitoring the development of epidemics on crops, but much work is in progress on the development of such techniques. For the future, aerial photography in conjunction with remote sensing have great potential for conducting surveys over large areas in a short space of time.

TABLE III   Calculation of loss in yield from survey data

Wheat—Cappelle Desprez

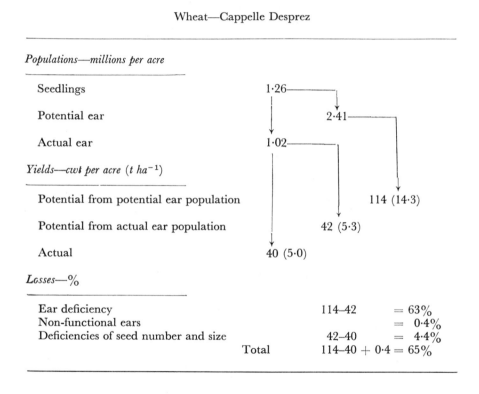

Populations—millions per acre			
Seedlings	1·26		
Potential ear		2·41	
Actual ear	1·02		
Yields—cwt per acre (t ha⁻¹)			
Potential from potential ear population			114 (14·3)
Potential from actual ear population		42 (5·3)	
Actual	40 (5·0)		
Losses—%			
Ear deficiency		114–42	= 63%
Non-functional ears			= 0·4%
Deficiencies of seed number and size		42–40	= 4·4%
Total		114–40 + 0·4	= 65%

VI. SYSTEMS APPROACH TO DISEASE-LOSS APPRAISAL AND MANAGEMENT

Reference has been made on several occasions in this review to the need to quantify the losses due to diseases within the context of the total production system. There is also an urgent need to develop disease-management schemes using the systems approach to utilize disease simulators in conjunction with disease-loss models to predict disease development, and intervene with economic control measures if necessary (James, 1974). Although the systems approach started as a philosophical science it has now evolved into a systems research with problem-solving capability which is dependent on the development of computer technology. Each system is defined by a conceptual boundary and is made up of sub-systems. Within the host–pathogen system there are two sub-systems, the pathogen and the host, and the interactions between the two are affected by exogenous variables like weather or fungicides, which can cross the conceptual boundary. At the same time endogenous variables, for example the yield of the crop and the propagules of the pathogen, will leave the system. Mihram (1972) considered systems research to consist of two major areas—systems analysis and systems synthesis. Systems analysis is that phase of system study that involves defining the system and its components, and specifying their interactive behaviour and interrelationships. Systems analysis is a quantitative process which in practice leads to the collection of data for a simulation (system) model (Anderson, 1972). Even if the exercise in system study ends at this point, analysis can reveal weak links in the system, as well as component processes in the system for which no information is available (Giese et al., 1975). The systems synthesis phase is concerned with using the knowledge gained from analysis to modify the original system or to design entirely new systems (Wright, 1971) and is therefore more concerned with the control and management functions of the system. Having briefly introduced the systems approach, its use for disease-loss appraisal studies will be examined and also the feasibility of applying it to develop disease-loss management systems.

A. DISEASE-LOSS APPRAISAL STUDIES

Almost without exception disease-loss models have been developed for single diseases whereas in practice crops are often attacked by more than one disease and are subject to many constraint factors other than disease. Indeed the inherent difficulty of even developing models for single diseases explains why little progress has been made with multiple-disease models. However in some cases, e.g. stem rust of cereals or late blight of potato, a single-model disease is adequate because most of the variability in yield is related to that particular disease. In general pathologists have been over-concerned with the pathogen component of the system without determining its relevance to other constraint factors in the production system. Wallace (1978) has recently reviewed some studies on disease with complex etiology, involving interactions between pathogens and other abiotic factors.

As long ago as 1948, Sallans applied multiple-regression analysis to study wheat production in Canada. He analysed the effect of five variables on wheat yield (Y) over 10 years; these were: rainfall during the cropping summer $(X1)$, rainfall during the preceding autumn and spring $(X2)$, average daily mean temperature during the cropping summer $(X3)$, percentage damage due to insects $(X4)$ and common root rot $(X5)$. The derived relationship between yield and the five variables was of the form

$$Y = 39 \cdot 91 + 1 \cdot 61 X_1 + 1 \cdot 12 X_2 - 0 \cdot 56 X_3 - 0 \cdot 15 X_4 - 0 \cdot 58 X_5.$$

Addition of the X_5 variable significantly increased the accuracy of the model, which explained 78% of total variation in yield. After examining the partial regression coefficients, Sallans (1948) concluded that common root rot was the major reason for yield reduction in wheat in his study area. In Colombia, Pinstrup-Andersen *et al.* (1976) conducted a similar study using a regression procedure to identify biotic and abiotic production constraints. They identified rust, bacterial blight and angular leaf-spot to be major constraints on bean yield, with their relative depressing effects being indicated at 16, 13 and 8% respectively. Figure 8 is a self-explanatory crop-loss profile indicating the relative importance of the crop production constraint factors monitored in the study. Sitepu and Wallace (1974) used a "synoptic" approach to diagnose retarded growth in apple by examining separately and interactively the correlation between size of apple trees and six factors— *Pythium* spp., *Phytophthora* spp., stylet-bearing nematodes, percentage clay, percentage soil moisture and soil pH. They found that tree growth was significantly correlated to soil pH, number of nematodes and the concentration of *Pythium* spp. in the soil.

Stynes (1975) conducted a more comprehensive study of wheat growth and production constraints on forty-two farms in Australia during 1972 and 1974. Various morphological and physiological plant records and soil determinations were recorded at four growth stages, and the final grain yield was measured. Symptoms of the diseases caused by *Gaeumannomyces graminis* and *Rhizoctonia solani* were assessed as well as damage caused by the nematodes *Heterodera avenae* and *Pratylenchus minyus*. Multivariate analyses were used in conjunction with principal component procedures to identify the possible variables responsible for the variability in growth and yield. Explanatory and predictive models were produced. The 1972 results showed that the efficiency of the root system and soil water were the main factors responsible for variation in yield. The pathogens and the nematodes were in part responsible for root inefficiency and accounted for 9–16% of the

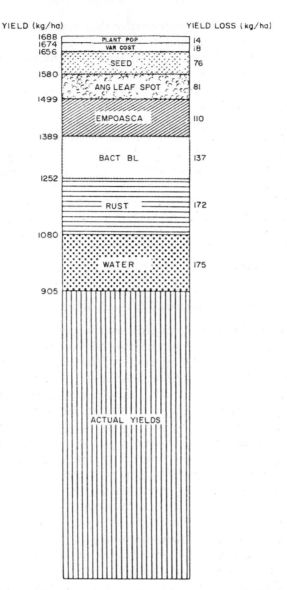

FIG. 8. A crop-loss profile showing the relative importance of different constraint factors on bean production in the Cauca Valley, Colombia. (After Pinstrup-Anderson *et al.*, 1976).

variation in growth. It is noteworthy that nematodes affected growth early in the season and had no effect on yield, whereas the fungal pathogens had no effect early in the season but had an important effect on yield. The models developed in 1972 were successfully fitted to data at all stages in 1974 except for grain yield. The misfit was due to a stem-rust epidemic in 1974 which was not present in 1972. In terms of yield variability, with the exception of the stem rust in 1974, *G. graminis* was the most important pathogen despite moderate populations of *H. avenae*. Stynes' "synoptic study" (1975) testifies to the merit of the systems approach, for quantifying the relative importance of various production constraints and identifying the variables which lend themselves to control and therefore present opportunities for increasing yields. The use of the synoptic study as the initial step in a crop-loss programme to identify priorities should be investigated more generally. If broadly applicable it would allow resources to be concentrated in the problem areas at the outset of programme development.

B. DISEASE-LOSS MANAGEMENT

When applying the systems concept to management, the property of the system which unifies its components—the functional objective of the system—is of paramount importance. The principal objective in the management of a crop agro-ecosystem is to maximize yield. If a pathogen is the major constraint, then the purpose of management is to minimize the effects of the constraint on the system objective (Teng *et al.*, 1977b). The means by which this can be achieved depends to a large extent on the time at which the pathogen infects the crop because as Norton (1976) noted, the number of options available to a farmer become more limited as the season progresses. Disease management through genetic or cultural manipulation (Robinson, 1976) is outside the scope of this chapter and discussion will concentrate on situations where an epidemic is developing, and is expected to cause significant yield loss in spite of these manipulations.

In applying systems thinking to management, the control function of management depends on a constant flow of information from the system to the manager, to enable him to evaluate the status of the system, the effects of his past decisions, and to make new decisions if necessary (Churchman, 1968). This control function of management has been compared by Wiener (1948) to that of a steersman, hence the term "cybernetics" (from the Greek meaning "steersman") to describe systems providing information feedback. In plant-disease management, the control function of management has the short term goal of maximizing profit with minimum cost; the minimum cost being attained by a rational use of fungicide. However, the rationalization of fungicide use is possible only if the amount of yield loss caused by disease is known, and this is the reason why disease-loss models must be incorporated into any disease-loss management system. The use of disease simulators to project increase in disease and to simulate the effect of a fungicide application, in conjunction with crop agro-ecosystem and disease loss models, should result in a rational disease-control system. The need for a rapid means of communicating data from the system to the manager, and translating this data into information also underlines the dependence of modern management schemes on electronic computers. Management information systems are well-developed for macrobiological systems like pig (Blackie and Anderson, 1974) and poultry (Blackie, M. J. pers. comm.) enterprises, possibly because the fundamental biological processes involved in those systems are less susceptible to the influence of exogenous variables. In contrast, pest–crop systems can be markedly affected by fluctuations in level of their exogenous variables and hence the stochastic element enters into any attempt to project ahead. Furthermore, management information systems appear to have been more successfully implemented on intensive enterprises, where small variations in the cost or quantity of a major input/output have a large effect on eventual profitability (Blackie, 1976). Cropping enterprises are extensive in nature, and this may be the reason for the few attempts at formulating management information systems for them. In the area of general pest management, Ruesink (1976) has reviewed progress made in adopting a systems approach to insect management. Simulation modelling is only one of the tools available to the scientist interested in applying systems techniques to management. Two other methods which have potential value are optimization (Shoemaker, 1973a,b,c) and the use of Bayesian Decision Theory (Carlson, 1970). However, both these methods, used on their own, are incapable of accounting for the dynamic nature of disease epidemics, particularly diseases which are not seasonally recurrent in epidemic proportions (Ruesink, 1976; Norton, 1976). However, when output from a simulation model is used in an optimization routine, a computer can assist the manager to decide on the best management strategy. An example of this sort of approach is work directed at optimal integrated control of alfalfa weevil (Fick et al., 1976; Shoemaker, 1976).

Dent (1974) urged the adoption of a "modular" approach towards developing practical systems models for management. The modular approach proposes that the system model should consist of submodels, each representing a component of the system, and that all the sub-models should then be linked together by an executive routine responsible for time-keeping and event advancement. In the USA, this modular approach has been developed and is in use; for example, the GASP-IV based alfalfa simulator, SIMED (Holt *et al.*, 1975) has been linked to an alfalfa weevil model to provide a real time, on-line pest management scheme (Giese *et al.*, 1975) in a plot area in Indiana. GASP-IV (Pritsker, 1974) is a multipurpose combined continuous discrete simulation language based on FORTRAN and can be simply described as an assembly of sub-routines and functions useful to modellers. Its availability means that there is no need for pathologists to become expert in systems analysis and computer programming. Another alfalfa simulator, ALSIM 1 (Fick, 1975) is being used as the crop component in an alfalfa-weevil management scheme where output from the combined pest-crop model is used as input for optimization (Fick *et al.*, 1976). In plant disease management, preliminary research in Canada was started to develop a scheme using a late blight simulator, PHYTOSIM, in conjunction with disease-loss models (James, 1974). In New Zealand, a barley leaf-rust simulation model, with a disease-loss sub-model built into its structure, is currently being evaluated for management (Teng *et al.*, 1977a). The predictive ability of the barley leaf-rust model has been ascertained from historical data; it forecasts a quantitative increase in disease, which is translated into yield loss by means of a multiple point disease-loss model (Teng, 1978b). In both the above examples, the systems are designed to prescribe each fungicide application on a cost/benefit basis commensurate with rational disease control.

A disease management scheme which is to make use of quantitative data must have an information system capable of agro-ecosystem surveillance, disease projection and yield loss estimation. The development of simulation models is a resource-demanding task (Blackie, 1978) and Krause and Massie (1975) have noted that in terms of implementation, a system may be more acceptable if it is based on existing prediction schemes, even though quantitative criteria may be absent. Krause *et al.* (1975) showed that a management information system based on prediction of favourable infection-periods of potato late-blight could result in the use of a significantly lower number of fungicide applications and absence of blight. We feel that disease-management information systems based on quantitative loss prediction are logical extensions of these qualitative schemes. The development of simulation models is time consuming and Arnold and Bennett (1975) have expressed the opinion that "cheap and nasty" models which biologists dislike because they are over-simplified, may be more useful and contribute more to improved agricultural practice than "expensive but accurate" models.

It may well be that progress in the development of disease-management systems can be accelerated, if tolerances are relaxed until experience has allowed us to refine our techniques.

VII. Concluding Remarks

We have attempted to demonstrate the need for quantifying production constraints associated with plant diseases as well as reviewing the progress already made in achieving this objective. In a world that is short of food, but is conscious of protecting the environment and utilizing finite resources responsibly, crop loss estimates can play a vital role by providing objective data for critically evaluating the use of resources. Although not yet accepted, it is suggested that a crop-loss appraisal programme should be a permanent feature of any national plant-protection programme, to continuously monitor changes in the dynamic production system. Such a programme would allow the economic importance of diseases in major crops to be monitored so that priorities could be revised regularly and limited resources used efficiently.

The difficulty of developing technology for estimating losses explains why so few disease-loss models have been developed. However, future model builders should benefit from studying the few but different types of models that have already been developed. Analysis of the host–pathogen system shows that epidemiological characteristics will probably dictate the type of model that will be appropriate. All the current disease–loss models describe the effect of one disease on yield but there is a critical need to develop models that will describe the effect of more than one disease and preferably include other yield constraint factors. The "synoptic approach" (Stynes, 1975) for quantifying the effect of abiotic and biotic constraint factors within the total production system looks encouraging and should be tested more widely to determine the breadth of its applicability. Similarly, the use of the single tiller technique should be further explored to establish its validity, so that full advantage can be taken of the economy of resources it offers. The successful example of the cereal disease surveys in England and Wales (James, 1969; King, 1977a,b) should stimulate plant pathologists to initiate similar surveys on crops of economic importance. Survey techniques will, we hope, be facilitated through developments in aerial photography and remote sensing that will simplify large scale disease surveillance.

Finally there is a need to accelerate the incorporation of disease-loss models into disease management schemes, utilizing the systems approach.

This will allow disease-loss models to be used for preventing losses due to disease. The system being developed by Teng *et al.* (1977a) for leaf rust of barley in New Zealand is a challenging development which will allow rational decision making in disease control. Such a development will not only lead to more economic disease control but will also minimize the use of fungicides on food crops. The systems approach requires a multi-disciplinary effort and this in itself will almost certainly acclerate progress in achieving the goals and objectives defined in this review.

References

A'Brook, J. and Heard, A. J. (1975). The effect of ryegrass mosaic virus on the yield of perennial ryegrass swards. *Ann. appl. Biol.* **80**,163–168.

Alexander, M. (1974). Environmental consequences of rapidly rising food output. *Agroecosyst.* **1**, 249–264.

Aluko, M. O. (1975). Crop losses caused by the brown leaf spot disease of rice in Nigeria. *Pl. Dis. Reptr.* **59**, 609–613.

Anderson, J. R. (1972). An overview of modelling in agricultural management. *Rev. Marketing and agric. Econ.* **40**, 111–122.

Anonymous (1947). The measurement of potato blight. *Trans. Br. Mycol. Soc.* **31**, 140–141.

Arnold, J. R. (1977). A use of computers in epiphytology—the SANITY system. *APPS Newsl.* **6**, 16–17.

Arnold, G. W. and Bennett, D. (1975). The problem of finding an optimum solution. *In* "Study of Agricultural Systems", (Dalton, G. E., Ed.), pp. 129–173. Applied Science Publishers, London.

Ausmus, B. S. and Hilty, J. W. (1973). Reflectance studies of healthy, maize dwarf mosaic virus-infected and *Helminthosporium maydis*-infected corn leaves. *Remote Sens. Environ.* **2**, 77–81.

Ayers, J. E., Nelson, R. R., Castor, L. L. and Blanco, M. H. (1976). Yield losses in corn caused by *Helminthosporium maydis* race T. *Pl. Dis. Reptr.* **60**, 331–335.

Barnett, V. (1974). "Elements of Sampling Theory." The English Universities Press, London.

Basu, P. K., Brown, N. J., Crete, R., Gourley, C. O., Johnston, H. W., Pepin, H. S. and Seaman, W. L. (1976). Yield Loss conversion factors for *Fusarium* root rot of pea. *Can. Pl. Dis. Surv.* **56**, 26–32.

Blackie, M. J. (1976). Management information systems for the individual farm firm. *Agric. Systems* **1**, 23–36.

Blackie, M. J. (1978). Modelling or muddling: some comments on the application of systems research techniques. *In* Proc. APPS Workshop Epidemiol. Crop Loss Assessment, Lincoln Coll., N.Z. **31**, 1–8.

Blackie, M. J. and Anderson, F. M. (1974). A planning and control system for an intensive farm enterprise: pig production. *Outlook Agric.* **8**, 42–46.

Brenchley, G. H. (1966). The aerial photography of potato blight epidemics. *Roy. Aeronaut. Soc.* **70**, 1082–1086.

Brooks, D. H. (1972). Observations on the effects of mildew, *Erysiphe graminis*, on growth of spring and winter barley. *Ann. appl. Biol.* **70**, 149–156.

Buchenau, G. W. (1975). Relationship between yield loss and area under the wheat stem rust and leaf rust progress curves. *Phytopathology* **65**, 1317–1318.

Burleigh, J. R., Eversmeyer, M. G. and Roelfs, A. P. (1972a). Development of linear equations for predicting wheat leaf rust. *Phytopathology* **62**, 947–953.

Burleigh, J. R. Roelfs, A. P. and Eversmeyer, M. G. (1972b). Estimating damage to wheat caused by *Puccinia recondita tritici*. *Phytopathology* **62**, 944–946.

Butt, D. J. and Royle, D. J. (1974). *In* "Epidemics of Plant Diseases: Mathematical Analysis and Modelling", (Kranz, J., Ed.), pp. 78–114. Springer-Verlag, Berlin.

Calpouzos, L., Roelfs, A. P., Madson, M. E., Martin, F. B., Welsh, J. R. and Wilcoxson, R. D. (1976). A new model to measure yield losses caused by stem rust in spring wheat. *Tech. Bull. Agric. Expl. Stn. Univ. Minnesota* No. **307**.

Carefoot, G. L. and Sprott, E. R. (1969). "Famine on the Wind: Plant Diseases and Human History." Angus and Robertson, London.

Carlson, G. A. (1970). A decision theoretic approach to crop disease prediction and control. *Am. J. agric. Econ.* **52**, 216–223.

Casey, P. (1978). Ground-based measurements of the reflectance factors of a diseased canopy. *In* Proc. APPS Workshop Epidemiol. Crop Loss Assessment, Lincoln Coll., N.Z. **5**, 1–2.

Chamberlain, N. H., Doodson, J. K. and Meadway, M. H. (1972). A technique for the evaluation of the resistance of barley varieties to infection with brown rust (*Puccinia hordei* Otth.) *J. Nat. Inst. Agr. Bot.* **12**, 440–444.

Chee, K. H. (1976). Assessing susceptibility of *Hevea* clones to *Microcyclus ulei*. *Ann. appl. Biol.* **84**, 135–146.

Chester, K. S. (1950). Plant disease losses: their appraisal and interpretation. *Pl. Dis. Reptr. Suppl.* **193**, 189–362.

Chiang, H. C. and Wallen, V. R. (1977). Detection and Assessment of Crop losses and insect infestations by aerial photography. Crop Loss Assessment Methods Supplement 2, 3.1.7/1–10 (looseleaf). FAO manual on the evaluation and prevention of losses by pests, diseases and weeds. Commonw. Agric. Bur., Slough, England.

Chiarappa, L., Gonzalez, R. H., Moore, F. J., Stickland, A. H. and Chiang, H. C. (1975). The status and requirements of the FAO International Collaborative Programme on crop loss appraisal. *FAO Pl. Prot. Bull.* **23**, 118–124.

Church, B. M. (1971). The place of sample survey in crop loss estimation. *In* "Crop Loss Assessment Methods. 2.2/1–12" (looseleaf) FAO manual on the evaluation and prevention of losses by pests, diseases and weeds. Commonw. Agric. Bur., Slough, England.

Churchman, C. W. (1968). "The Systems Approach." Dell, New York.

Cobb, N. A. (1892), Contribution to an economic knowledge of the Australian rusts (Uredinae). *Agric. Gaz. N.S.W.* **3**, 60–68.

Cochran, W. G. (1963). "Sampling Techniques." Wiley, New York.

Colwell, R. N. (1956). Determining the prevalence of certain cereal crop diseases by means of aerial photography. *Hilgardia* **26**, 223–286.

Cooke, B. M. and Brokenshire, T. (1975). Assessment keys for halo spot disease on barley, caused by *Selenophoma donacis*. *Trans. Br. Mycol. Soc.* **65**, 318–321.

Cramer, H. H. (1975). Economic aspects of plant protection. Proc. Sem. d'Etud. Agriculture et Hygiène des Plantes. Gembloux (Belg.) 507–518.

Dent, J. B. (1974). Application of systems concepts and simulation in agriculture. Misc. publication, School of Agriculture, Univ. of Aberdeen.

Doling, D. A. and Doodson, J. K. (1968). The effect of yellow rust on the yield of spring and winter wheat. *Trans. Br. Mycol. Soc.* **51**, 427–44.

Downs, S. W. Jr. (1974). Remote sensing in agriculture. *NASA Tech. Memo.* NASA TM X-64803. Alabama.

Draper, N. R. and Smith, H. (1966). "Applied Regression Analysis." Wiley, New York.

Emge, R. G. and Shrum, R. D. (1976). Epiphytology of *Puccinia striiformis* at five selected locations in Oregon during 1968 and 1969. *Phytopathology* **66**, 1406–12.

Eversmeyer, M. G. and Burleigh, J. R. (1970). A method of predicting epidemic development of wheat leaf rust. *Phytopathology* **60**, 805–811.

Eversmeyer, M. G., Burleigh, J. R. and Roelfs, A. P. (1973). Equations for predicting wheat stem rust development. *Phytopathology* **63**, 348–51.

Eyal, Z. and Brown, M. B. (1976). A quantitative method for estimating density of *Septoria tritici* pycnidia on wheat leaves. *Phytopathology* **66**, 11–14.

Fick, G. W. (1975). ALSIM 1 (Level 1) Users' Manual. Dept. of Agronomy, Mimeo 75–20, N.Y. State College of Agriculture and Life Sciences, Cornell University, Ithaca, N.Y.

Fick, G. W., Shoemaker, C. A., Helgesen, R. G. and Lowe, C. C. (1976). Alfalfa weevil research—crop, insect and management modelling. *In* "ARS Publication n. NC-52 Rep. 25th Alfalfa Improvement Conf." p. 18–19.

Food and Agriculture Organization of the United Nations. (1967). Papers presented at Symposium of crop losses. FAO,UN, Rome.

Food and Agriculture Organization of the United Nations (1971). Crop loss assessment methods; FAO manual on the evaluation and prevention of losses by pests, diseases and weeds. Commonw. Agric. Bur., Slough, England.

Fry, W. E. (1977). Integrated control of potato late blight—effects of polygenic resistance and techniques of timing fungicide applications. *Phytopathology* **67**, 415–420.

Gaskill, J. O. and Schneider, C. L. (1966). Savoy and yellow vein diseases of sugarbeet in the Great Plains in 1963–64–65. *Pl. Dis. Reptr.* **50**, 457–459.

Gaunt, R. E. (1978). Crop physiology: disease effects and yield loss. *In* Proc. APPS. Workshop Epidemiol. Crop loss Assessment. Lincoln Coll., N.Z. **9**, 1–12.

Gausman, H. W. (1974). Leaf reflectance of near infrared. *Photogrammetric Engng.* **40**, 183–191.

Geh, S. L. and Ting, W. P. (1973). Loss in yield of groundnuts affected by groundnut mosaic virus disease. *MARDI Res. Bull.* **1**, 22–28.

Giese, R. L., Peart, R. M. and Huber, R. T. (1975). Pest management: a pilot project exemplifies new ways of dealing with important agricultural pests. *Sci.* **187**, 1045–1052.

Gorter, G. J. M. A. (1974). Methods of assessing cucurbit powdery mildew (*Sphaerotheca fuliginea*) in terms of fungicide evaluation. *S. Afr. J. Sci.* **70**, 7–9.

Grainger, J. (1947). The ecology of *Erysiphe graminis* DC. *Trans. Br. Mycol. Soc.* **31**, 54–65.

Grainger, J. (1967). Methods for use in economic surveys of crop disease. Background papers prepared for the FAO Symposium on Crop Losses. pp. 49–74, FAO, UN, Rome.

Griffiths, E., Jones, D. G. and Valentine, M. (1975). Effects of powdery mildew at different growth stages on grain yield of barley. *Ann. appl. Biol.* **80**, 343–49.

Hampton, R. O. (1975). The nature of bean yield reduction by bean yellow and bean common mosaic virus. *Phytopathology* **65**, 1342–1346.

Hansen, M. H., Hurwitz, W. N. and Madow, W. G. (1953). "Sample Survey Methods and Theory." Wiley, New York.

Harlan, J. R. (1976). The plants and animals that nourish man. *Sci. Am.* **235**, 89–97.

Harper, F. R., Nelson, G. A. and Pittman, V. J. (1975). Relationship between leaf roll symptoms and yield in Netted Gem Potato. *Phytopathology* **65**, 1242–1244.

Hide, G. A., Hirst, J. M. and Stedman, O. J. (1973). Effects of black scurf (*Rhizoctonia solani*) on potatoes. *Ann. appl. Biol.* **74**, 139–148.

Holt, D. A., Bula, R. J., Miles, G. E., Schreiber, M. M. and Peart, R. M. (1975). Environmental physiology, modeling and simulation of alfalfa growth: I. Conceptual development of SIMED. *Res. Bull.* **907**, Agric. Exp. Stn., Purdue University.

Horsfall, J. G. and Barratt, R. W. (1945). An improved grading system for measuring plant diseases. *Phytopathology* **35**, 655.

Hosford, R. M. Jr and Busch, R. H. (1974). Losses in wheat caused by *Pyrenophora trichostoma* and *Leptosphaeria avenaria* f.sp. *triticea*. *Phytopathology* **64**, 184–187.

International Food Policy Research Institute (1977). Food needs of developing countries: projections of production and consumption to 1990. *Res. Rep.* **3.** (Washington, D.C.).

Jackson, H. R. (1972). Black and White infrared photography of plant disease symptoms (macro). *J. Biol. Photogr. Ass.* **40**, 138–162.

Jackson, H. R. and Wallen, V. R. (1975). Microdensitometer measurements of sequential aerial photographs of field beans infected with bacterial blight. *Phytopathology* **65**, 961–968.

Jackson, H. R., Hodgson, W. A., Wallen, V. R., Philpotts, L. E. and Hunter, J. (1971). Potato late blight intensity levels as determined by microdensitometer studies of false-color aerial photographs. *J. Biol. Photogr. Ass.* **39**, 101–106.

James, W. C. (1969). A survey of foliar diseases by spring barley in England and Wales in 1967. *Ann. appl. Biol.* **63**, 253–263.

James, W. C. (1971a). An illustrated series of assessment keys for plant diseases, their preparation and usage. *Can. Pl. Dis. Surv.* **51**, 39–65.

James, W. C. (1971b). A manual of disease assessment keys for plant diseases. *Can. Dep. Agric. Publication* **1458.**

James, W. C. (1971c). Importance of foliar diseases of winter wheat in Ontario in 1969 and 1970. *Can. Pl. Dis. Surv.* **51**, 24–31.

James, W. C. (1974). Assessment of plant diseases and losses. *Ann. Rev. Phytopathology* **12**, 27–48.

James, W. C. (1979). Crop Loss Assessment. *In* "Plant Pathologist's Pocketbook" (2nd Edn.). Compiled by C.M.I., London.

James, W. C. and Shih, C. S. (1973a). Relationship between incidence and severity of powdery and mildew and leaf rust on winter wheat. *Phytopathology* **63**, 183–187.

James, W. C. and Shih, C. S. (1973b). Size and shape of plots for estimating yield losses from cereal foliage diseases. *Exp. Agr.* **9**, 63–71.

James, W. C., Jenkins, J. E. E. and Jemmett, J. L. (1968). The relationship between leaf blotch caused by *Rhynchosporium secalis* and losses in grain yield of spring barley. *Ann. appl. Biol.* **62**, 273–288.

James, W. C., Callbeck, L. C., Hodgson, W. A. and Shih, C. S. (1971). Evaluation of a method used to estimate loss in yield of potatoes caused by late blight. *Phytopathology* **61**, 1417–1476.

James, W. C., Shih, C. S., Hodgson, W. A. and Callbeck, L. C. (1972). The quantitative relationship between late blight of potato and loss in tuber yield. *Phytopathology* **62**, 92–96.

James, W. C., Shih, C. S., Callbeck, L. C. and Hodgson, W. A. (1973). Interplot inteference in field experiments with late blight of potato (*Phytophthora infestans*). *Phytopathology* **63**, 1269–1275.

Johnson, R. and Taylor, A. J. (1976). Spore yield of pathogens in investigations of the race-specificity of host resistance. *Ann. Rev. Phytopathology* **14**, 97–119.

Jones, D. G. and Cooke, B. M. (1969). The epidemiology of *Septoria tritici* and *S. nodorum* I. A tentative key for assessing *Septoria tritici* infection on wheat heads. *Trans. Br. Mycol. Soc.* **53**, 39–46.

Jones, D. G. and Davies, J. M. L. (1969). A comparison of field inoculation methods with *Cercosporella herpotrichoides* (Fron) on spring barley. *J. Agr. Sci.* **73**, 437–444.

Jones, D. G. and Rowling, R. D. W. (1976). The reaction of two spring wheat varieties exposed to epidemics of *Septoria nodorum* and *S. tritici* of varying intensity and duration. *J. Agr. Sci.* **87**, 401–406.

Kanemasu, E. T. (1974). Seasonal canopy reflectance patterns of wheat, sorghum and soyabean. *Remote Sens. Environ.* **3**, 43–48.

Kanemasu, E. T., Schimmelpfennig, H., Chin Choy, E., Eversmeyer, M. G. and Lenhert, D. (1974a). ERTS-1 data collection systems used to predict wheat disease severities. *Remote Sens. Environ.* **3**, 93–97.

Kanemasu, E. T., Niblett, C. L., Manges, H., Lenhert, D. and Newman, M. A. (1974b). Wheat: its growth and disease severity as deduced from ERTS-1. *Remote Sens. Environ.* **3**, 255–260.

Keed, B. R. and White, N. H. (1971). Quantitative effects of leaf and stem rusts on yield and quality of wheat. *Aust. J. Exp. Agric. Anim. Husb.* **11**, 550–555.

Kelber, E. (1975). Möglichkeiten der Entwicklung von Befalls-Verlust-Realtionen für Pflanzenkrankheiten aus Sundärdaten. Diss. Univ. Giessen. PhD. Thesis.

King, J. E. (1972). Surveys of foliar diseases of spring barley in England and Wales 1967–70. *Pl. Path.* **21**, 23–35.

King, J. E. (1976). Relationship between yield loss and severity of yellow rust recorded on a large number of single of stems of winter wheat. *Pl. Path.* **25**, 172–177.

King, J. E. (1977a). Surveys of diseases of winter wheat in England and Wales, 1970–1975. *Pl. Path.* **26**, 8–20.

King, J. E. (1977b). Surveys of foliar diseases of spring barley in England and Wales, 1972–75. *Pl. Path.* **26**, 21–29.

Kingsolver, C. H., Schmitt, C. G., Peet, C. E. and Bromfield, K. R. (1959). Epidemiology of stem rust: II (Relation of quantity of inoculum and growth stage of wheat and rye at infection to yield reduction by stem rust.) *Pl. Dis. Reptr.* **43**, 855–862.

Kirby, R. S. and Archer, W. A. (1927). Diseases of cereal and forage crops in the United States in 1926. *Pl. Dis. Reptr. Suppl.* **53**, 110–208.

Koutsoyiannis, A. (1973). "Theory of Econometrics: an Introductory Exposition of Econometric Methods." MacMillan, London.

Kranz, J. (1970). Schätzklassen für Krankheitsbefall. *Phytopathol. Z,* **69**, 131–139.

Kranz, J. (1975). Crop loss appraisal. Proc. IV. Congr. Mediterranean Phytopathological Union, Zadar.

Krause, R. A. and Massie, L. B. (1975). Predictive systems: modern approaches to disease control. *Ann. Rev. Phytopathology* **13**, 31–47.

Krause, R. A., Massie, L. B. and Hyre, R. A. (1975). Blitecast: a computerized forecast of potato late blight. *Pl. Dis. Reptr.* **59**, 95–98.

Kuhn, C. W. and Smith, T. H. (1977). Effectiveness of a disease index system for evaluating corn for resistance to maize dwarf mozaic virus. *Phytopathology* **67,** 288–291.

Kumar, R. and Silva, L. (1974). Statistical separability of spectral classes of blighted corn. *Remote Sens. Environ.* **3,** 109–116.

Large, E. C. (1952). The interpretation of progress curves for potato blight and other plant diseases. *Pl. Path.* **1,** 109–117.

Large, E. C. (1954). Growth stages in cereals: illustration of the Feekes scale. *Pl. Path.* **3,** 128–129.

Large, E. C. (1966). Measuring plant disease. *Ann. Rev. Phytopathology* **4,** 9–28.

Large, E. C. and Doling, D. A. (1962). The measurement of cereal mildew and its effect on yield. *Pl. Path.* **11,** 47–57.

Large, E. C. and Doling, D. A. (1963). Effect of mildew on the yield of winter wheat. *Pl. Path.* **12,** 128–130.

Latin, R. X. and MacKenzie, D. R. (1976). The application of multiple point methods for forecasting yield losses caused by late blight. *Proc. Am. Phytopathology Soc.* **3,** 307. (Abstr.)

MacKenzie, D. R. and Petruzzo, S. E. (1975). Generalized equation for estimating tuber yield losses due to late blight of potato. *Proc. Am. Phytopathogy Soc.,* **2,** 101. (Abstr.)

MAFF (1976). Manual of Plant Growth States and Disease Assessment Keys. Pl. Path. Lab., MAFF Harpenden, Herts.

Main, C. E., Nusbaum, C. J., Lucas, G. B. and Chaplin, J. F. (1973). Tobacco quality related to severity of foliar disease. *2nd Int. Congr. Pl. Path.* **0590.** (Abstr.)

Manzer, F. E. and Cooper, G. R. (1967). Aerial photographic methods of potato disease detection. *Maine Agric. Exp. Stn. Bull.* **646.**

Marsh, R. W., Byrde, R. J. W. and Woodcock, D. (1977). "Systemic Fungicides." 2nd Edn. Longman, New York.

Melchers, L. E. and Parker, J. H. (1922). Rust resistance in winter wheat varieties. *U.S.D.A. Bull.* **1046.**

Melville, S. C. and Lanham, C. A. (1972). A survey of leaf diseases of spring barley in South-west England. *Pl. Path.* **21,** 59–66.

Mihram, G. A. (1972). "Simulation: Statistical Foundations and Methodology." Academic Press, New York and London.

Millar, C. S. and Colhoun, J. (1969). Fusarium diseases of cereals IV. Observations on *Fusarium nivale* on wheat. *Trans. Br. Mycol. Soc.* **52,** 57–66.

Mogk, M. (1974). Automatic data processing in analyses of epidemics. *In* "Epidemics of Plant Diseases: Mathematical Analysis and Modelling." (Kranz, J., Ed.), pp. 55–77. Springer-Verlag, Berlin.

Moore, W. C. (1943). The measurement of plant diseases in the field. *Trans. Br. Mycol. Soc.* **26,** 28–35.

Morrison, R. A. and Boyd, R. N. (1973). "Organic Chemistry." Allyn & Bacon, Boston.

Mundy, E. J. (1973). The effect of yellow rust and its control on the yield of Joss Cambier winter wheat. *Pl. Path.* **22,** 171–176.

Nelson, L. R., Holmes, M. R. and Cunfer, B. M. (1976). Multiple regression accounting for wheat yield reduction by *Septoria nodorum* and other pathogens. *Phytopathology* **66,** 1375–1379.

Newell, L. C. and Tysdal, H. M. (1945). Numbering and note-taking systems for use in the improvement of forage crops. *J. Am. Soc. Agron.* **37,** 736–749.

Nie, N. H., Hull, C. H., Jenkins, J. G., Steinbrenner, K. and Bent, D. H. (1975). "SPSS: Statistical Package for the Social Sciencies." 2nd edition. McGraw-Hill, New York.

Norton, G. A. (1976). Analysis of decision making in crop protection. *Agro-ecosyst.* **3**, 27–44.

Olofsson, B. (1968). Determination of the critical injury threshold for potato blight (*Phytophthora infestans*). *Medd. Waxtskyddsanst* Stockholm, **14**, 81–93.

Peterson, R. F., Campbell, A. B. and Hannah, A. E. (1948). A diagrammatic scale for estimating rust intensity on leaves and stems of cereals. *Can. J. Res.* **C26**, 496–500.

Pinstrup-Andersen, P., Londono, N. de and Infante, M. (1976). A suggested procedure for estimating yield and production losses in crops. *PANS* **22**, 359–365.

Polley, R. W. and King, J. E. (1973). A preliminary proposal for the detection of barley mildew infection periods. *Pl. Path.* **22**, 11–16.

Powell, N. L., Garren, K. H., Griffin, G. J. and Porter, D. M. (1976). Estimating Cylindrocladium black rot disease losses in peanut fields from aerial infrared imagery. *Pl. Dis. Reptr.* **60**, 1003–1007.

Pritsker, A. A. B. (1974). "The GASP IV Simulation Language." Wiley, New York.

Rayner, R. W. (1961). Measurement of fungicidal effects in field trials. *Nature* **190**, 328–330.

Redman, C. E. and Brown, I. F. (1964). A statistical evaluation of the Barratt and Horsfall rating system. *Phytopathology* **54**, 904.

Richardson, M. J. (1971). Yield losses in wheat and barley—1970. *Scot. Agric.* **50**, 72–77.

Richardson, M. J. (1975). 1974 cereal disease and yield loss survey. A report of the study of 96 wheat and 162 oat crops. Dep. Agric. Fish. Scotl. E. Craigs, Edinburgh.

Richardson, M. J., Jacks, M. and Smith, S. (1975). Assessment of loss caused by barley mildew using single tillers. *Pl. Path.* **24**, 21–26.

Richardson, M. J., Whittle, A. M. and Jacks, M. (1976). Yield-loss relationships in cereals. *Pl. Path.* **25**, 21–30.

Ride, J. P. and Drysdale, R. B. (1971). A chemical method for estimating *Fusarium oxysporum* f. *lycopersici* in infected tomato plants. *Physiol. Pl. Path.* **1**, 409–420.

Ride, J. P. and Drysdale, R. B. (1972). A rapid method for the chemical estimation of filamentous fungi in plant tissue. *Physiol. Pl. Path.* **2**, 7–15.

Robinson, R. A. (1976). Plant Pathosystems. *In* "Advanced Series in Agricultural Science 3." Springer-Verlag, Berlin.

Romig, R. W. and Calpouzos, L. (1970). The relationship between stem rust and loss in yield of spring wheat. *Phytopathology* **60**, 1801–1805.

Romig, R. W. and Dirks, V. A. (1966). Evaluation of generalized curves for number of cereal rust uredospores trapped on slides. *Phytopathology* **56**, 1376–1380.

Ruesink, W. G. (1976). Status of the systems approach to pest management. *Ann. Rev. Entomology* **21**, 27–44.

Saari, E. E. and Prescott, J. M. (1975). A scale for appraising the foliar intensity of wheat diseases. *Pl. Dis. Reptr.* **59**, 377–380.

Sallans, B. J. (1948). Interrelations of common root rot and other factors with wheat yields in Saskatchewan. *Sci. Agric.* **28**, 6–20.

Salter, P. J. and Goode, J. E. (1967). Crop responses to water at different stages of growth. Commonw. Agric. Bur., Slough, England.

Scarborough, B. A. and Smith, S. H. (1977). Effects of tobacco- and tomato ringspot viruses on the reproductive tissues of Pelargonium × hortorum. *Phytopathology* **67,** 292–297.

Schaller, C. W. (1963). The effect of mildew and scald infection on yield and quality of barley. *Agron. J.* **43,** 183–188.

Scheider, C. L. and Safir, G. R. (1975). Infrared aerial photography estimation of yield potential in sugarbeets exposed to blackroot disease. *Pl. Dis. Reptr.* **59,** 627–631.

Schneider, R. W., Williams, R. J. and Sinclair, J. B. (1976). *Cercospora* leaf spot of cowpea: models for estimating yield loss. *Phytopathology* **66,** 384–388.

Schwarzbach, E. (1975). The pleiotropic effects of the ml-o gene and their implications in breeding. Barley Genetics III. Proc. 3rd Int. Barley Genetics Symp., Garching.

Semeniuk, W. and Ross, J. G. (1942). Relation of loss smut to yield of barley. *Can. J. Res.* **20**(c), 491–500.

Shearer, B. L. and Wilcoxson, R. D. (1976). The distribution of Septoria species on winter wheat plants sprayed with fungicides. *Plant Dis. Reptr.* **60,** 990–994.

Shoemaker, C. (1973a). Optimization of agricultural pest management. I. Biological and mathematical background. *Math. Biosci.* **16,** 143–175.

Shoemaker, C. (1973b). Optimization of agricultural pest management. II. Formulation of a control model. *Math. Biosci.* **17,** 357–365.

Shoemaker, C. (1973c). Optimization of agricultural pest management. III. Results and extensions of a model. *Math. Biosci.* **18,** 1–22.

Shoemaker, C. A. (1976). Optimal integrated control of alfalfa weevil, *Hypera postica* (Gyllenhal) Coleoptera: Curculionidae. Paper presented at the Joint EPPO/IOBC Conf. on Systems Modelling in Modern Crop Protection, Paris.

Singh, B. R. and Singh, D. R. (1975). Brinjal mosaic incidence and effect on yield. *Indian J. Farm. Sci.* **3,** 117–118.

Sitepu, D. and Wallace, H. R. (1974). Diagnosis of retarded growth in an apple orchard. *Aust. J. Exp. Agric. Anim. Husb.* **14,** 577–584.

Slope, D. B. and Etheridge, J. (1971). Grain yield and incidence of take-all (*Ophiobolus graminis* Sacc.) in wheat grown in different crop sequences. *Ann. appl. Biol.* **67,** 13–22.

Snedecor, G. W. (1957). "Statistical Methods." 5th edn. Iowa State College Press, Ames, Iowa.

Steadman, J. R., Kerr, E. D. and Mumm, R. F. (1975). Root rot on bean in Nebraska: primary pathogen and yield loss appraisal. *Pl. Dis. Reptr.* **59,** 305–308.

Stover, R. H. (1971). A proposed international scale for estimating intensity of banana leaf spot (*Mycosphaerella musicola* Leach). *Trop. Agric.* Trinidad, **48,** 185–196.

Strandberg, J. (1973). Spatial distribution of cabbage black rot and the estimation of diseased plant populations. *Phytopathology* **63,** 998–1003.

Sturgeon, R. J. (1974). Chemical and biochemical aspects of fungal cell-walls. *In* "Plant Carbohydrate Biochemistry" (Pridham, J. B., Ed.), v. 10, pp. 219–233.

Stynes, B. A. (1975). A synoptic study of wheat. Ph.D. Thesis, University of Adelaide, South Australia.

Sukhatme, P. V. and Sukhatme, B. V. (1970). "Sampling Theory of Surveys with Applications." Asia Publishing House, London.

Tatum, L. A. (1971). The southern corn leaf blight, epidemic. *Sci.* **171,** 113–1116.

Teng, P. S. (1975). A quantitative assessment of padi foliar diseases in the Tanjong Karang Irrigation Scheme, Selangor, *Malaysian Agric. J.* **50,** 78–99.

Teng, P. S. (1978a). Sample surveys for disease-loss estimation. *In* Proc. APPS

Workshop on Epidemiology and Crop Loss Assessment, Lincoln Coll. N.Z. **36**, 1–11.

Teng, P. S. (1978b). System simulation in disease management: barley leaf rust as a case study. *In* Proc. APPS Workshop on Epidemiology and Crop Loss Assessment Lincoln Coll. N.Z. **32**, 1–10.

Teng, P. S. and Close, R. C. (1977). Spectral reflectance of healthy and leaf rust-infected barley leaves. *APPS Newsletter* **6**, 7–9.

Teng, P. S., Blackie, M. J. and Close, R. C. (1977a). A simulation analysis of crop yield loss due to rust disease. I. Model development and experimentation. *Agric. Systems* **2**, 189–198.

Teng, P. S., Blackie, M. J. and Close, R. C. (1977b). Systems analysis as a strategy for agroecosystem management: the barley leaf rust epidemic. *In* Proc. Int. Symposium on Microbial Ecology, Dunedin, N.Z.

Thomas, T. H. (1974). Investigations into the cytokinin-like properties of benzimidazole-derived fungicides. *Ann. appl. Biol.* **76**, 237–41.

Thorne, G. N. (1973). Physiology of grain yield of wheat and barley. *Rep. Rothamsted Exp. Stn.* **5**, 25.

Toppan, A., Esquerre-Tugaye, M. T. and Touze, A. (1976). An improved approach for the accurate determination of fungal pathogens in diseased plants. *Physiol. Pl. Path.* **9**, 241–251.

Van der Plank, J. E. (1963). "Plant Diseases: Epidemics and Control." Academic Press, New York and London.

Van der Plank, J. E. (1967). Spread of plant pathogens in space and time. *In* "Airborne Microbes, 17th Symp. Soc. General Microbiol. Imperial College, London." pp. 227–246. Cambridge University Press.

Wal, A. F. van der and Cowan, M. C. (1974). An ecophysiological approach to crop losses exemplified in the system wheat, leaf rust and glume blotch. II. Development, growth, and transpiration of uninfected plants and plants infected with *Puccinia recondita* f. sp. *triticina* and/or *Septoria nodorum* in a climate chamber. *Netherlands J. Pl. Path.* **80**, 192–214.

Wallace, H. R. (1978). The diagnosis of plant diseases of complex etiology. *Ann. Rev. Phytopathology* **16**, 379–402.

Wallen, V. R. and Jackson, H. R. (1971). Aerial photography as a survey technique for the assessment of bacterial blight of field beans. *Can. Pl. Dis. Surv.* **51**, 163–169.

Wallen, V. R. and Philpotts, L. E. (1971). Disease assessment with IR-color. *Photogrammetric Engng.* **37**, 443–446.

White, L. Jr. (1967). The historical roots of our ecologic crisis. *Sci.* **155**, 1203–1207.

Wiener, N. (1948). Feeback and oscillation. *In* "Cybernetics: or Control and Communications in the Animal and the Machine." Ch. 4. Wiley, New York.

Wood, R. K. S. (1967). "Physiological Plant Pathology." Blackwell Scientific Publishers, Oxford.

Wright, A. (1971). Farming systems, models and simulation. *In* "Systems Analysis in Agricultural Management." (Dent, J. B. and Anderson, J. R., Eds.), pp. 17–33. Wiley, New York.

Wright, N. S. (1970). Combined effects of potato viruses X and S on yield of Netted Gem and White Rose potatoes. *Am. Potato J.* **47**, 475–78.

Wu, L. C. and Stahmann, M. A. (1975). Chromatographic estimation of fungal mass in plant materials. *Phytopathology* **65**, 1032–1034.

Yates, F. (1960). "Sampling Methods for Census and Surveys." 3rd edn. Griffin, London.

Zadoks, J. C. (1972). Methodology of epidemiological research. *Ann. Rev. Phytopathology* **10**, 253–276.

Zadoks, J. C., Chang, T. T. & Konzak, C. F. (1974). A decimal code for the growth stages of cereals. *EUCARPIA Bull.* no. **7**. Also in *Weed Research* **14**, 415–421.

Zarkovitch, S. S. (1966). "Quality of Statistical Data." FAO, Rome.

Subject Index